GENDERED MILITARISM IN CANADA

GENDERED MILITARISM IN CANADA

Learning Conformity and Resistance

Nancy Taber, Editor

THE UNIVERSITY OF ALBERTA PRESS

Published by
THE UNIVERSITY OF ALBERTA PRESS
Ring House 2
Edmonton, Alberta, Canada T6G 2E1
www.uap.ualberta.ca

LIBRARY AND ARCHIVES CANADA CATALOGUING IN PUBLICATION

Gendered militarism in Canada : learning conformity and resistance / edited by Nancy Taber.

Includes bibliographical references and index.
Issued in print and electronic formats.
ISBN 978-1-77212-084-4 (paperback).—ISBN 978-1-77212-107-0 (epub).—
ISBN 978-1-77212-108-7 (kindle).—ISBN 978-1-77212-109-4 (pdf)

1. Educational sociology—Canada. 2. Militarism—Social aspects—
Canada. 3. Sex role—Canada. I. Taber, Nancy, 1971-, editor

LC191.8.C2G45 2015   306.430971   C2015-906538-0
                                            C2015-906539-9

First edition, first printing, 2015.
Printed and bound in Canada by Houghton Boston Printers, Saskatoon, Saskatchewan.
Copyediting by Angela Wingfield.
Proofreading by Joanne Muzak.
Indexing by Adrian Mather.

The University of Alberta Press is committed to protecting our natural environment. As part of our efforts, this book is printed on Enviro Paper: it contains 100% post-consumer recycled fibres and is acid- and chlorine-free.

The University of Alberta Press gratefully acknowledges the support received for its publishing program from the Government of Canada, the Canada Council for the Arts, and the Government of Alberta through the Alberta Media Fund.

This book has been published with the help of a grant from the Canadian Federation for the Humanities and Social Sciences, through the Awards to Scholarly Publications Program, using funds provided by the Social Sciences and Humanities Research Council of Canada.

Government of Canada / Gouvernement du Canada

Canada Council for the Arts / Conseil des Arts du Canada

Alberta Government

CONTENTS

FOREWORD

THE WINDOWS OF MY OFFICE at Mount Saint Vincent University overlook the Bedford Basin, where I have frequently observed military vessels and Sea King helicopters engaged in practice manoeuvres. On the drive into Halifax I see uniformed naval officers at the crosswalks, I see the fenced army base across from Citadel Hill (an 18th-century army base that is now a Parks Canada site), and I see tanks stored in the old red stone armoury across from the Halifax Commons. Like most Haligonians, even though I have always been a civilian, these symbols of military presence are woven into the fabric of my everyday life in this small Canadian city.

As the daughter of an American World War II veteran I have always had respect for members of the military, even though as a feminist and a mother I believe firmly that societies need to work toward peace through means other than war. As a critical adult educator and a Canadian I am concerned with the ways in which we explore difficult issues of militarism and peace in a country that has traditionally prided itself on its peacekeeping role.

This book, edited by my colleague (and former Sea King navigator) Nancy Taber, provides rich insights into the ways in which militarism shapes and permeates our everyday lives, far beyond the casual glance out my office window—"Oh, look, submarine!" It delves into a number of difficult and thorny questions that affect all of us as citizens and as educators. The concept of militarism is taken up not just in terms of issues pertaining to war and military service, but also in the manner that violence connected to militaristic beliefs permeates many of our day-to-day experiences, as can be seen in the recreational activities of computerized gaming. Important topics that have been underexplored, such as the connection between militarism and ability or disability, are considered. A critical thread woven throughout the book is a gender analysis that examines particularly the way discourses around masculinity and femininity (as well as race and heteronormativity) can provide insights into many of the ways in which militarism shapes our everyday experiences and normative assumptions.

One of the main objectives for critical adult educators is to provoke their learners into questioning their taken-for-granted understanding about the world around them. In doing so, learners may begin to examine the messages that are communicated to them through the mass media, government policies and promotions, and within educational systems. Individuals may begin to reflect upon their past experiences, their interactions with others, and information that they may have previously accepted unquestioningly that shapes their beliefs and value systems. This critical questioning can be an uncomfortable process at times, but it is an important aspect of encouraging adults to think carefully about what it means to be an active and engaged learner and citizen.

Readers will find that this book challenges them to question how militarism infiltrates many aspects of their daily life as Canadians, exploring topics ranging from the evolution of social media such as Facebook to the ways in which traditional fairy tales are taken up and sometimes reconstituted in popular culture. The Canadian focus of this text is unique, yet important, as it challenges the perception of Canadians as "peacekeepers." In a world characterized by globalization and mobilities, it also draws attention to complex issues around citizenship and inclusion, when many people are seeking refuge in countries such as Canada. The text also explores our role as Canadians in international development and aid programs, which are often linked to considerations around militarism.

In addition to contributions from well-established scholars such as Shahrzad Mojab and the editor, Nancy Taber, the book includes a number of different research contributions from emerging scholars. The stories that they share, and the questions that they raise, provide many important topics for adult educators to ponder and debate. This is an insightful contribution to the ongoing debates around citizenship, inclusion, and learning in Canadian adult education.

Patricia Gouthro

PREFACE

AS A SCHOLAR WHOSE RESEARCH and teaching focus on gender, militarism, and learning I have often found it difficult to find materials that centre on all three concepts, particularly in relation to Canada. There are some notable instances in which scholars explore the topics of women, war, and learning (see Mojab, 2011, for an international example). However, it has generally been necessary to build on work that connects gender and militaries (e.g., Goldstein, 2001; Higate, 2003); gender, militaries, and militarism (e.g., Enloe, 2007); and militarism and education (e.g., Giroux, 2008). Furthermore, much of this work is positioned within the United States. Although the United States certainly connects to the Canadian context, Canada is a unique country with its own history, geography, politics, education system, and cultures. This book arises from my desire to have a cohesive volume of work that centres on Canada with respect to gender (and intersecting oppressions) as a societal construct;

militarism as an overarching concept that includes belief systems and that positions violence or conflict as connected to but not equated with war and militaries; and learning, from a lifelong perspective that includes compulsory education and the variety of contexts addressed in adult education. I wanted a volume that would directly address the common misconceptions that these issues only affect people in other countries, that Canada is an unproblematically peaceful and equitable country nationally, and that Canada's international involvement is always beneficial.

The intended audience for this book is feminist, adult, and teacher educators in universities, and their students. Additionally, it may be of interest to community educators and activists, as well as to those who explore gender, militarism, and learning in other contexts and capacities.

Nancy Taber

ACKNOWLEDGEMENTS

I WOULD LIKE TO ACKNOWLEDGE the work of the chapter authors who have contributed to this volume. Their scholarship provides an important societal critique of the ways in which gender and militarism intersect in the daily learning of Canadians. In June 2014 the chapter authors who focus on adult education presented their work in a symposium at the Canadian Association for the Study of Adult Education (CASAE) conference.[1] My thanks to those who presented at and attended the symposium.

This book has been published with the help of a grant from the Federation for the Humanities and Social Sciences, through the Awards to Scholarly Publications Program, using funds provided by the Social Sciences and Humanities Research Council of Canada. Funding was also received from the Brock SSHRC Institutional Grant, Special Purpose— Subvention for Scholarly Books.

NOTE

1. N. Taber, N., Haddow, A., Lane, L., Magnusson, J., & Mojab, S. (2014). Pushing the boundaries of adult education: The intersection of learning, militarism, and gender in Canada. In D. Plumb (Ed.), *Proceedings of the Canadian Association for the Study of Adult Education 2014 Conference*. St. Catharines, ON: Brock University.

INTRODUCTION

Learning, Gender, and Militarism

Nancy Taber

WHEN I WRITE ABOUT LEARNING, gender, and militarism, I am reminded that my scholarly positioning is connected to my own personal experiences. Therefore, I begin this introductory chapter with a discussion of my own route to this area of study. I then introduce theories of gendered militarism and explain their importance in the Canadian context, discuss learning as a public pedagogy through the example of fairy tales, and give an overview of the chapters to follow.

Gendered Militarism: Theory and the Canadian Context

Despite my military background, my entry into the scholarly exploration of gender and militarism was rather unexpected for me. I grew up in a military family, joining the military myself when I was 17 years old.

As I have written extensively about my experiences elsewhere (Taber, 2005, 2007), they will be briefly summarized here. Our military family moved often, and my sister and I attended several different schools. Upon completion of high school I decided to apply to military college to earn my undergraduate degree in political science. After graduation I became an air navigator, serving on Sea King helicopters as a tactical coordinator in the air force. In general, I quite enjoyed serving in the military and was proud to do so. Gradually, however, I began to question first my place in the military and then the military's place in society. This questioning stemmed from my experiences as a woman in a male-dominated institution. Always having to be on my toes, knowing I was somehow different, was an undercurrent throughout my service despite my overall success. Near the end of my short service contract (four years of university plus nine years of service) I studied for a master's degree in adult education. It was at this point that I began to problematize the enactment of gender in the military.

After leaving the military, I began my doctorate, wanting to focus on gender but not quite sure of the context. I knew only that I had no intention of doing any work with the military. Other students were rather astonished at this, thinking that the military would be a perfect research context for me. Eventually I also came to this realization and started looking into women's service in the military. At the beginning of my research I found that the work of Cynthia Enloe helped me to understand the interconnections between militaries and society and introduced me to the concepts of militarism and militarization:

> Thinking about militarization allows us to chart the silences. It enables us to see what is not challenged or, at the very least, what is not made problematic: elevating a good soldier to the status of a good citizen; expanding NATO in the name of democratization; seeing JROTC [Junior Reserve Officer Training Corps] as simply a program to enhance school discipline; imagining Carmen Miranda's wartime movie roles as nothing more than harmless comedies. The silence surrounding militarization is broken when

> military assumptions about, and military dependence on, gender are pushed up to the
> surface of public discussion. (Enloe, 2000, p. 32)

Reading this quotation, I began to see how my life in the military intersected with gendered militarism in society, eventually leading to my questioning of the military itself as an institution. My dissertation focused on the way in which military institutional ruling relations were implicated in the daily lives of mothers in the military. In my exploration I analyzed my own experiences as connected not only to military policy documents but also to children's books written for military families and newspaper articles. Over the years I have continued to research military contexts but have also broadened the focus on militarism in society as a whole.

Historically, the service of Canadian women has been restricted to that of nursing sisters (beginning in the late 1800s), women's only units (World War II), and support roles (initially with mandatory release upon marriage or pregnancy). It was not until 1989, when I joined the military, that all occupations were open to women, except service in submarines (Dundas, 2000). The final submarine restriction was lifted in 2000 (Canada, 2013). It is important to note that these changes were precipitated by Canadian commissions that investigated women's status in the country and by legislation that guaranteed equal rights. The Canadian context was legally supportive of women's integration.

However, women are still in the minority in the Canadian military, comprising only 15 per cent in the Regular and Primary Reserve forces combined (Canada, 2013). Such a low representation in the military indicates as much about the country as a whole as it does about the military itself. I am not arguing that more women *should* join the military, but I am demonstrating that Canadian lives are affected by gender and militarism in complex ways that go beyond equal rights legislation, just as they go beyond the military.

Often, when I state that I research militarism, it is assumed that I simply mean militaries. In my experience people have difficulty separating the concept of militarism from the context of the military. Militarism, as defined by Enloe (2007), is present when citizens "adopt militaristic values (e.g., a belief in hierarchy, obedience, and the use of force) and priorities as one's own, to see military solutions as particularly effective, to see the world as a dangerous place best approached with militaristic attitudes" (p. 4). She gives examples of everyday objects that demonstrate how militarism is present in everyday life, such as soup cans containing *Star Wars* pasta; the naming of the bikini after the atoll that was all but destroyed by American military testing; and camouflage fashion. These examples demonstrate how the military as a national institution is connected to, but does not encompass, everyday experiences of militarism.

A discussion of the Canadian government's current commemoration of wars can help to illuminate these connections with respect to Canada's military history and contemporary understandings. In 2014 the Canadian government began commemorating the passage of 100 years since the start of World War I. It has also recently celebrated the two hundredth anniversary of the War of 1812 and has launched a new program called Operation Distinction, an "initiative [that] spans all the way to 2020, which will mark the 75th anniversary of the Second World War's Victory in Europe Day and Victory over Japan Day" (Chase, 2014, para. 4). In this way the government and the Department of National Defence are actively working to bring the Canadian military, and its participation in war, into the daily lives of Canadians, to the tune of $83 million. Typically it does so in an uncritical way that glamorizes the military. It is often stated that the military action by Canadians was and is necessary for the freedom of the country.

In a newspaper article drawn from his recent book, *Canada in the Great Power Game: 1914–2014*, Gwynne Dyer (2014), a noted historian, contests the notion that war and freedom are inextricably linked. He states that, in relation to World War I in particular, and contemporary wars in general, "we were never in any danger." He adds, "To make sense of so much pain and loss, we simply had to believe the war had been about something important. In fact, it had to be a crusade against evil itself, for nothing else could justify violent death on such a scale." The attitude that war is necessary and important colours the ways in which Canada's military history is viewed and current military actions are interpreted. Such a dedication to representing the military in an unproblematically positive way, through "public education, ceremonies, events and remembrance partnerships" (Chase, 2014, para. 2), is an apt demonstration of how a nation's military influences its citizens' experiences of militarism. Perhaps this privileging of war contributed to my recent sighting of two boys in a nearby park, dressed completely in military camouflage, playing war with toy guns. It was very eerie because in some parts of the world this is a daily sight, but it is certainly not "play," and the guns are not toys. For these two boys, though, it was simply part of their weekend enjoyment. They were not in the military but were engaged in overtly militaristic play.

The Canadian government's backing of a proposal to build the Never Forgotten National Memorial in Cape Breton, Nova Scotia, is another example of militarism. It aims to promote the military in a sentimental way by "pouring concrete over a pristine arm of pink granite that extends into the sea" (J. Taber, 2014), on land that is purportedly protected in a national park. The monument will be 30 metres tall with a parking lot for 300 vehicles. Various parts of the monument will be named after the national anthem. It is intended to open for celebrations of Canada's 150th birthday, and it is hoped that it will increase tourism to the area. A charity has been established in order to raise money for the $25 million to $60 million project, and Parks Canada is donating the land. In sum, the profit to be earned from tourism is positioned as more important than the environment; "charity" money will go toward a monument; Canada's birthday will be marked with a military memorial; and a statue of a grieving woman, "Mother Canada," will hold out her arms to dead (male) soldiers buried in France who were killed by enemy others. As Enloe (2007) wrote, "militarization and the privileging of masculinity are both products not only of amorphous cultural beliefs but also of deliberate decisions" (p. 33). The decision to fundraise millions of dollars in order to militarize the land, the anthem, and Canada's birthday are indeed deliberate. Joni Mitchell's song lyrics come to mind: "they paved paradise and put in a parking lot." The public pedagogy of the Canadian government is teaching citizens about valued national ideas.

Public Pedagogy: An Example of Fairy Tales

Canadians engage with gendered militarism daily in an ongoing learning relationship. In a "pedagogical project of everyday life" (Luke, 1996, p. 1) citizens are not passive consumers but active participants, accepting and resisting, advancing and preventing militarism. Learning occurs with and without the presence of specific teachers and educational programs; living life itself is a "public pedagogy" (Sandlin, Schultz, & Burdick, 2009). Children, youth, and adults learn in various interconnected spaces, with their learning at one stage of life connected to that at other stages. For example, some of my recent research has explored the way that gendered militarism is learned through fairy tales (Taber, 2013a, 2013b; Taber, Woloshyn, Munn, & Lane, 2013). Fairy tales are often viewed as made for children; yet their complex history indicates that they are engaged by all age groups. Adults read fairy tales to children and take children to movies based on traditional and revised tellings. Recent fairy-tale television programs and movies have been made specifically for adults. Furthermore, adults' own interactions with fairy tales are connected to their experiences with the genre as children. Interestingly, fairy tales are often viewed as benign. As such, they are an excellent example for my argument here.

The findings of my research into two television programs made for adults that mix various fairy and folk tales, *Grimm* and *Once Upon a Time*, indicate that, although women are gaining increasing agency and strength as main protagonists, "good still triumphs over evil while hegemonic masculinity saves the day" (Taber, 2013a, para. 28). Violence is viewed as necessary against enemy "others" who are beyond understanding and undeserving of empathy. However, the programs do provide excellent points of entry for discussions of the ways in which gender and militarism are portrayed. In a collaborative study about fairy tales in general and Snow White in particular (Taber et al., 2013), my co-researchers and I wanted to build on the idea that fairy tales are sites of learning. We created a media group not only to understand how female college students interacted with gender but also to use fairy tales as a basis from which to assist them in engaging in a gendered critique of the artifacts and daily life. We found that participants critiqued traditional versions of the Snow White character for being too passive (which they connected to their childhood recollections of her), yet when shown what they viewed as a stronger version in the film *Snow White and the Huntsman*, they wanted the Huntsman to be tougher in order to save Snow White. They were generally uncomfortable with Snow White saving herself and wanted a traditional happily-ever-after wedding at the end. We continued on with the group, exploring superheroes and the supernatural, using the media group as a way to connect their learning in daily life as women and college students to their engagement in a societal critique. Using fairy tales, then, is one way in which educators can explore pedagogies of everyday life.

Overview of Chapters

This book stems from the idea that learning is lifelong; it views education from a broad perspective and aims for societal critique. The authors explore various reasons Canadian educators should be concerned with examining the intersection of learning, militarism, and gender. As a whole, the authors delineate the ways in which gender and militarism are embedded in the daily learning of Canadians. Although those who critique military actions have often been labelled unpatriotic and enemies of democracy (McKay & Swift, 2012), the book demonstrates that it is our social and educative responsibility, as citizens and educators, to challenge militaristic thinking. The authors aim to raise awareness of gendered militarism in order to critique it, pushing the boundaries of education theory, research, and practice.

Care was taken to ensure that the authors represented various Canadian demographics: they are students, emerging scholars, and established scholars. Although currently located in various Canadian provinces such as Ontario, Manitoba, and Saskatchewan, they hail from other countries such as Iran and Yugoslavia as well as several other Canadian provinces. They have worked, researched, taught, and built networks in countries such as Iran, Iraq, Palestine, Turkey, Kosovo, South Korea, Jamaica, Nepal, Ethiopia, South Africa, Chile, and the United States. The authors are men and women with intersecting positionalities, refugees or immigrants to Canada, and Canadian-born, who identify as LGBTQ (lesbian, gay, bisexual, transgender, queer), straight, working-class, and privileged. They approach militarism by centring on militarism itself or connecting concepts such as militaries, conflict, war, violence, and cyberbullying.

The authors variously focus on gender, race, class, colonialism, and imperialism (as relates to capitalist financialization), heteronormativity, and ability. A notable gap is the lack of a chapter from an Aboriginal perspective. I had an author who was originally interested but had to decline based on other commitments. It is my hope that I will be able to include such work in the future. The chapters include conceptual arguments and empirical research, as well as an ethnodrama. The volume is organized according to the educational context of the chapters, examining informal and everyday contexts as well as institutionalized ones. Chapters 1 through 3 explore various forms of popular culture such as gaming, social networking, films, and television programs. Chapters 4 and 5 focus on embodied discourses relating to ideal citizens and ideal bodies, respectively. Chapters 6 and 7 examine links between Canada and international contexts. Chapter 8, which examines Yugoslav-Canadian mothers' experiences of teaching, also connects to Chapters

9 and 10, which focus on aspects of compulsory schooling. A summary of each chapter follows. The volume is bookended by chapters about war games: the first concerns online alternative reality games; the last, sports and schooling, serving to demonstrate the interrelationships between various learning contexts.

In Chapter 1, "War of Gender Games," Jamie Magnusson and Shahrzad Mojab argue for making visible the invisible social relations embedded in concepts of "capitalist financialization, patriarchy, and militarized gender learning." They analyze an online alternative reality game called *Urgent EVOKE*, which was created by the World Bank Institute. Gamers are asked to participate in missions intended to change the world by "empowering" youth, specifically in relation to Africa. In their chapter Magnusson and Mojab focus on the missions about women's rights. They argue that the game, ostensibly about empowering women, conflates equality with the economy and further supports a heteronormative, colonial, and militarized world of inequality.

Chapter 2, "Militarizing or Anti-Militarizing Facebook: Resisting and Reproducing Gendered Militarism Online," by Laura Lane, explores how social networking sites (SNS) are online spaces in which gender and militarism are learned, supported, and resisted. Using two Facebook pages—the Canadian Armed Forces (formerly the Canadian Forces) and the Women's International League for Peace and Freedom—as contrasting "educational spaces," she analyzes the way in which the online visuals, user comments, and terms of use mirror off-line realities. Lane thus concludes that SNS are powerful sites of learning that must continue to be problematized. Educators should critique gendered militarism online while understanding the transgressive potential of SNS.

In Chapter 3, "Popular Media, Pedagogy, and Patriarchy: Gender, Militarism, and Entertainment in Canada," Andrew Haddow discusses popular culture as a whole and then focuses on films, television programs, and gaming. Drawing on a large body of literature about popular culture in Britain and the United States, he explores the pedagogical implications of this content for the Canadian context. Haddow argues that Canadians interact with American media content on a daily basis and that much of Canadian programming reflects that of the United States. He then turns to critical media literacy, detailing how educators can encourage a critique of the ways in which gender and militarism are represented in popular culture, "in order to dismantle the systems of oppression that maintain a structure of militarization and patriarchy."

In Chapter 4, "Official (Masculinized and Militarized) Representations of Canada: Learning Citizenship," I explore how Canadian citizenship documents perform pedagogically to idealize a certain form of citizenship. Using feminist discourse analysis, I analyze government-created citizenship documents such as study guides, passports, and educational web pages. Although discourses of equal rights are present, images of masculinized militarism prevail overall. The privileging of men, masculinity, militaries, and militarism in the citizenship documents reflects that in Canadian society. I conclude that, as the government is "creating a very particular education of the Canadian public, so must educators work to problematize these discourses of citizenship, offering alternative understandings and ways to learn about Canadian 'ideals' that are pluralistic, critical, and complex."

Chapter 5, "A Critical Discussion on Disabled Subjects: Examining Ableist and Militaristic Discourses in Education," by Mark Anthony Castrodale, explores the notion of "ideal" bodies. He details the manner in which the interdisciplinary nature of critical disability studies (CDS) supports his Foucauldian analysis of the construction of ability and gender with respect to militarism. Castrodale focuses on militarized masculinity and the ideal body. He explores the advancement of prosthetic medicine by military cyborg technologies, which arguably improve the mobility of those with disabilities while at the same time normalizing certain forms of ability. Castrodale discusses how a CDS-informed pedagogy can help educators and students to problematize societal notions of ability.

In Chapter 6, "Uncovering Rainbow (Dis)Connections: Sexual Diversity and Adult Education in the Canadian Armed Forces," the book turns to examine the experiences of international aid workers. Robert Mizzi begins with a narrative of his own experiences with military recruiters, explaining that he was immediately marginalized owing to his "effeminate mannerisms," which discouraged him from joining. He examines the military policies with respect to the LGBTQ community that have changed over the years, ostensibly becoming more inclusive while in practice changing little. Mizzi then describes his research in Kosovo, exploring the use of military personnel to train aid workers, which served to privilege certain forms of masculinity and militarism.

Chapter 7, "The Complexities of Gender Training in Contexts of Conflict and Peacebuilding," by Cindy Hanson, continues in this vein, focusing on the way that gender training is conceptualized and delivered with respect to Canada's domestic and international commitments. She argues that gender training is too often superficial, treating all women as the same, promoting Western values, and ignoring the social context. Hanson details and analyzes the training itself, including anecdotes and "suggesting critical points of intervention for the field of gender training." She calls for radical changes to the training of facilitators and the design and development of programs.

In Chapter 8, the context of compulsory schooling is introduced as Snežana Ratković discusses "Militarism, Motherhood, and Teaching: A Yugoslav-Canadian Case." Drawing from her research with refugee women teachers from Yugoslavia, she focuses on two participants in particular who were dealing with tensions in their lives as mothers and teachers. Ratković shows how certain myths of motherhood intersected with their lives in Yugoslavia, presenting bilingual poems of their experiences of conflict, immigration, and teaching. In Canada not only were their credentials devalued, but they themselves were marginalized as they were marked as different. Ratković's chapter demonstrates the operation of gendered militarism "across cultures, ideologies, and societies."

In Chapter 9, "An Invisible Web: Examining Cyberbullying, Gender, and Identity through Ethnodrama," Gillian Fournier presents an ethnodrama about teenage girls' experiences with and understandings of cyberbullying. Using drama as a social intervention to engage her participants in a variety of activities, Fournier argues that cyberbullying is a complex phenomenon that should be addressed by educators and schools. She has arranged her data into an ethnodrama, providing an artistic representation of her participants' perspectives.

Chapter 10, "War Games: School Sports and the Making of Militarized Masculinities," by Roger Saul, explores compulsory schooling from the perspective of physical education. He uses cultural studies of sport, masculinity studies, and equity studies to examine the "uncritical championing of sports' individual and social benefits to the lives of young people" in general, and boys in particular. Saul demonstrates that sports are rooted in military traditions, an "impoverished view of masculinity" is privileged in school sport, and many are thus excluded from school life. He ties his argument to specific examples of the intersection of race, masculinity, and militarism in popular representations of black, male, student athletes in Canada.

The Conclusion, "Final Thoughts and Connecting Threads," connects the themes presented throughout the other chapters. In particular, I explore how, despite Canada's claim to be a gender-equitable nation, militarism continues to function in ways that protect inequality. The privileging of certain forms of masculinity and femininity is tied to militaristic values that portray the masculine as tough protectors, and the feminine as those protected. Those who are different are marginalized and othered. The book demonstrates that, in order to make change, one must take a wide view of gender and militarism. Canadians can and do resist gendered militarism, but more must be done. The authors in this book point the way.

REFERENCES

Canada. National Defence. (2013). *Backgrounder: Women in the Canadian Armed Forces.* Retrieved from www.forces.gc.ca

Chase, S. (2014, June 16). Ottawa spends more on military history amid criticism over support for veterans. *Globe and Mail*. Retrieved from www.theglobeandmail.com

Dundas, B. (2000). *A history of women in the Canadian military*. Montreal: Art Global.

Dyer, G. (2014, August 9). What if the Kaiser had won the war? *Globe and Mail*. Retrieved from www.theglobeandmail.com

Enloe, C. (2000). *Maneuvers: The international politics of militarizing women's lives*. Berkeley: University of California Press.

Enloe, C. (2007). *Globalization and militarism: Feminists make the link*. Lanham, MD: Rowman & Littlefield.

Giroux, H.A. (2008). Education and the crisis of youth: Schooling and the promise of democracy. *The Educational Forum, 73*(1), 8-18.

Goldstein, J. (2001). *War and gender*. Cambridge: Cambridge University Press.

Higate, P. (Ed.). (2003). *Military masculinities: Identity and the state*. Westport, CT: Praeger.

Luke, C. (1996). Introduction. In C. Luke (Ed.), *Feminisms and pedagogies of everyday life* (pp. 1-27). Albany: SUNY Press.

McKay, I., & Swift, J. (2012). *Warrior nation: Rebranding Canada in an age of anxiety*. Toronto: Between the Lines.

Mojab, S. (Ed.). (2011). *Women, war, violence, and learning*. London: Routledge.

Sandlin, J.A., Schultz, B.D., & Burdick, J. (Eds.). (2009). *Handbook of public pedagogy: Education and learning beyond schooling*. New York: Routledge.

Taber, J. (2014, March 8). The battle over "Mother Canada": Proposal for 30-metre tall war monument creates "a lot of rancour and anger" along Cape Breton's Cabot Trail. *Globe and Mail*, A13.

Taber, N. (2005). Learning how to be a woman in the Canadian Forces / Unlearning it through feminism: An autoethnography of my learning journey. *Studies in Continuing Education, 27*(3), 289-301.

Taber, N. (2007). *Ruling relations, warring, and mothering: Writing the social from the everyday life of a military mother* (Unpublished doctoral dissertation). University of South Australia, Adelaide.

Taber, N. (2013a). Detectives, bail bond "persons," and fairy tales: A feminist antimilitarist analysis of gender in *Grimm* and *Once Upon a Time*. *Gender Forum: An Internet Journal for Gender Studies, 44*, art. 2, http://www.genderforum.org/index.php?id=731

Taber, N. (2013b). Mulan, western military mothers, and gendered militarism: The warrior myth of equality. In J.M. Aston & E. Vasquez (Eds.), *Masculinity and femininity: Stereotypes/myths, psychology, and role of culture* (pp. 95-110). New York: NOVA Science.

Taber, N., Woloshyn, V., Munn, C., & Lane, L. (2013). Exploring fairy tales in a college
women's media group: Stereotypes, changing representations of Snow White, and
happy endings. *Canadian Association for the Study of Adult Education (CASAE) 2013
conference*. Victoria, BC: University of Victoria.

1 ✖ ✖ ✖ ✚ ✖

WAR OF GENDER GAMES

Jamie Magnusson and Shahrzad Mojab

ADULTS LEARN WAYS OF BEING, doing, and living and in a variety of settings and spaces. The learning takes diverse forms, is continuous, and is constantly evolving the self and the mode of social connectivity. We open this chapter by explaining what is visible when we scan the complexity of this world, its pace, and its innumerable choices, but, we aim to go deeper in our exploration of the relationship between modes and spaces of learning, and the actual context in which they take place. This context is racialized and genderized patriarchal capitalism. To take this leap we ask, is repeating what is *visible* adequate for understanding the social relations that result in the condition of subjugation and disparity for the majority of humanity? Do we not need to go deeper to make visible the *invisible* social relations that prepare the ground for the production, perpetuation, and the maintenance of these relations?

In this chapter we aim to uncover the essence of learning in the computer game *Urgent EVOKE*, designed and implemented by the World Bank Institute (WBI).[1] In particular, we unpack the gender "empowerment" component of the game with the intention of theorizing the relations between capitalist financialization, patriarchy, and militarized gender learning. We begin with an introduction to the World Bank's recent investment in gamified learning as a major initiative, and show the historical traces to war-gaming and futurology. Although global in perspective, this investment in gamified learning has important implications for learning gendered militarism in Canada. First, Canada's ruling class is invested in global financial accumulation, which requires the state to free resources by disinvesting in the social welfare state, which in turn sets the stage for financialized privatization, including areas such as health care, education, and the carceral state. Among the hardest hit by these strategies are youth, who are also the most avid gamers in Canada. The World Bank narratives of accumulation through militarized and financialized crisis containment, as we outline below, become an ideology consumed by Canadian gamers.

Second, recent studies show that, within Canada, video gaming has become important not only culturally but also economically. For example, the Entertainment Software Association of Canada (ESA) reports that Canada has the third-largest gaming industry in the world (behind Japan and the United States) and that Canada's video game industry contributes $2.3 billion to the nation's gross domestic product (ESA, 2013). Fifty-eight per cent of Canadians are gamers, and of these, 48 per cent are women (ESA, 2013). Statistics Canada reports that since 1998 Canadians have been watching less television and spending more time on the computer (Statistics Canada, 2010). Currently, 71 per cent of youth reported playing games on their mobile devices (Rogers Communications, 2012a, 2012b). Of Canadian online users aged 16 to 24, 57 per cent reported playing online games (Statistics Canada, 2013). According to the most recent Rogers Innovation Report (Rogers Communications, 2012b), Canadians spend more time on a smart phone or tablet than they do on eating, engaging in personal hygiene, or being active (see Lane, Chapter 2 of this volume, for a discussion of online learning and gender with respect to Facebook). The 2012 Rogers Innovation Report gives interesting statistics about Canadian women and digital technology: 67 per cent cannot imagine their lives without digital technology, 56 per cent report that staying connected with technology is important to their well-being, and 71 per cent report that they would feel out of touch without this technology (the corresponding statistics for Canadian men are 49, 39, and 53 per cent, respectively; Rogers Innovation Report, 2012a). This comparative data reveals the emerging importance of personal-device technology and social media in shaping the sociality of women's lives as well as men's lives, interrupting the idea of the Internet as a male technological space.

Third, the above statistics do not fully capture the cultural significance of gaming within the Canadian context. For example, the University of Waterloo (Stratford Campus) houses the Games Institute, which organizes the gamification hub that has gamification of education as its primary innovation activity. While public schools continue to erode as a result of state disinvestment, significant proportions of youth—particularly racialized youth—are dropping out, and gamified learning is being constructed as the way of the future. Gamification is seen as a viable "fix" for school dropout rates that have become a national public education crisis. The kind of game offered by the World Bank, then, is increasingly seen as the future of education in the Canadian context (see Mizzi, Chapter 6, and Hanson, Chapter 7, in this volume for additional explorations of the ways in which international organizations are connected to Canadian learning). The financial promise of "big data" mining is closely connected to gamification of education, gamification of health care, gamification of organizations, and so on. There has even been outraged online discussion over the Israeli Defense Forces blog, which has gamified its war on Hamas by offering "badges" and "promotion through the ranks" to those who visit the blog multiple times and share its content on social media. Given Canada's political, educational, and financial connection with the World Bank Institute, and given that Canadians are poised to enter an unprecedented era of digital connectivity and gamification, *Urgent EVOKE* represents an important site through which to explore the gamification of learning gendered militarism in the Canadian landscape.

Fourth, the project evaluation report published on the game reveals that Canadian players were in fact active participants. For example, a Canadian player posted one of the 36 winning "evokations" in the category of "Education and Information Dissemination." Moreover, an *Urgent EVOKE* wiki entitled "Calling All Teachers" drew discussion from teachers internationally, including from Canada. Canadian teachers are potentially drawn to the game as a curriculum module for high school and college courses.

In the subsequent sections of the chapter we provide an overview of the game *Urgent EVOKE* and reveal step by step the way in which the game is invested in finance capital. We explain how the financialization of capitalism is inseparable from the gendered and racialized militarization of everyday life. Within the Canadian landscape *Urgent EVOKE* significantly steps up the learning of gendered militarism via gamification. Finally, we offer our own vision of adult education rooted in feminist praxis that, in the words of Paula Allman (2001/2010), is "critical" and "revolutionary."

Gaming Fictions and Economic Imaginaries

On March 3, 2010, the World Bank Institute announced the launch of the online alternative reality game (ARG) *Urgent EVOKE*, which was described in a press release as "a crash course in changing the world." A massive multiplayer game, it is "designed to empower young people all over the world, but especially in Africa, to solve urgent social problems such as hunger, poverty, disease, conflict, climate change, sustainable energy, lack of health care and education." Extending far beyond edutainment, the intent of the game's developers is to leverage seemingly endless passion and available time for gaming in order to cultivate a globally networked, gamified citizenry that is adept in new social media for producing social innovation in "the real world." Jane McGonigal, gaming guru and project leader, claims that as a planet we spend three billion hours per week playing video games. "Reality is broken," she claims in a recent book of the same title, "and we need to make it more like a game" (McGonigal, 2011). This chilling quotation reveals the egregious alienation from the complexities of the real-world problems that are produced through militarism, and sets up a kind of gaming narrative that flows from the logic of "war games."

McGonigal is the director of Games Research and Development at the Institute for the Future (IFTF), a spin-off from the RAND Corporation. General Henry H. Arnold, US Air Force commander, established RAND in 1948, with financial assistance from the Ford Foundation, as a think tank for the long-term strategic planning of future weapons (http://www.rand.org/). Among its achievements, RAND is credited with some of the early work that laid the foundations for computers, the Internet, artificial intelligence, and the development of war-gaming. The institute came into existence in 1968, again with the assistance of the Ford Foundation. IFTF's website explains that the organization "brings people together to make the future—today" (http://www.iftf.org/what-we-do/). Its arsenal of practical tools includes "collaborative forecasting and serious gaming" and involves activities that are described as follows: "From intimate workshops to global online games, we have a tool kit of frameworks, processes, and platforms to tap the best insights of groups to imagine—and create—the futures they want for their organizations and communities and the world." McGonigal's current project involves creating a globally networked gaming environment to produce real-time "forecasting" data, which ingeniously harnesses the social lives of gamers as unpaid labour for the purpose of capital accumulation based on the lucrative possibilities available through the push for big data within finance capitalism. The mission as outlined on IFTF's website provides an interesting segue to the World Bank Institute and its investment in McGonigal's game to the tune of $622,000 (Gable & Dabla, 2010).

In April 2011 the World Bank Group announced the launch of E-Institute. Led by the World Bank Institute, it is a virtual learning space set up to address the professional development needs of self-motivated learners who, according to the website information, are increasingly constricted in terms of budget and time, which prevents their travel to central locations for "high quality, hands on learning" (https://einstitute.worldbank.org/ei/node/103). The audience targeted by the E-Institute initiative includes the usual stakeholders such as policy-makers and private sectors, but most emphatically "youth." According to information on the E-Institute website, "learning activities can take the form of structured learning via self-paced and virtually facilitated e-Courses, as well as immersive learning experiences using *Second Life* and serious games." *Second Life* is a three-dimensional immersion online gaming environment "where everyone you see is a real person and every place you visit is built by people just like you" (http://secondlife.com/whatis/?lang=en-US).

The project *Urgent EVOKE*, then, was the prelude to a major initiative on the part of the World Bank Institute to develop online mediated opportunities to mobilize social innovation on some of the most serious issues confronting the world at the moment. *Urgent EVOKE*, in fact, served as a spectacular media event, anticipating the E-Institute initiative, complete with a TED Talk, CNN coverage, interviews, articles in e-zines, and a book launch. The event itself, an alternative reality, massive online multiplayer game, complete with an animated trailer (normally used to whip up audience interest in a blockbuster Hollywood movie), is presented as a graphic novel featuring hip young racialized women who were represented as smart, courageous, and forward-thinking African protagonists; it was targeted at youth and with laudable sophistication in making the game attractive to young women. *Urgent EVOKE* ran from March to May 2010, and an evaluation of the game was released on December 13, 2010, called *Project Evaluation: EVOKE*

(Gable & Dabla, 2010). We draw upon the results and the recommendations of this document in our presentation and analysis of the game in the section below.

Gender Games: The Illusion of Equality and the Reality of Violence

EVOKE should be seen as occupying a unique and potentially important niche in the broad array of donor-driven and national programs for development. EVOKE's impact stems primarily from two key factors: the establishment of a diverse, global social network focused on social and economic challenges, and a powerful blend of fiction and reality. (*Project Evaluation: EVOKE*, 2010, p. 7)

In this section we describe the game *Urgent EVOKE* in order to understand the way in which gaming can be a vehicle to learn gendered, market-based militarism. Our presentation will focus on aspects of the game that are particularly relevant to women. We will try to recreate the experience of "the gamer." In the beginning, we are invited into the game via a captivating movie trailer (http://vimeo.com/9094186). Narrated by a central character named Alchemy, the trailer begins "in the heart of Africa," the geographical representation of which is part of the game's corporate logo.

When Alchemy chooses to speak to his secret network, he projects a computerized image of a talking African mask and speaks English with an African accent. Using this image, Alchemy invites us to join him and his secret network in a game that teaches collaboration, creativity, local insight, courage, entrepreneurship, knowledge networks, resourcefulness, spark, sustainability, and vision. He explains that "humanity needs our help" and that we will participate by involving ourselves in the ten missions over ten weeks that comprise the game "EVOKE: A crash course in changing the world." Completing the ten-week course earns a certificate, and the top contenders are invited to a world summit in Washington, DC, to workshop and also meet potential business mentors. In fact, *Urgent EVOKE* is spun as "free job training for the job of inventing the future," thereby folding gaming into futurology, or the active production of economic imaginaries. As the invitation into the game unfolds, graphic images of the "global slump" (McNally, 2011) flash in front of our eyes, thereby creating a sense of moral urgency. According to *Program Evaluation: EVOKE*, "6,618 players completed at least a single mission or quest," "142 players completed all ten missions and quests," and "286,219 visits to EVOKE took place during the run-time of the game" (pp. 13, 16).

The game itself is presented as an online graphic novel illustrated by Jacob Glaser, a well-known name to consumers of graphic novels and animation. The first instalment of the graphic novel begins with a narrative that justifies or normalizes the use of local actors to facilitate opening access to public resources, so that the non-local "network" can move in and secretly "solve" a food-crisis problem. Alchemy reminds the local actor—a head of state—that the network does not officially exist and that it will solve the local problem, but in a way that is "strictly off the books." Alchemy continues the episode by asserting to the head of state, "You'll quietly facilitate local resources and access to public land. **We'll** provide the imagination" (bold in original). With this assertive act· of dispossession and enclosure of public lands, the crash course begins.

The two main protagonists in the first instalment are smart, progressive women who are tactically connected to the secret network as problem-solving heroes. The first is a Black-African professor named Ember who, when we are introduced to her, is giving a lecture on "the social problems caused by the mass migration of 2016." She stops the lecture to answer an urgent communication from Alchemy, who directs her to a crisis in Tokyo involving a food shortage. She leaves immediately, explaining that she will tell her husband she will be late for dinner. The second is an Asian-African woman named Eureka who appears to work as a scientist or engineer in a high-tech lab environment. When she answers her communication from Alchemy, she begins packing some equipment and says that she can leave for Tokyo in one hour. We can see, then, that exquisite attention to narrative detail was invested into making the graphic novel and the crash course enticing to young women. The image of action-oriented women problem-solvers is a gaming narrative consumed by young men and women alike and constructs a particular vision of women as active global citizens. In a later section our analysis shows how the narrative strategy of the game constructs an image of gender empowerment while simultaneously reproducing racialized gender ideologies consistent with patriarchal capitalism.

The game epitomizes the World Bank's obsession with simplicity—that is, reducing complex and contradictory economic, political, and social realities to problem-solving techniques. It also resembles the bank's overall colonial and religious missionary discourse, in particular the evangelical approach to missionary deeds (Hibou, 1998). "EVOKE Powers" include 10 skills and abilities to "tackle the world's toughest problems" (they read as the 10 commandments!): collaboration, courage, creativity, entrepreneurship, local insight, knowledge share, resourcefulness, spark, sustainability, and vision.

With this introduction we would like to skip ahead to a chapter in the graphic novel organized around the theme "Empowering Women." The episode begins with a startling graphic representation in the foreground of Middle Eastern women wearing head scarves, and in the background are frightening images of armed men in army fatigues. We learn that a woman named Sareh has been kidnapped because of her outspoken advocacy for women's rights. The kidnapping was executed by "a stateless group called Al-Hamsa" who are "fringe radicals wanting nothing more than a Taliban-style regime."[2] On some of the images Sareh's name and the word *free* appear in the background, written in the Arabic alphabet, which can be read by speakers of Dari, Pashtu, Kurdish, or Persian, among others using this script. Therefore, the game certainly evokes the logic of women's rescue similar to that used by the Bush administration in the war on Afghanistan and Iraq (Abu-Lughod, 2002; Mojab, 2010). The "mission" is taking place in an Islamic society in which women do not have equal rights. Individual women, young and older generations, in praise of Sareh's daring act of speaking up, address the importance of education and employment for women. Sareh is eventually rescued, which marks the beginning of the actual mission. First, the fact is stated: "Out of 128 economies around the world, only 20 have equal rights for women." Let us note that, in this factual statement, nations, countries, or societies are replaced by "economies." Therefore the mission is to "help empower women: raise your voice in support of equal rights and economic opportunity."

There are three steps in the mission: learn, act, and imagine. The Urgent EVOKE (i.e., a player) starts by first "learning" about women's rights and opportunities worldwide. This learning takes place through a direct link to extensive resources produced by the World Bank such as *Women, Business, and Law* (2010 World Bank Report). Urgent EVOKE (UE) is invited to join WomenWatch: "WomenWatch is a real-time news feed covering women's rights. Created by the United Nations, it can help you track the progress toward gender equality—and discover the obstacles we still face. This week, your mission is to join the WomenWatch: Find a story that inspires you, and create your own follow-up investigation." Alchemy, the mission leader, states (taken from the United Nations Population Fund's statement on empowering women): "Equality between men and women exists when both sexes are able to share equally in the distribution of power and influence; have equal opportunities for financial independence through work or through setting up businesses; enjoy equal access to education and the opportunity to develop personal ambitions." He says that there are three ways to empower women: economic, educational, and political (in this order). The "act" is to "help empower one girl or woman with better access to education or economic opportunity." The following quotation is indicative of the game's text:

Make a small donation that can change another person's life forever. There are 100 ways to support women's equal opportunities and rights via Global Giving. Invite your friends, family, classmates, and neighbors to team up this week. Set aside time to explore the opportunities at Global Giving and pick a social innovation YOU want to help support—and then work together to make a life-changing donation. How much good can you do in a week? If you can raise $30 USD, you can buy 500 bricks to build one classroom wall for a new girl's science lab in Uganda. If you can raise 72 ZAR, you can train two young girls as peer leader-educators in Bangladesh. If you can raise 22 EURO, you can buy feed and vaccine for an entire year for 1 woman's poultry business in Ghana. OR: If you can't make a donation this week, spread the word: Use Facebook and Twitter to inspire your friends beyond the EVOKE network to support women's equal rights and opportunities. Tell them about your favorite Global Giving venture.

Your objective: Work with friends, family, classmates or neighbors to make a contribution to a social venture focused on empowering girls and women. Tell a story about your efforts to donate, or to raise awareness, in a blog post, video, or photo essay.

The third segment requires UE to "imagine" a future. Players are asked to "picture how all these changes might come together and tell us about a future where the girls and women you supported in 2010 are significantly more empowered than they are today. What is it like, and how did it come to pass?" "Bonus Resources" are provided to assist the UE to "imagine how different life might be for girls and women in the future." The link presented takes the UE to the page of "Women's Rights" on the site of "Global Issues: Social, Political, Economic and Environmental Issues That Affect Us All." At the time that this chapter was written, the page had been last updated on March 2010. It contained a wide range of issues from work, discrimination, and poverty to reproductive rights, population, children, militarization, violence, Beijing +5 and Beijing +15, media, and climate change. Another bonus resource is the link to the "Women's Rights" page of Freedom House. Freedom House is a US-based non-governmental organization that was established in 1941 to defy the spread of communism. It endorsed the Marshall Plan and the establishment of the North Atlantic Treaty Organization. Today Freedom House, as stated on its website, "is a strong voice for a US foreign policy that places the promotion of democracy as a priority" (http://www.freedom-house.org/content/our-history#.UuxuTPtjOfM).

What we have mapped out about the "Empowering Women" episode only scratches the surface of the materials available for further in-depth reading of each page. The commentaries and discussions among the Urgent EVOKEs and the 11 "game runners" provide excellent materials for analysis. "Game runners' responsibilities included assigning points and providing feedback to the players' game inputs, answering questions about the game, encouraging players, facilitating players interactions and game inputs, creating active discussion, and keeping the game moving forward smoothly" (*Program Evaluation: EVOKE*, 2010, p. 10). But what should we do with this knowledge? What is the World Bank problematique in addressing gender equality?

The Game of Accumulation and Imperialism

> One effect of EVOKE's fiction/reality intermarriage was to blur the boundary between current real-world development activities and the fictional mission-assignments.... In practice, EVOKE's fictional/imaginative elements freed younger or less experienced players from the "burden" of feasibility stemming from policies and protocols, donor agencies, national governments and other sources—and from the sheer difficulty of success. (*Program Evaluation: EVOKE*, 2010, p. 37)

In this section we present some of the complex connections between the emerging interest in serious gaming as shown earlier, and the new face of imperialism as structured through the militarized relations of financialized capitalism. Focusing on women for a moment, these gaming initiatives capture the social lives of youth who are immersed in gaming narratives that organize the gendered and racialized relations necessary to reproduce financialized accumulation regimes. Alternative reality games such as *Urgent EVOKE* are played in real-life spaces, but the gaming activities of these real-life spaces are coordinated through the

social interventions offered by globalized online collaboratives, productive of a real-time flow of doings within the gamer's own life space and
its actualities. The narratives structuring these collaboratives in terms
of particular problems (i.e., crises) that invite social innovation originate
in the World Bank's predatory gesture to create entrepreneurial opportunities from real-world crises generated by militarized capitalism in the
first place—crises whose violences have an uneven impact on racialized
and indigenous women (Smith, 2005). These crises supply the chapter-by-
chapter storylines in Urgent EVOKE's online graphic novel. For example,
the chapters, from first to last, focus on food security, power (energy
crises), water crisis, the future of money, empowering women, urban
resilience, indigenous knowledge, and crisis networking. Successful
innovations are those that solve a problem and create opportunities
for financial investment, earning the gamers points and opportunities
to connect with investors and business mentors. These investors and
business mentors, primarily located within the geographic epicentre
controlling the flow of financialized capital, are poised to scoop innovations that they could never have developed themselves because they
lack the local knowledge and the situated experiences of the gamers.
No wonder the World Bank is fascinated by the possibilities of serious
gaming.

A big question in all of this is, in what ways does playing Urgent
EVOKE foster the learning of gendered militarism in the Canadian
context? In order to answer this question it is necessary to understand
the links between the financialization of neoliberal capitalism and the
new face of imperialism through the global militarization of everyday
life. One can define financialization as the emergent dominance of
money capitalism, as distinct from commercial and industrial capitalism (although these are all intricately connected), in the world economic
system. The topic can be as complex as it sounds, but the kernel of it is
that the bulk of capital accumulation today occurs through what Marx
referred to as "the money circuits" (Marx, 1978/1992, pp. 110–144), which
include interest-bearing capital (e.g., accumulating through predatory

debt) and rent (e.g., accumulating through land dispossession and speculative real estate), all of which are pulled into the orbits of stock market
dynamics as well as unregulated trading venues (e.g., the shadow bank-
ing sector) that offer speculative investment opportunities: the so-called
casino economy (McNally, 2011). That is, it can be more lucrative to invest
money in the money circuit, for example taking out a loan at 1 per cent
interest and investing it in a credit market that garners 20 per cent interest, than to invest in building more factories (Harvey, 2003, 2010).

There are two features of finance capital that are important to understand in relation to the new face of imperialism. First, as capital
accumulation became increasingly financialized, the historical tendency for this accumulation process to become concentrated into fewer and
fewer hands began to unfold (Bellamy Foster, 2007, 2010). The battle cry
of "Occupy" was that the movement represented the voices of the 99 per
cent who were increasingly in debt servitude, dispossessed of housing,
and either unemployed or working multiple low-wage, temporary jobs
as migrant or nomadic workers, in contrast to the 1 per cent who owned
all the wealth. In fact, the picture is more complex than the social-
movement narrative suggests. As neoliberal policy and the financialization process worked together, we saw evidence of a significant public
disinvestment in the social welfare state and civic infrastructure, and a
significant *investment* in a militarized carceral state on the one hand and
nationally organized homeland security on the other. The militarization
of everyday life offers considerable opportunities for private investment
to speculate on the successive enclosure and commodification of what
constitutes "the safe life" or "the secure life." That is, the response of
the ruling elite, primarily the financial class, has been to speculate on
security or risk management or, in other words, to find ways to make
money by parasitically feeding off a global slump that is proliferating
"unsafe spaces" in which to live. Gamers in the Canadian context, then,
are being schooled in a particular imperializing narrative of economic
democracy that obscures the very real dangers that financial capitalism poses, and creates an easier pathway for the capitalist nation-state

to pursue deleterious policies that offer nationalist support to a global accumulation process.

The second feature, flowing from the last point, is that as wealth accumulation becomes so concentrated, forming monopolies and oligopolies, it becomes necessary to use militarized imperial force as a means by which to protect the class interests of the ruling elite. Ellen Meiksins Wood's writings in *Empire* (2003) provide a comprehensive historical account of this process, culminating in what she (and others) describes as the political economy of permanent war. Wood's argument is that the intensification of global monopoly finance is dependent on a hierarchically arranged, globally networked system of nation-states controlled from an imperial epicentre over which, in this historical moment, the United States has consolidated considerable power via the internationally configured "weapons-dollar / petro-dollar" accumulation regime. Nation-states stay in line by investing heavily in their own regimes, including nationally organized military as well as militarized citizenry environments through policing, surveillance, criminalization of the racialized poor, and carceral facilities (see Taber, Chapter 4 of this volume, for a discussion of how Canadian citizenship is taught through a masculinist, militarist lens). The political economy of permanent war entails a war on the "the poor world" (Bhattacharyya, 2005) and is achieved through continually innovating technologies of containment and control. The militarization of everyday life succeeds in conflating most spheres with military strategy, including health, education, and environmental and social crises (Cooper, 2008). Hence, the militarization of everyday life is inextricably woven into the financialization of everyday life and the speculative opportunities to accumulate capital through the militarized containment of crises, militarized aid, and militarized development (Magnusson, 2013a, 2013b).

The historical evolution from RAND Corporation's war games to IFTF's focus on gaming to the World Bank's new investment in serious gaming reveals the hidden imperial relations that are organizing the bank's agenda to "gamify life" and social innovation as a means to produce the speculative opportunities presented by crises in food, water, global conflict, energy, health, environment, climate, urban decay, erasure of indigenous knowledges, and by the reproductive crises that result from the mass disruption of family, thereby threatening the role of women in community life. The integration of war games into futurology accomplished by the RAND Corporation succeeds in reproducing an economic imaginary, or futures, that consolidates the imperial power of the financialized weapons-dollar regime. The IFTF has successfully folded gaming into a new iteration of futurology, namely militarized financialization, thereby reproducing a new configuration of the weapons-dollar regime grounded in monopoly finance capital. By extending the integration of gaming and futurology to the activities of the World Bank, with its role in international finance and militarized development, the consolidation and reproduction process continues. The popularity of the movie *The Hunger Games* may in fact express the deep resonance that occurs when recognition, fear, and diminishing hope converge as a profound sympathetic response to being immersed in a world of war games that eliminates the distinction between gaming fiction and warring.

In the world of war games women occupy a special, central role. First, they are most affected by the violences of patriarchal militarized economies. This impact is evidenced in terms of the way women are economically and politically positioned within waged labour and, in addition, experience exploitation by producing goods and services for free (i.e., super-exploitation that forces women to simultaneously perform waged and unwaged labour). Second, women's forced participation in migrant labour via violent dispossession (through the production of wars, social crises, environmental crises, and outright land theft) represents the new colony of surplus labour for the financialized economy. Gendered migrant labour is specifically targeted for surveillance, containment, and criminalization within the current economic landscape and represents emergent contours of gendered and racialized imperialism and militarism. Moreover, disinvestment in the social welfare state frees up state resources that are then used to subsidize monopoly capital, but this redirection increasingly requires super-exploitation and imperialism as a permanent structural feature of financialization. All of this is to say that monopoly finance capital can only thrive as an accumulation regime to the extent that violence and exploitation of women intensifies on a global scale. Thus, the *appearance* of equality and democracy constructed through *Urgent EVOKE*'s episode on empowering women contrasts sharply against the *essence* of creating the condition of militarized insecurity, subjugation, and violence.

Learning Gendered Militarism

Historically, the World Bank's development projects aimed at empowering women have systematically attempted to put what is viewed as an underutilized resource—women's labour—to the service of global accumulation regimes (see Hanson, Chapter 7 in this volume, for an exploration of gender equality and inequality training). Most critics are quick to point out that the World Bank in this regard is propagating super-exploitation as described earlier. Super-exploitation necessitates imperialism as illustrated in many ways, but one case in point is the severe regulation of sexuality required of heteronormative patriarchy that has historically accompanied (colonial) capitalist nation-building projects; homosexuality has historically been criminalized, LGBTQ people are terrorized, and so on (see Mizzi, Chapter 6 this volume, for a discussion of LGBTQ issues with respect to international conflict training). Even briefly experiencing a life outside the strict parameters of heteronormative patriarchy leads to vicious attacks upon young women, including sanctioned "corrective" rape, imprisonment, and murder. This, then, is not empowerment; it is a contradiction. The ideology of economic freedom is contradicted by the actualities of super-exploitation, and the ideology of social freedom is contradicted by the actualities of the violence perpetuated on the women who step outside of normativity to create autonomous lives, including the sanctioned rape we see in many global contexts such as India (Puri, 2004), South Africa (Nel & Judge, 2008), and the Canadian military (e.g., WIN, 1999, p. 48). The ideology of social freedom is also empirically contradicted by the dramatic increases in women's carceration rates under monopoly finance capital (Sudbury, 2005), and by the exponential increases in the numbers of women who are forced to become migrant labourers and are ultimately criminalized and contained. These are the actualities of women's lives under capitalist relations of imperialism emergent within the logic of monopoly finance capital (Mojab, 2012).

The carceral state, in terms of waging a war against the domestic or the migrant poor, requires gendered militarism. *Urgent EVOKE* is not simply a game; it is a war game sponsored by the World Bank Institute that builds upon the historical experiences of RAND's war-gaming and encourages the learning of not just everyday militarism but the gendered and racialized everday militarism that is required to reproduce an economic imaginary characterized by monopoly finance (see Saul, Chapter 10 of this volume, for an examination of the intersection of sports, war, and schooling). From this perspective, the focus on empowering Middle Eastern women is not merely arrogantly hypocritical but actively feeds into powerful social and cultural narratives constructed by imperialist nations to legitimize the weapons- and petro-dollar financialized accumulation regime.

Where to Go?

We started this chapter with a powerful dialectical metaphor of essence and appearance to map out the visible relations embedded in the World Bank Institute's *Urgent EVOKE* game. This dialectical conceptualization enabled us to go deeper and wider to expose the invisible patriarchal, colonialist, and imperialist relations in the game. The game is presented to us as an objective, scientific, alternative learning space about equality, freedom, or democracy. Our contention is that, both in its mode of presentation and in its content, it is a learning experience that dehistoricizes colonization, capitalism, patriarchy, and imperialism. It also delinks the women's global cry for equality and freedom from patriarchal capitalism and instead presents these categories in dualistic or binary constructions of East or West, freedom or tyranny. Bannerji calls this construction "ideological knowledge production": knowledge production that creates dehistoricized myths of progress or democracy and an ideological construction to obstruct the possibilities of knowing in a socio-historical way (Bannerji, 2011).

From the point of view of capital, women who organize their activities in terms of what benefits them and their families and communities are "underdeveloped" and constructed as backward at best (e.g., think of racist characterizations of indigenous women) or as criminals at worst (e.g., "squatters," "dead beats"). Recently Dorothy Smith (2012) called for a new wave to the women's movement that begins precisely with organizing lives according to the everyday actualities of the benefits to women and their communities. The futurology narratives of *Urgent EVOKE* construct a monologic economic imaginary that is dependent on gendered militarism and super-exploitation; however, a feminist revolutionary narrative begins with the actualities of women's lives and considers, "what is best for us and our communities?" We need feminist adult-learning projects that feed the social and political processes connecting the actualities of what is beneficial to us to community livelihoods that promote relational existences that are mutually nourishing rather than hierarchical, destructive, and exploitive. We are calling for a revolutionary feminist pedagogy that is sufficiently radical to take apart even its own hierarchies and ruling structures. A Marxist feminist project along these lines may consider the ways to disengage from alienated economic imaginaries (exchange value) and to organize our lives along the lines of what is useful and satisfactory to us (use value). What would these pedagogies look like?

If we consider gaming as a potential site to encourage youth activism, perhaps a starting place in thinking through revolutionary possibilities might be Bakthin's *Dialogical Imagination* as read and interpreted by Dorothy Smith (1999). For Bakhtin, the novel represented the most fertile literary genre in that it provided access to and interaction with a hybrity of life genres and their cultural expressions. In contrast, *Urgent EVOKE* is not dissimilar to Bakhtin's description of "epics," wherein each game instalment appears as an "open-ended" game but is in actuality "utterly closed," and each player's performance is but an "epic," reproducing absolute, valorized, and hierarchized categories of what is good (collaboration, courage, entrepreneurship, etc.) that are distanced temporally and spatially from gamers' actual lives. Mojab and Carpenter (2012) have named this kind of learning that occurs through "distanced" or "alienated" frames, "learning by dispossession" because the learning that occurs dispossesses the learner of her or his own personal experiences and lived actualities in order to construct an economic imaginary that in fact leads to material dispossession. The World Bank Institute is using a gaming pedagogical genre constructed through narrative strategies of the "epic" in order to achieve "learning by dispossession."

> The epic world is constructed in the zone of an absolute distanced image, beyond the sphere of possible contact with the developing, incomplete and therefore re-thinking and re-evaluating present. (Bakhtin, 1981, p. 17)

Ironically, the futurology project inherent in this game is rooted in an absolute and closed past characterizing capitalist modernity and its epic narratives. There is no contact with the re-thinking and re-evaluating "present" in terms of the lived actualities of women's lives. Just as the novel for Bakhtin represented the literary form wherein authors could speak from any of a multiplicity of speech or action genres, to talk back to the distantly constructed past and re-evaluate and re-invent the present, are there similar pedagogical genres that disintegrate the absolute epic past into a re-thinking of present actualities and future possibilities for women?

> From the very beginning the novel was structured not in the distanced image of the absolute past but in the zone of direct contact with inconclusive present-day reality. At its core lay personal experience and free creative imagination. (Bakhtin, 1981, p. 39)

This brings us back to the actualities of our lives, and the possibility of pedagogical genres that allow us to re-evaluate and talk back to the epic narratives of the past in the context of an incomplete and open-ended present. Sites of adult learning grounded in a multiplicity of social movements are perhaps uniquely positioned to introduce such revolutionary feminist pedagogies that are connected to women's movements originating in the diverse particularities of women's experiences but organized around patriarchal capitalism as an anti-imperialist, anti-colonial project. As Bannerji suggested in an interview, "you can use the category 'woman' and then you can talk about the specificity of the lives and the experiences of different women in social relations. There can surely be a women's movement organized around patriarchy in which we mutually become aware of race and class" (interview with Erin Gray, Tom Keefer, and John Viola, 2005). The multiplicity of women's social movements arising out of the particularities of women's lives can read like a novel or, taken together, serve as pedagogical genres that allow us to take up patriarchy from very different historical circumstances, speak back to the past, and re-invent the present in ways that are meaningful to us. Thinking through the multiplicity of women's experience and reading the experience in a particular historical formation, such as capitalism, pushes us to sharpen our feminist, anti-racist, and anti-capitalist praxis. Concurring with Paula Allman (2007), we argue that "human praxis has the potential to exist in two very different and opposed forms" (Allman, p. 34). One form, Allman argues, is "uncritical" and "reproductive," which "supports and facilitates the necessary developments and as a consequence the reproduction of capitalist social relations as well as the given conditions of humanity's existence." The other form is "critical" and "revolutionary" praxis that "requires the simultaneous and complementary transformation of both self and society." We acknowledge, as did Allman, that this is not an easy process, and neither form—revolutionary or reproductive praxis—can be imposed on people. Thus, it is our responsibility as feminist, anti-racist, and anti-capitalist educators to introduce learners, with care and clarity, to the options available to them to imagine and build a better world for themselves and humanity.

NOTES

1. While writing this chapter, we became aware of another, excellent analysis of this game by David Waddington (2013), who unpacks the irony of the World Bank's investing in a game that turns impending world crises into money-making opportunities. Our chapter rounds out this analysis by providing a feminist, anti-racist understanding of the imperialist relations that organize the World Bank Institute's investment in online learning and gaming.

2. *Al-Hamsa* is a coined word, intended to remind one of Hamas, the Palestinian Islamic organization that has been governing the Gaza Strip since 2007 and which the United States considers a terrorist group.

REFERENCES

Abu-Lughod, L. (2002). Do Muslim women really need saving? Anthropological reflection in cultural relativism and its others. *American Anthropologist, 104*(3), 73-90.

Allman, P. (2001/2010). *Critical education against global capitalism: Karl Marx and revolutionary critical education.* Westport, CT: Bergin & Garvey.

Allman, P. (2007). *On Marx: An introduction to the revolutionary intellect of Karl Marx.* Rotterdam, Netherlands: Sense Publishers.

Bakhtin, M. (1981). *The dialogic imagination: Four essays.* Austin: University of Texas Press.

Bannerji, H. (2011). *Demography and democracy: Essays on nationalism, gender, and ideology.* Toronto: Canadian Scholars' Press.

Bellamy Foster, J. (2007). The financialization of capitalism. *Monthly Review, 58*(11). Accessed online.

Bellamy Foster, J. (2010). The financialization of accumulation. *Monthly Review, 62*(5). Accessed online.

Bhattacharyya, G. (2005). *Traffick: The illicit movement of people and things.* London: Pluto.

Cooper, M. (2008). *Life as surplus: Biotechnology and capitalism in the neoliberal era.* Seattle: University of Washington Press.

Entertainment Software Assocation of Canada. (2013). Essential facts about the Canadian videogaming industry. http://theesa.ca/wp-content/uploads/2013/10/Essential-Facts-English.pdf

Gable, E., & Dabla, A. (2010). *Project evaluation: EVOKE*. http://siteresources.worldbank.org/ EDUCATION/Resources/ProjectEVOKE-evaluation-final-16oct11.pdf

Gray, E., Keefer, T., & Viola, J. (2005). Singing in dark times: The politics of race and class; An interview with Himani Bannerji. *Upping the Anti, 2*. http://uppingtheanti.org

Harvey, D. (2003). *The new imperialism*. Oxford: Oxford University Press.

Harvey, D. (2010). *The enigma of capital*. London: Profile Books.

Hibou, B. (1998). *Économie politique du discours de la Banque mondiale en Afrique sub-saharienne: Du catéchisme économique au fait (et méfait) missionaire*. Texte préparé pour le Joint Committee on African Studies of the Social Science Research Council, Centre d'études et de recherches internationales, Fondation nationale des sciences politiques. http://www.sciencespo.fr/ceri/sites/sciencespo.fr.ceri/files/etude39.pdf

Magnusson, J. (2013a). Biosurveillance as a terrain of innovation in an era of monopoly finance capital. *Policy Futures in Education, 11*(6), 745-754.

Magnusson, J. (2013b). Precarious learning and labour in financialized times. *Brock Education: A Journal of Educational Research and Practice, 22*(2), 69-83.

Marx, K. (1978/1992). *Capital: A critique of political economy, Volume II* (David Fernbach, Trans.). London: Penguin Books in association with *New Left Review*.

McGonigal, J. (2011). *Reality is broken: Why games make us better and how they can change the world*. New York: Penguin Books.

McNally, D. (2011). *Global slump: The economics and politics of crisis and resistance*. Oakland, CA: PM Press.

Meiksins Wood, E. (2003). *Empire of capital*. London: Verso.

Mojab, S. (Ed.). (2010). *Women, war, violence, and learning*. London: Routledge.

Mojab, S. (2012). Education and/in imperialism. In S. Carpenter & S. Mojab (Eds.), *Educating from Marx: Race, gender, and learning* (pp. 167-190). New York: Palgrave.

Mojab, S., & Carpenter, S. (2011). Learning by dispossession: Democracy promotion and civic engagement in Iraq and United States. *International Journal of Lifelong Learning, 30*(4), 549-563.

Nel, J.A., & Judge, M. (2008). Exploring homophobic victimization in Gauteng, South Africa: Issues, impacts, and responses. *Acta Criminologica, 21*(3). http://www.unisa.ac.za/contents/faculties/humanities/psy/docs/doc5%20neljudge.pdf

Puri, J. (2004). *Women, body, desire in post-colonial India: Narratives of gender and sexuality*, London: Routledge.

Rogers Communications. (2012a). Rogers innovation report: Technology and relationships. http://redboard.rogers.com

Rogers Communications. (2012b). Rogers innovation report: Youth, parents, and technology." http://slidesha.re/NiMl42

Smith, A. (2005). *Conquest: Sexual violence and American Indian genocide.* Boston: South End Press.

Smith, D. (1999). *Writing the social: Critique, theory, and investigations.* Toronto: University of Toronto Press.

Smith, D. (2012, October). The politics and practice of feminist research. Invited lecture for the Centre for the Study of Women and Education, OISE, University of Toronto.

Statistics Canada. (2010). *General social survey: Time use.* http://www.statcan.gc.ca

Statistics Canada. (2013). Canadian Internet, Internet use, by age group, Internet activity, sex, level of education and household income (CANSIM table 358-0153). *Canadian Internet Use Survey.* http://bit.ly/1dhrrew

Sudbury, J. (2005). *Global lockdown: Race, gender, and the prison-industrial complex.* New York and London: Routledge.

Waddington, D.I. (2013). A parallel for the World Bank: A case study of *Urgent EVOKE*: An educational alternative reality game. *International Journal of Technologies in Higher Education, 10*(3), 42-56.

WIN. (1999). Canada: Rape cases shake up the army. *WIN News,* Winter, 42. *Academic OneFile.* Retrieved on March 19, 2014, from http://go.galegroup.com

2 ✖ ✖ ✖ ✚ ✖

MILITARIZING OR
ANTI-MILITARIZING FACEBOOK

Resisting and Reproducing Gendered
Militarism Online

Laura Lane

EMERGENCES OF DIGITAL communicative technology and social
network sites have changed the way people learn as knowledge rapidly
and extensively reaches populations (Apple, 2006; Boon & Sinclair, 2009;
Van Doorn, 2010). Social network sites such as Facebook support Internet
user knowledge production and dissemination by offering a platform for
engagement with peers (Boyd & Ellison, 2007). Depending on the ways
in which these spaces are used, social network sites such as Facebook
thus stand to offer sites for liberatory knowledge production but may
also further reproduce broader social norms. These social norms include
gender and militarism.

As society encourages differential socialization of males and females,
heteronormative gender roles that reproduce gender inequalities are
reinforced (J. Butler, 1999; Myers & Raymond, 2010; Paechter, 2003). These
gender inequalities generally position men as protectors and women as

caregivers, further supporting roles and representations necessary to maintain militarism (Enloe, 2007; Cockburn, 2013). Militarism is not isolated to uniformed officers and direct military involvement; it pervades civilian life in subtle and non-threatening ways that make it difficult to "uproot" (Enloe, 2000, p. 3). With rapid globalization through communication technology, militaristic attitudes and contingent masculinities and femininities become represented on Facebook. Importantly, users are not just passively influenced by social norms; they can actively construct or reconstruct cultural contexts and gendered social realities through participation online (Greenhow & Robelia, 2009; Sassen, 2002). Facebook thus has the potential to "enable the emergence of new cultures of interaction between cyberspace and the larger social order" (Sassen, 2002, p. 377) as users may have new opportunities to contribute to and challenge knowledge and information.

The increasing popularity of Facebook signals a need to critically analyze the representation of gender and militarism in new media and social contexts. In this chapter I discuss the learning and resisting of gender and militarism through Facebook. First, I discuss social networking sites as a digital adult-education space. I then outline current literature that discusses the ways gender and militarism are reproduced and challenged in digital contexts. I then analyze contrasting examples of gender and militarism in the Facebook pages of the Canadian Army and the Women's International League for Peace and Freedom (WILPF). I conclude by discussing complexities of transformative digital engagement.

Digital Contexts and Adult Education

Adult education has been framed as a social movement focusing on collective adult learning for social change (Nesbit, 2013). Concerns over adult education as a social movement in Canada arise as adult learning is increasingly institutionalized through various community programs and new academic disciplines (Field, 2013; Selman & Selman, 2009). Furthermore, shifts towards digital contexts for learning risk maintaining individualism and limiting social action (Field, 2013; Nesbit, 2013).

Despite scepticism of the future directions for adult education in Canada, it is important to caution against deterministic attitudes towards technology because digital critics must consider the technology as well as the constructors of digital spaces (Jack, 2009; Kutz-Flamenbaum, 2012). Importantly, digital contexts facilitate alternative and self-directed or social learning, which can support critical contexts for adult education. Within social network sites, such as Facebook, users learn to interact with others, derive meaning of their own and other users' interactions, and construct their self-representation. In relying on peer interaction for digital engagement, social network sites support the community building and collaborative engagement (Peppler & Solomou, 2011) necessary for adult-education contexts that support critical dialogue and political action. Unfortunately, users often rely on these sites for communicative rather than political purposes (Boyd, 2008), thus missing opportunities for social movement engagement (Greenhow, 2010).

Notably, Taber (2013) critiques the learning of gender through militarism, detailing the military as a site for adult learning. She argues that, through participation in militaristic environments, both uniformed and civilian people learn gender representations relative to militarized experiences. Connecting Taber's (2013) Canadian analysis of adult learning through the military with social networking sites for adult education, I argue that Facebook can extend the learning of gender and militarism. With increased access to information through technology, users of Facebook may become saturated with information and representations of ideal women, men, civilians, and soldiers. Furthermore, users of these spaces build upon ideal representations by engaging in discourses that are often supportive and sometimes disruptive of these norms. Facebook as a space for adult education may therefore support both reproductive and transformative discourses related to militarism and gender.

Militarism and Gender: Resistance and Regulation Online

Sex and gender have been socially constructed as a regulatory system (J. Butler, 1993, 1999) and a "significant dimension of power" (Cockburn, 2010, p. 145). Judith Butler (1999) argues that non-adherence to normative definitions and representations of gender are more inclusive than binary systems, yet society continues to maintain heteronormative gender binaries through "the heterosexual matrix." In connecting sex and gender with compulsory heterosexuality, "the naturalization of both heterosexuality and masculine sexual agency are discursive constructions nowhere accounted for but everywhere assumed" (J. Butler, 1999, p. 58). Gender and sexuality are thus invisibly embedded in society through structures such as language, science, knowledge, history, biology, social codes, and performance, where they are left unquestioned and unchallenged.

Gender naturalization is further reinforced through militaristic environments in which normative gender roles and discourses are necessary to support war-related objectives and national defence (Enloe, 2000). Importantly, even "the category of sex belongs to a system of compulsory heterosexuality that clearly operates through a system of compulsory sexual reproduction" (J. Butler, 1999, p. 150). As such, language and symbolic representation shapes the ways that gender is understood (J. Butler, 1999; Howard & Prividera, 2008). Gender discourses are further emphasized in war and militaristic contexts where men are associated with being strong soldiers who protect weak, nurturing women (Howard & Prividera, 2008; Segal, 2008). Sex and gender are connected with militarism and war through their mutual adherence to patriarchal values and phallocentric discourse (Cockburn, 2010; Howard & Privdera, 2008).

Discourse implicates enactments of gender because "'sex' not only functions as a norm, but is part of a regulatory practice that produces the bodies it governs" (J. Butler, 1993, p. 1). Militarism requires that heteronormativity and gender inequalities are normative and contingent on gender (J. Butler, 1999; Enloe, 2007; Myers & Raymond, 2010; Paechter,

2003). For example, in order for men to be maintained in combat roles, they must be perceived as stronger and more violent than women. Women thus are constructed as the weak and protected. Furthermore, these gender roles play out through the ways of dealing with conflict and through the policies that are implemented because "many decisions have not only gendered *consequences* but gendered *causes*—that is, causes flowing from presumptions or fears about femininity or masculinity" (Enloe, 2007, p. 17, italics in original). Additionally, those in positions of power converge upon many axes of privilege including race, gender, ability, and class, maintaining such positions through political allegiance and military support (Enloe, 2000). Militarist values thus become contingent upon the ways in which these listed qualities are valued and represented.

In addition to the ways in which militarism supports heteronormative gender representation, gender also influences engagement within physical and social spaces (Cranny-Francis, Waring, Stavropoulos, & Kirkby, 2003) with direct implications for militarism. The same gender binaries that support women as weak and nurturing further influence the coding of space as women are often associated with domestic or private spaces and are excluded from political or public spaces (Cranny-Francis et al., 2003). This is also the case for digital spaces that support off-line gender divides between domestic and public spheres (Bowen, 2009; Herbst, 2009; Jack, 2009). These divides have consequences for political engagement online and off-line because "young women are under-represented in many conventional forms of political practice and often use new technologies in under-valued ways" (Harris, 2008, p. 481), with their use being "perceived as frivolous or problematic because of their association with youth and femininity" (p. 488).

Dominant views of masculinity and femininity uphold patriarchal social systems in which men largely make public decisions, and women are often silenced. In devaluing women's public political engagement, men can operate in influential political roles. These political roles often call for militaristic masculinities that further maintain patriarchal systems (Enloe, 2008). Undervaluing women's informal political engagement online supports "contained empowerment" (Newsom & Lengel, 2004), where transformative and critical conversation online does not support wider social transformation beyond the conversations within the site. Additionally, this engagement is subject to surveillance where conversations can be viewed, challenged, or discouraged by other users. Furthermore, such conversations are subject to the policy of the particular social networking site, such as Facebook where comments can be removed for being too disruptive, and pornographic or violent content can be regulated.

Any regression from the rules of the website may put the poster in the position of being denied access. For example, Facebook banned images of a breastfeeding woman under policies that prohibited pornographic content (Hern, 2013). Similarly, Facebook administrators banned a mother's access to the site after she had posted a photograph of her newborn son who had a physical defect (Dillon, 2014). These images were considered to have violated the policy prohibiting violent images (Dillon, 2014). These instances of upholding policy encourage women to align their self-representation with dominant values of acceptable body representation.

Beyond gender expectations for engagement, digital spaces are also male-dominated at structural levels of coding and website development (Herbst, 2009). The language of the Internet is a series of complex codes that are used to create web pages, often by men (Herbst, 2009). These web pages, such as Friendster and Facebook, are also regulated according to their male web-page creators (Herbst, 2009). As such, "the maintenance of virtual spaces—thus the question of access, or the censuring of speech—is subject to a male perspective of behavioral norms" (Herbst, 2009, p. 146).

While men dominate digital infrastructure through proficiency in coding, they also dominate the blogosphere, with their blogs being more frequently viewed and highly rated than those of female bloggers (Jack, 2009). For women, blogging is often associated with domestic work as it can be done from the home with domestic-focused blogs, which are often undermined in comparison to male-written political blogs (Daniels, 2012). In perhaps a worrisome response to male privileging in digital spaces, women have resorted to taking on either gender-neutral or masculine names when discussing politically charged issues (Herbst, 2009). While women use these names as a means to be taken seriously in political debates and to avoid online harassment, their doing so reiterates the strength of patriarchal hierarchies online (see Haddow, Chapter 3 of this volume, for a concomitant discussion of the ways that women's participation is constrained with respect to online gaming). Identity construction and corresponding engagement online are thus policed by peer-user responses that reflect and uphold wider social values of gender.

Technology is connected to a knowledge society because, "in order for women to benefit equally from the possibilities of the knowledge society, they need to participate in it actively from a position of independence, choice, capabilities, and action" (Hafkin & Huyer, 2006, p. 1). Accordingly, agency must be promoted so that women can become active constructors and disseminators of knowledge within technological spaces (Hafkin & Huyer, 2006). In order to support women's voices and develop a feminist presence, women are also developing collaborative online communities to challenge patriarchy and to advocate for peace. An example of a women's peace movement is the Machosom Watch program (Kutz-Flamenbaum, 2012) that monitors border-crossing practices on the Israeli-Palestine border. In this program a group of women dedicate their time to observing the practices and communicating them online in an effort to uphold safe crossing for women.

Challenging online patriarchal hierarchies, some women contribute to political discussions and advance their understanding of political issues. Harell (2009) argues that Canadian women have increased their political participation with support from informal social networks such as conversations between peers or volunteering. Challenging suggestions of contained empowerment and frivolousness, these informal social networks may support increased interest in politics while also offering resources for women to learn about politics (Harell, 2009). Despite the barriers to traditional forms of political engagement, such as "gender gaps in resources, networks and engagement" (Harell, 2009, pp. 4-5), women seem to be bridging gender gaps through digital forms of political participation. As Giroux (2011) argues, "the new media—embodied, for example, by the blogosphere—has enormous potential for enhancing public discourse by making power visible, articulating dissenting views, and bringing strangers and communities together" (p. 24). Social networking sites may thus support democratic dialogue promoted through peer interaction (Burwell, 2010) and subversive identity performance (J. Butler, 1999) through self-representation on social networking sites, thus challenging the very militaristic gender norms that the dialogue may also serve to reproduce.

Contrasting Examples of Gender and Militarism or Anti-Militarism on Facebook

To discuss contrasting representations of war and gender on Facebook, I compare the Facebook pages of the Canadian Army and the Women's International League for Peace and Freedom. These two pages exemplify the ways in which Facebook can simultaneously reproduce and disrupt gendered militarism. Both sites are clear in their standpoints relative to war, use Facebook as a platform to convey information, and support user dialogue. Specifically, the Canadian Army page is used to reproduce and reinforce discourses of masculinity and femininity through predominant representations of men as strong protectors and women as caregivers and homemakers. Alternately, WILPF seeks to be transformative in representing women's experiences as central to war and peace, with notably absent representations of normative gender representations. Both men and women are represented as engaged in dialogue to promote peace.

Reproducing Militarism

Facebook increases the visibility of individuals by exposing private aspects of individuals' lives, such as personal relationships, life events, and daily routines and practices. With information being widely distributed and accessible, users can be monitored and influenced by wider corporate and political systems such as the Canadian military. Along with an increase in social surveillance, the Internet can be seen as having been "hijacked by corporate interests" (Giroux, 2011, p. 26) as users are exposed to propaganda through multimedia texts and user dialogue. Furthermore, Facebook reproduces heteronormative gender representations in alignment with dominant notions of masculinity and femininity. These dominant notions are emphasized in representations of war where, in militaristic climates, "media, via gendered narratives, support the military's hegemonic structure" (Howard & Prividera, 2008, p. 288).

The Government of Canada (Canada, 2014) recognizes that women in the Canadian military "have been fully integrated in all occupations and roles for over 20 years" (para. 3). Women constitute 12.4 per cent of the Canadian Army (Canada, 2014), and some do engage in combat missions. Despite women's participation in these missions, discourses on Facebook represent the continued prevalence of men in combat and women in domestic roles.

Connections between Facebook, gender, and militarism further emphasize the military's "full-scale occupation of the entertainment industry" (Turse, 2008, p. 116). Canadian involvement in the entertainment industry ranges from the non-theatrical film propaganda of Canadian military expeditions (Lester, 2013), to the funding of films that positively portray soldiers (Turse, 2008), to the development of Department of National Defence videos for YouTube (RCAFIMAGERY, 2014). Video games such as *Call of Duty* promote the military for civilian users and train members of the Canadian National Defence (Brewster, 2013). This extensive military reach now includes Facebook "invad[ing] new media territory" (Turse, 2008, p. 170) for recruitment and support. Not only are violence and allegiance to militaristic values promoted in these media sites, but also these values are promoted by the representation of women as sexualized and men as brutish. These representations support men in violent roles as the fighters and protectors, while women are positioned as protected or prostituted in war contexts (Enloe, 2007).

The Canadian military has a strong presence on Facebook with a page for the Canadian Army Reserve (Canadian Army, 2014), community pages for members of Canadian Armed Forces (Canadian Armed Forces, 2014), and media pages for the *Canadian Military Family Magazine* (*Canadian Military Family Magazine*, 2014). These Canadian military pages promote normative gender expectations that are reliant on discourses of masculinity and strength juxtaposed against femininity and caregiving with little room for critical commentary from other Facebook users.

The slogan "Strong, Proud, Ready" on the Canadian Army's Facebook page is stamped on a backdrop of two androgynous soldiers dressed in camouflage-print clothing and wearing helmets that obscure their faces (Canadian Army, 2014). Together the soldiers are firing a rocket launcher into a forest. The Canadian Army's Facebook page states that the Canadian Army is internationally known for "soldier's courage, integrity and discipline" (Canadian Army, 2014). Through these images and words the Canadian Army promotes discourses in alignment with dominant notions of masculinity through depicting strength and obedience with connections to violence. Furthermore, the photographs are predominantly images of men in combat, aiming weapons, hugging female civilians, greeting civilian wives, or engaging in exercise. Alternately, the few female soldiers in the photographs are shown shaking hands with other military members, caring for young children, and maintaining military equipment. These differences in gender representations in Canadian Army images re-articulate the military as a masculine field. Women's involvement reflects traditional feminine roles, such as caregivers and housekeepers, while the men are the country's strong, violent protectors (Enloe, 2007).

The Canadian Army's Facebook page can be used to convey information about the military to the wider public. Beyond a site for supporting a military-focused community, Facebook is also used by the Canadian Armed Forces for recruitment through messages sent directly to the inboxes of Facebook users (B. Butler, 2012) and through advertisements added to user profiles (Villiard & Moreno, 2012). Facebook advertisements are crafted to target specific user-identified information (Facebook, 2014b), targeting young women for wedding advertisements, and young men for military employment. These advertisements encourage Facebook users to visit the army's official website and participate in the Facebook site.

If users decide to participate in the Facebook page, they will receive updates on recent military events and missions such as the military's status in Afghanistan and soldier commemoration. Followers of this Facebook page can post on it, and, while some show levels of criticality, most are supportive and echo their pride for their soldiers and Canada (see Taber, Chapter 4 of this volume, for a connecting example of the reverence given to military service, with respect to citizenship). Uniquely, the Canadian Army outlines terms of acceptable use in addition to those outlined by Facebook Inc. The Canadian Army states that "comments may be removed at the Canadian Army's discretion," thus surveilling and regulating critical discussion (Canadian Army, 2014).

Transformative Potential

Although tensions remain evident in perceptions of social network use, gender, and technology, research remains hopeful as to the liberatory potential of social network sites. In their discussion of female blogging communities, both Bowen (2009) and Jack (2009) are optimistic for women's engagement as acts of resistance and transformation within digital spaces. Bowen (2009) argues that, through blogging and continued engagement in digital spaces, "women can articulate bodies of knowledge based on their own experiences and perceptions, and in so doing, subvert and redefine extant discourses" (p. 311). Women's blogging can thus challenge patriarchal hierarchies that privilege male users over female users, and can undermine topics associated with domesticity and femininity.

Perhaps a major caveat to digital engagement is that user engagement is subject to site-specific terms of agreement. With men dominating digital infrastructures and being the primary developers of Facebook, feminist organizations must still work within the very broader patriarchal systems that they are challenging. As such, acceptable use of Facebook may vary depending on how the dialogue and discourse aligns with or diverges from that of website developers, and on the fact that the content that Facebook administrators find problematic is thus subject to removal from Facebook. Despite structural limitations, groups such as WILPF continue to use Facebook for social activism.

Although Facebook can be used to promote participation in democratic dialogue, it is often underutilized and overlooked by researchers and site users. Some feminist organizations are beginning to use these sites to challenge militarism and promote peace. This is particularly important for women who are often left out of conversations regarding politics and military (Enloe, 2007). The WILPF is a notable example of bringing together women from around the world and within Canada. In doing so, they consider and critique local and global impacts of militarism.

Juxtaposing the layout and discourses within the Canadian Army's Facebook page, WILPF displays its logo of a dove and the female gender symbol. These two symbols clearly represent women and peace, which directly reflect their objectives and organization title. Behind the logo is a silhouette of a veiled person (presumably a woman), against a backdrop of words (*women, participation, gender, voices, negations, inclusive*); the words *Syria* and *Peace* with the caption "Peace includes women: Geneva II talks" (WILPF, 2014) are the largest and foremost. The page description states that the organization is "a women's anti-war organization"; "since 1915 WILPF has been working for peace, disarmament and human rights" (WILPF, 2014).

Unlike the Canadian Army's, this website does not detail its own acceptable-use policy. Instead, free and critical speech is supported; however, this engagement is still subject to Facebook's own user policy, which ultimately overrides decisions made by WILPF regarding acceptable content (Facebook, 2014a). As such, content that is perceived by Facebook administrators to be pornographic or violent is subject to removal.

By contrast to the pictures of uniformed officers on the Canadian military page, those on WILPF's Facebook page show both men and women speaking in large, formal group settings, presumably about issues related to peace advocacy and anti-militarism. As such, engagement with peace is not limited to women but can also include men, with representations of each reflecting peace and leadership. Other photographs include women from various racial and cultural backgrounds, with text captions advocating education, empowerment, and peace. These images not only advocate peace but also demand that women's experiences be central to discussions for peace. This is apparent in their postings of examples of women's experiences and updates regarding international peace summits.

WILPF has the ability to access a wide range of audiences through Facebook and to campaign for peace through advertisements and personal messaging, thereby exemplifying both the disruptive and the reproductive possibilities for Facebook as a social networking site. WILPF's images of women participating in political discussions support discourses of women as active agents for peace and social change rather than as compliant and domesticated. Furthermore, images of men in these scenarios are not distinctly gendered, because some men are shown as participating in the same conversations, in similar roles as women and without clear associations with violence.

Conclusion

Social networking sites such as Facebook stand to offer alternate sites for knowledge construction and critical debates that advance feminist anti-militarist objectives. These same transformative sites also risk advancing militarism and reinforce patriarchal hierarchies on which militarism is contingent (see Fournier, Chapter 9 of this volume, for a discussion of gender and cyberbullying). Social movement groups such as WILPF exemplify transformative uses for social networking sites. The use of Facebook to challenge dominant systems of power can support Enloe's (2007) call for the exploration of the ways in which diverse women's lives can be demilitarized (see Magnusson and Mojab, Chapter 1 of this volume, for a discussion of how social movement learning can critique racialized and gendered representations in alternative reality online games). Facebook can provide a space for sharing experiences that uncover the reasons for militarization and the impacts of such militarism. Exploring experiences through organizations such as WILPF, and facilitated through Facebook, uncovers connections between gender and militarism and allows for investigation into the ways in which global, local, and personal militarism are constructed (Enloe, 2007). Through this process, one can begin to resist and possibly dismantle militarizing structures such as those represented in the Canadian military Facebook page (Enloe, 2007). In particular, social network sites such as Facebook can offer spaces in which militarism can be discussed and challenged across international borders and despite restricted access to physical spaces for political engagement (Lonkila, 2008).

Debates regarding the effectiveness of social networking sites for social justice often prove futile because technology is not deterministic, and users of such technology are active constructors of digital spaces. As such, it is important to understand how social networking sites can be used for both militaristic and anti-militaristic purposes. With this understanding, pervasive systems of militarism become visible and can then be dismantled. Furthermore, digital contexts are increasingly being analyzed as educational tools that support the formal education objectives of transmitting knowledge, without considering ways in which communities of adults facilitate their own learning and construct alternate knowledges. In this regard, it is worthwhile to quote Hall (2012): "When one combines the learning resources available via Twitter, Facebook, web sites, blogs, wikis and even image sites such as Tumblr or Instagram, we have living social movement encyclopedias, but ones that are 'written' by each one of us as we choose what and where to read" (p. 137). As such, social network sites are not limited to culturally reproductive, socially transmissive objectives. Instead, social network sites operate in complex ways that can offer forums to support adult education and to advance feminist and anti-militarist social movements.

REFERENCES

Apple, M. (2006). *Educating the "right" way: Markets, standards, god, and inequality* (2nd. ed.). New York: Routledge.

Boon, S., & Sinclair, C. (2009). A world I don't inhabit: Disquiet and identity in Second Life and Facebook. *Educational Media International, 46*(2), 99–110.

Bowen, D.S. (2009). E-criture feminine: Women's online diaries and the new female discourse. In K. Blair, R. Gajjala, & C. Tully (Eds.), *Webbing cyberfeminist practice: Communities, pedagogies, and social action* (pp. 309–326). New York: Hampton Press.

Boyd, D. (2008). Can social network sites enable political action? *International Journal of Media & Cultural Politics, 4*(2), 241–244.

Boyd, D.M., & Ellison, N.B. (2007). Social network sites: Definition, history, and scholarship. *Journal of Computer-Mediated Communication, 13*(1), 220–230.

Brewster, M. (2013, December 22). Canadian military looks at video games for training. *Toronto Star.* Retrieved from www.thestar.com

Burwell, C. (2010). Rewriting the script: Toward a politics of young people's digital media participation. *Review of Education, Pedagogy & Cultural Studies, 32*(4/5), 382–402.

Butler, B. (2012, December 20). Facebook messaging changes could let paid advertisements into users' inboxes. *Network World.* Retrieved from http://go.galegroup.com.proxy. library.brocku.ca

Butler, J. (1993). *Bodies that matter: On the discursive limits of "sex."* New York: Routledge.

Butler, J. (1999). *Gender trouble: Tenth anniversary edition.* London: Routledge.

Canada. National Defence. (2014). Women in the Canadian Armed Forces. Retrieved from www.forces.gc.ca

Canadian Armed Forces. (2014). Canadian Armed Forces. *Facebook*. Retrieved January 21, 2014, from https://www.facebook.com/CanadianForces/timeline

Canadian Army. (2014). Canadian Army. *Facebook*. Retrieved January 21, 2014, from https://www.facebook.com/CANArmy

Canadian Military Family Magazine. (2014). *Facebook*. Retrieved January 21, 2014, from https://www.facebook.com/CanadianMilitaryFamilyMagazine

Cockburn, C. (2010). Gender relations as causal in militarization and war. *International Feminist Journal of Politics, 12*(2), 139-157.

Cockburn, C. (2013). War and security, women and gender: An overview of the issues. *Gender & Development, 21*(3), 433-452.

Cranny-Francis, A., Waring, W., Stavropoulos, P., & Kirkby, J. (2003). *Gender studies: Terms and debates*. New York: Palgrave Macmillan.

Daniels, J. (2012). *BlogHer* and *Blogalicious*: Gender, race and the political economy of women's blogging conferences. In R. Gajjala & Y. Ju Oh (Eds.), *Cyberfeminism 2.0*. New York: Peter Lang.

Dillon, J. (2014). Facebook bans pictures of baby born with defect. *Fox 25*. Retrieved March 31, 2014, from www.okcfox.com

Enloe, C. (2000). *Maneuvers: The international politics of militarizing women's lives*. Berkeley: University of California Press.

Enloe, C. (2007). *Globalization and militarism: Feminists make the link*. Toronto: Rowman & Littlefield.

Facebook. (2014a). Facebook policies. Retrieved January 2014 from https://www.facebook.com/policies

Facebook. (2014b). How to build your audience on Facebook. Retrieved January 21, 2014, from https://www.facebook.com/advertising/how-it-works

Field, J. (2013). Adult education as a social movement: Inspiring change or fading dream? *Adults Learning, 24*(4), 34-35.

Giroux, H.A. (2011). The crisis of public values in the age of the new media. *Critical Studies in Media Communication, 28*(1), 8-29.

Greenhow, C. (2010). Youth as content producers in a niche social network site. *New Directions for Youth Development, 2010*(128), 55-63.

Greenhow, C., & Robelia, B. (2009). Informal learning and identity formation in online social networks. *Learning, Media, and Technology, 34*(2), 119-140.

Hafkin, J.N., & Huyer, S. (2006). *Cinderella or cyberella? Empowering women in the knowledge society*. Bloomfield, CT: Kumarian Press.

Hall, B. (2012). A giant human hashtag: Learning and the Occupy Movement. In B. Hall, D. Clover, J. Crowther, & E. Scandrett (Eds.), *Learning education for a better world: The role of social movements* (pp. 127-139). Boston: Sense Publishers.

Harell, A. (2009). Equal participation but separate paths? Women's social capital and turnout. *Journal of Women, Politics & Policy, 30*(1), 1-22.

Harris, A. (2008). Young women, late modern politics, and the participatory possibilities of online cultures. *Journal of Youth Studies, 11*(5), 481-495.

Herbst, C. (2009). Masters of the house: Literacy and the claiming of space on the internet. In K. Blair, R. Gajjala, & C. Tulley (Eds.), *Webbing cyberfeminist practice: Communities, pedagogies, and social action* (pp. 135-152). Cresskill, NJ: Hampton Press.

Hern, A. (2013, October 22). Facebook's changing standards: From beheading to breastfeeding images. *The Guardian.* Retrieved March 31, 2014, from http://www.theguardian.com

Hooley, T. (2009). Facebook, social integration, and informal learning at university: "It is more for socialising and talking to friends about work than for actually doing work." *Learning, Media and Technology, 34*(2), 141-155.

Howard, J.W., & Prividera, L.C. (2008). The fallen woman archetype: Media representations of Lynndie England, gender, and the (ab)uses of US female soldiers. *Women's Studies in Communication, 31*(3), 287-311.

Jack, J. (2009). We have brains: Reciprocity and resistance in a feminist blog community. In K. Blair, R. Gajjala, & C. Tulley (Eds.), *Webbing cyberfeminist practice: Communities, pedagogies, and social action* (pp. 327-343). Cresskill, NJ: Hampton Press.

Kutz-Flamenbaum, R. (2012). Mobilizing gender to promote peace: The case of Machsom Watch. *Qualitative Sociology, 35*(3), 293-310.

Lester, P. (2013). Four cents to sea: 16 mm, the Royal Canadian Naval Film Society, and the mobilization of entertainment. *Film History, 25*(4), 62.

Lonkila, M. (2008). The Internet and anti-military activism in Russia. *Europe-Asia Studies, 60*(7), 1125.

Malone, M. (2012). Tweeting history: An inquiry into aspects of social media in the Egyptian revolution. In B. Hall, D. Clover, J. Crowther, & E. Scandrett (Eds.), *Learning education for a better world: The role of social movements* (pp. 169-182). Boston: Sense Publishers.

Myers, K., & Raymond, L. (2010). Elementary school girls and heteronormativity: The girl project. *Gender & Society, 24*(2), 167-188.

Nesbit, T. (2013). Canadian adult education: A critical tradition. In T. Nesbit, S.M. Brigham, N. Taber, & T. Gibb (Eds.), *Building on critical traditions: Adult education and learning in Canada.* Toronto: Thompson Educational.

Newsom, V., & Lengel, L. (2004). *The culture of computing: Gender online as contained empowerment.* Conference papers, Feminist Scholarship Division of the International Communication Association, New Orleans, LA.

Paechter, C. (2003). Learning masculinities and femininities: Power/knowledge and legitimate peripheral participation. *Women's Studies International Forum, 26*(6), 541.

Peppler, K.A., & Solomou, M. (2011). Building creativity: Collaborative learning and creativity in social media environments. *On the Horizon, 19*(1), 13-23.

RCAFIMAGERY. (2014). RCAFIMAGERY - YouTube. Retrieved from https://www.youtube.com/user/RCAFIMAGERY

Sassen, S. (2002). Towards a sociology of information technology. *Current Sociology, 50*(3), 365.

Segal, L. (2008). Gender, war, and militarism: Making and questioning the links. *Feminist Review, 88*, 22-35.

Selman, G., & Selman, M. (2009). The life and death of the Canadian Adult Education movement. *Canadian Journal of University Continuing Education, 35*(2), 13-28.

Taber, N. (2013). Learning war through gender: Masculinities, femininities, and militarism. In T. Nesbit, S.M. Brigham, N. Taber, & T. Gibb (Eds.), *Building on critical traditions: Adult education and learning in Canada.* Toronto: Thompson Educational.

Turse, N. (2008). *The complex: How the military invades our everyday lives.* New York: Picador.

Van Doorn, N. (2010). The ties that bind: The networked performance of gender, sexuality, and friendship on MySpace. *New Media & Society, 12*(4), 583-602.

Villiard, H., & Moreno, M.A. (2012). Fitness on Facebook: Advertisements generated in response to profile content. *Cyberpsychology, Behavior, and Social Networking, 15*(10), 564-568.

Women's International League for Peace and Freedom. (2014). Women's International League for Peace and Freedom. *Facebook.* Retrieved January 21, 2014, from https://www.facebook.com/wilp

3 ✖ ✖ ✖ ✦ ✖

POPULAR MEDIA, PEDAGOGY, AND PATRIARCHY

Gender, Militarism, and Entertainment in Canada

Andrew Haddow

WITH THE ADVENT AND SPREAD of the Internet, media and popular culture are disseminated at unprecedented levels of speed and permeation. Television programs, films, music, and advertisements are available online, and, as such, "many people, including children and youth, are now consuming media across platforms, often simultaneously" (Hoechsmann & Poyntz, 2011, p. 6). As the following chapter will show, it is crucial to regard popular media and culture as pedagogical and educational because there is potential to both reinforce dominant patriarchal and militaristic beliefs and also find opportunities for social and ideological resistance. While Canada has its own popular culture and media, Canadians live and negotiate with the influence of the United States on a regular basis. In a time when the United States and Canada have become highly militarized, this is especially troubling.

A wide acceptance of military culture and the militarization of daily life is made possible, in part, by conscious and unconscious ideologies in popular culture and the media—the main way in which civilians at home are exposed to wars (Taber, 2013, p. 143). This has a negative impact on the democratic principles of citizenship and can be particularly detrimental to the lives and experiences of women and men owing to the violent and oppressive associations that masculinity has within military culture. This chapter will borrow the idea of Enloe's (2007) conceptual flashlights, with those of *militarization* and *patriarchy* being particularly useful, and adding one of *learning* or *pedagogy*.[1] My analysis will demonstrate the educational dimensions of popular culture and entertainment, the use of these phenomena towards the militarization of citizens, the damaging outcomes for the learning of gender, and the complex way that the creation and consumption of media can be used as a form of resistance. While much of the work below deals with popular media of US origin, I will argue that these artifacts have significant influence on the Canadian imaginary. My intent is not to devalue Canadian popular culture but to provide a holistic examination of the Canadian experience. I believe that, by focusing on gender, militarism, and learning together, this chapter and this book at large will work towards addressing a significant gap in Canadian research and literature. A contextualization will be presented regarding, first, the Canadian relationship to foreign media and, second, popular culture in general. The following sections deal with the relationship of popular media to militarism and gender and with the potential for media and fiction to be utilized as sites of ideological protest and resistance, before concluding with a discussion on the importance of media literacy. The fostering of a culture of feminist curiosity (Enloe, 2007) and critical media literacy in Canada and the United States is integral to the education of both youth and adults in order to dismantle the systems of oppression that maintain the structures of militarization and patriarchy.

A Canadian Perspective

As mentioned at the outset of this chapter, the Canadian experience is saturated with popular media and culture of US origin. Once again, this is not to say that Canadian culture and media is not unique, significant, and worthy of its own study. However, the statistics prove that to study Canadian media consumption one must examine American media. At the time of writing, of the top 30 television programs, only eight were of Canadian origin (BBM, 2014). The weighting of this top 30 is also significant because no Canadian programming appeared in the top 10, and the bulk of the Canadian content in the list was news, sports, or reality television (BBM, 2014). Likewise, the top 10 DVD and Blu-ray rentals included no Canadian films or programs (Nielsen Videoscan, 2014). While Canadians have their own unique context in which they fashion meaning from popular media, it is clear that they are indeed overwhelmed by American content.

It has been a long struggle for the Canadian Radio-television and Telecommunications Commission (CRTC) to regulate the amount of Canadian content broadcast across the country. Currently the CRTC regulates that "not less than 60% of the broadcast year and not less than 50% of the 6 p.m. to midnight evening broadcast period must be devoted to Canadian programs" (CRTC, 1999). A famous example of these measures from the 1980s concerns the Canadian Broadcast Corporation (CBC) and the sketch-comedy program Second City Television (SCTV), in which the producers were asked to add an additional two minutes of Canadian material to the program (Durkee, 1982). Comedian and SCTV star Rick Moranis, in a 1982 interview with *People* magazine, recalls, "Our first reaction...was, the show is done in Canada and we're Canadian; isn't that enough?" (Durkee, 1982). Humorously, Moranis and co-star Dave Thomas created the popular sketch "The Great White North," in which the pair, dressed in flannel, parkas, and ski caps, cook Canadian bacon, drink beer, and discuss current events in exaggerated Canadian accents

(Durkee, 1982). This helps to illuminate the tensions between popular media and the politics of nationhood, culture, and Canadian identity. It appears as though the CRTC and CBC have historically been on the defensive against the hegemony and domination of American media and culture, seeking to carve out a space for Canadian content and, deeper still, identity among the airwaves.

Popular Culture: A Contextualization

Before popular culture is discussed any further, it must be defined. Historically, as explained by Danesi (2012), the term came into use in the 1950s, a postwar period "which gave people in the mass...considerable buying power, thus propelling them into the unprecedented position of shaping trends in fashion, music, and lifestyle through the market-place....By the end of the decade a full-blown pop culture, promoted by a savvy media-technology-business partnership, had materialized" (p. 2). With the widespread saturation of the television in American homes developing at the same time (Danesi, 2012), popular culture in this sense implies a connection to mass media and to entertainment. According to Aronowitz (1989), "what we call 'popular culture' has become technologically mediated....We can no longer...distinguish what really counts as a popular form from the electronically produced culture that is consumed as records, television programs, or movies" (p. 199). The individual, according to these authors, seems to take on the role of both a shaper and a consumer of popular culture.

Regardless of the agency of the individual in influencing the trends of popular culture, the act of consuming media such as film or television carries a great ideological significance. Scholars like Ellsworth (1989) remind us that a "film needs viewers to give it its meaning" and that "viewers are not passive recipients of an already meaningful message" (p. 58). Therefore, the process of meaning making within popular culture is undertaken by both the creators and the receivers or consumers. Although writing before the widespread adoption of the Internet, White (1989) claims that television occupies "a position of hegemonic centrality in the habits of everyday life. It is also the most overdetermined cultural apparatus, negotiating a complex range of economic, institutional, social, and cultural practices and interests" (p. 176). The potential for television, films, and media at large to shape, reinforce, or even challenge dominant ideological discourse cannot be overstated. After quoting a study by Mattleart (1985) in an analysis of the children's program *Sesame Street*, Ellsworth's (1989) article reads, "One may legitimately ask whether the true educational message of 'Sesame Street' doesn't reside in this initiation into the consumer universe" (as cited in Ellsworth, 1989, p. 60). The educational value of such programs, therefore, reaches far beyond the *ABC*s.

Writing about pedagogy and film, Giroux (2004) addresses this idea further when he states that "symbolic capital and political power now reinforce each other through a public pedagogy produced by media that have become handmaidens to dominant elites and corporate ruling interests" (p. 120). One of the predominant goals of the education system is to foster citizenship in students, and within the neoliberal context citizenship has become entwined with consumerism (Ferguson, 2011) (see Taber, Chapter 4 of this volume, for a further discussion of discourses of citizenship). Writing about neoliberal ideology in the Canadian classroom, Ferguson (2011) suggests that "such a 'consumer citizen' identity... contradicts and has the potential to overwhelm more democratic ideals of citizenship that schools have traditionally fostered" (p. 138). In an article regarding adult learning Gouthro and Holloway (2013) explain that "a neoliberal framework devolves responsibilities for education onto the learner and minimizes government accountability for redressing social inequities" and that "this focus on individualism frequently disadvantages women, particularly those who have minority status or who come from a working class background" (p. 42). Before looking specifically at the effects on and representations of women in the media, I will adopt a lens of militarization to focus on the role of popular culture in the spread of militaristic attitudes.

Popular Culture and Militarism

The current generation can be defined not only by the increasing abundance of technology and the (relative) freedom and instantaneity of information but also, in the case of the United States, by an unprecedented level of military spending and the spread of militaristic values in the lives of citizens. In his book *The New American Militarism*, Bacevich (2005) states that "the United States spends more on defense than all other nations in the world together" (p. 17). While dwarfed in comparison to the United States, Canadian military spending has closely followed US military expenditure trends between 1947 and 2010, except during the era of the Vietnam War (Robinson, 2011, p. 6). To explain this common trend, Robinson (2011) suggests that "the degree of synchronization between the two budgets could be seen as evidence of the degree to which the two countries have had shared perceptions of their common interests, the military threats they face, and the way to respond to those threats" (p. 6).

This highlights the similarities between US and Canadian military culture. While unique in its own right, Canada has nevertheless undergone a similar cultural militarization to that of the United States. There has been a shift away from peacekeeping operations and humanitarian efforts towards armed conflict, particularly in the wake of the Afghanistan mission (Robinson, 2011). This has worrying implications not only in relation to Canada's foreign policy but also at home. Enloe (2007) teaches that "ordinary citizens can become militarized whenever they start to think that the world is so dangerous that the necessarily slow processes of legislative hearings, compromise, and open voting don't match the sense of speed and urgency—and maybe secrecy— they have come to think are needed to address those alleged dangers" (p. 5). How does an "ordinary citizen" come to see the world this way? In Canada there has been an effort to shift the way that the public imagine their country and history towards what McKay and Swift (2012) call a "warrior nation." In the thick of the war with Afghanistan the Canadian government "was promoting a return to romantic notions of military exploits," treating the public "not so much as a rational citizenry, but as a persuadable mass market" (McKay & Swift, 2012, p. 9).

Popular culture and media have become very much entwined with the promotion of militaristic attitudes. These notions have great implications for public pedagogy and popular culture, "instilling the values and the aesthetic of militarization through a wide variety of pedagogical sites and cultural venues. From video games to Hollywood films to children's toys, popular culture is increasingly bombarded with militarized values, symbols, and images" (Giroux, 2008, p. 46). The popular video game *America's Army*, which has been available via a free download or free CD-ROM since its release, is used to entertain soldiers and to recruit youth at home (Giroux, 2008, p. 48) (see Magnusson and Mojab, Chapter 1 of this volume, for an exploration of alternative reality games). In Canada, as McCready (2010) explains, popular media like the television program *The Border* and the radio show *Afghanada* work towards "normalizing militarization as an integral aspect of Canadian culture" (p. 33). This militaristic influence in the lives of civilians encourages what Ben-Porath (2006) has termed "belligerent citizenship," under which the role of the state is to physically protect citizens, civil liberties become limited, patriotic solidarity is a required attitude, and deliberation and social criticism are supressed (pp. 11-15). While all of these tenets are disturbing, the final one has significant repercussions for women, who become subordinate and "protected" (Enloe, 2007, p. 60). Furthermore, women and femininity are often represented as a threat to military or masculine success and therefore to the safety of soldiers and civilians (Cohn & Weber, 1999, p. 466). Along with the popular acceptance of military culture, masculinity and violent behaviour become associated with each other and normalized in public discourse (Giroux, 2008, p. 49).

This militaristic attitude, within a broader culture of patriarchy, has also contributed to the misrepresentation of women in popular culture in ways that negatively influence how they see their identity.

Television and Film: A Feminist Perspective

As has been shown above, popular culture and the media can contribute to both the formal and the informal education of consumers and citizens. In addition to the culture of militarism that is being propagated through popular mediums, the way in which women are represented in popular culture has severe implications for both male and female viewers and can reinforce the oppressive system of patriarchy. Enloe (2007) characterizes patriarchy as a system of beliefs that upholds the idea that women and men have natural roles to play in society, men being the stronger and more rational income earners, and women the natural homemakers and caregivers (p. 67). While the West has undergone several waves of feminism in the last century, women are still routinely oppressed by patriarchy, as evidenced by their portrayal in the media.

The documentary film *Miss Representation* by Siebel Newsom (2011) excellently links the educational influences of popular culture to the oppression and limitation of women within Western society. Although the documentary is almost entirely US focused, the consumption patterns of Canadian viewers and consumers make Siebel Newsom's (2011) central arguments very relevant to this discussion. Including television, movies, magazines, and time spent online, teenagers spend approximately 10 hours and 45 minutes each day consuming media (Siebel Newsom, 2011). The film presents the argument that girls are taught from an extremely young age to care about their bodies and looks through stereotyping and objectification, which shape their perception of their role in society. Siebel Newsom refers to this as a culture of self-objectification among women in the United States. This relates to the low percentage of women in positions of power in the country relative to their population; according to the film, women account for 51 per cent of the population in the United States but make up only 17 per cent of Congress (Siebel Newsom, 2011).

The situation in Canada is only slightly better, with women occupying only 24.7 per cent of seats in Parliament, and, while representation is proportionally higher within the Senate at 36.3 per cent, the average is still far below the global 30 per cent critical mass goal (Cool, 2011). With women currently making up 50.4 per cent of the population (Statistics Canada, 2010b), this minimum should be set considerably higher in order for accurate (by gender, at least) democratic representation. Once again, with the current trends of militarization within Western culture, one must keep in mind Ben-Porath's (2006) concept of the belligerent citizen. She writes that "deliberation and disagreement are widely regarded as threats to the security effort, and the more real and pressing the security threat becomes, the narrower the limits of acceptable perspectives in public debate" (p. 15). Issues of gender equality, such as the achievement of the parliamentarian benchmark or fairer representation in the media, can be generally seen as unimportant in dominant discourse.

The under-representation of women in Western popular media is a serious problem. Women represent roughly 37 per cent of characters on mainstream television, and women over 45 years of age make up only 15 per cent (Siebel Newsom, 2011). It is clear that there is an unequal bias in the media to privilege men and their stories as important, and women (particularly older women) as irrelevant to Western culture and society. The more power that women achieve (the film presents Hillary Clinton and Sarah Palin as examples), the stronger is the resistance to them within a patriarchal society (Siebel Newsom, 2011). Resistance to women in a *male space* can be seen in the American military, in which female soldiers are often subjected to sexual harassment and rape by their male counterparts (Enloe, 2007, pp. 106-107). Anita Sarkeesian of the *Feminist Frequency* blog has been subjected to much symbolic violence for her entrance into video-game discourse, as discussed in the following section.

Video Games: Contested Space

Although she has been writing and making feminist-centred content about popular media for quite some time, Sarkeesian took to the crowd-funding website Kickstarter in 2012 for help to create a series about female stereotypes within video games, which premiered on YouTube the following year (Hicks, 2013). Her series, entitled *Tropes vs. Women in Video Games*, illuminates how female characters in games have long been delegated to passive roles like the damsel in distress and how they are often sexually objectified (Sarkeesian, 2013a). This reinforces the assumption that gamers are a predominantly male demographic, but, similar to the statistics above regarding women in television, this is not the case. According to the Entertainment Software Association of Canada (ESA, 2013), women make up 46 per cent of gamers, compared to 45 per cent in the United States (ESA, 2013). Similar to the statistics cited above from Siebel Newsom (2011), the under-representation of women in video games is undemocratic and serves to gender the politics of video games.

To build further on the idea that video games reinforce stereotypes of gender, one can examine the reports produced by the Entertainment Software Association of Canada (2013). First of all, it is worth noting that the infographics of the Canadian report, which detail average game-developer salaries, the contribution of the game industry to the Canadian gross domestic product, and the permeation of various gaming platforms in Canadian homes, are all illustrated with recogniz-ably male humanoid figures. Only the data that deals specifically with female games is illustrated by figures wearing dresses. This reinforces game developers, gamers, and, more broadly, Canadian citizens as male by default (see Lane, Chapter 2 of this volume, for an exploration of the preponderance of male online developers and the perception of the Internet as a male space). Later, in the section titled "Gamer Profiles," the Entertainment Software Association of Canada breaks down the habits of male and female gamers, separated again by age group.

Across all age groups, males are reported to have a preference for action, adventure, role-playing, and shooter games (ESA of Canada, 2013). By contrast, the report states that female gamers prefer more arcade, educational, puzzle, and card games. These consumption trends are congruent with the militarized gender roles described by Enloe (2007), in which man, the "'natural protector' is the person who has not just the physical strength or the collective physical resources to wield definitive power but who—allegedly—is most capable of thinking in a certain way: more 'strategically,' more 'rationally'" (pp. 60-61). Female gamers, however, appear to have a quieter, more studious, and domestic gamer profile, similar to the "protected" role within broader patriarchal culture (Enloe, 2007). The above statistics help to demonstrate that the politics of video games are informed by heteronormative and hypermasculine ideals.

To return to the idea of a backlash against empowered women, one must examine the way in which Sarkeesian's video series was antici-pated and received by the online community of, assumingly, male gamers. Sarkeesian was met with "waves of misogynistic comments, from the standard threats of rape to barely ironic demands that she 'get back in the kitchen'" (Hicks, 2013). This capitulated in the creation of an in-browser Flash game in which players attacked Anita Sarkeesian until "her face [became] bruised and bloodied beyond recognition" (Hicks, 2013) (see Fournier, Chapter 9 of this volume, for an exploration of the gendered violence of cyberbullying). The sheer violence of this reac-tion can be linked to the militarized notions of masculinity discussed earlier and to the legitimation of masculine violence against those who question or disrupt the status quo. Sarkeesian responded to the game in a piece written for the *Toronto Standard*, urging readers to "remember that this 'game' is a symptom of our deeply misogynist culture (both online and offline)" (Sarkeesian, 2012). This virtual violence, ideologically, is not far removed from the sexual assault "epidemic" in the United States Army (Enloe, 2007, p. 85). Both instances represent an invasion of male space by female presence. Despite the seemingly limitless potential for media and popular culture to have negative educational impacts on Western culture, there is simultaneously a space for resistance to this dominant ideology through both the consuming and the creating of media.

Fiction: The Potential for Transformation and Resistance

To help illuminate the way in which the educational influence of popular culture can have a positive effect towards critiquing notions of militarized masculinity and limited gender roles, the transformative potential of fiction is discussed below. In a study conducted with a group of women across a diverse range of ages and socio-cultural backgrounds, Jarvis (2006) analyzed their responses to romantic fiction novels. She notes that the way in which this genre is often disregarded and not taken seriously suggests that the books' "emphasis on feelings, love, and relationships [is] shameful...connected to the way some feminist critics see the romance as a subversive form that resists a dominant social tendency to belittle those areas of life, such as marriage and the family, with which women are often associated in favor of the public sphere" (p. 42).

In the group led by Jarvis, this type of fiction was used to guide students through a transformational learning experience in critiquing patriarchal culture. Her students were able to critique the heteronormative stereotypes present in the fiction and were able to "read texts as a series of signs with shifting but often preferred or dominant meanings" (2006, p. 74). Fiction, even when it embodies dominant stereotypes and discourse, can create a space for transformational learning in which readers can learn to see and critique ideology. Jarvis, however, stresses the importance of the role of a critically minded teacher in guiding such transformation. In 2013, Taber, Woloshyn, and Lane documented the experiences of four young Canadian girls who participated in a book-club reading of *The Hunger Games*. The hope was that such a massively popular work of fiction could be used towards encouraging feminist sociological critique in students. Similar to Jarvis (2006), Taber et al. (2013) encourage teachers and youth workers to adopt a critical lens when reading popular fiction. The researchers hope, "through such repeated opportunities for structured critique[,] that youth may gain some sense of agency for social change" (p. 1035).

Jarvis and Burr (2011) conducted a project to research the effects of the popular program *Buffy the Vampire Slayer* (*BTVS*) on transformative education. While the authors admit that it is up to the viewer to make her or his own meaning (p. 166), some media, "like *BTVS*, are constructed in ways that make them more likely than others to challenge existing sociolinguistic and moral–ethical frames of reference, to create dissonance, to offer alternative perspectives to accepted social beliefs and culturally approved aspirations, and to illuminate contemporary dilemmas" (p. 169).

In a culture that is becoming increasingly militarized and in which Ben-Porath's (2006) concept of belligerent citizenship is a reality, the role of fictional works such as *Buffy the Vampire Slayer* in encouraging social criticism is invaluable. Jarvis (2006) argues that such programs that present "moral dilemmas, sophisticated character development, [and a] reversal of stereotypes and audience expectations" are more likely to initiate a transformational educational experience (p. 169). However, it must be noted that such subversive and empowering heroines can also be entangled in gendered and militaristic values.

The ways in which subversive female hero characters can still reinforce patriarchal gender tropes are discussed by O'Reilly (2005). Similar to Wonder Woman's being forced to prove her heroism, unlike male heroes, Buffy underwent examination in several episodes to validate her super powers and worthiness (O'Reilly, 2005). The programs, therefore, subtly reinforce heroism and strength as male traits that females can only possess unnaturally. Indeed, "when faced with the Watchers Council's trials, Buffy initially regresses from powerful action hero to frightened young woman" (O'Reilly, 2005). *Buffy the Vampire Slayer*'s titular heroine can also be seen to promote militarized values because the series constantly promotes violence as a justified means of resolving narrative conflicts.

Another example of this complex relationship is the way in which lesbian characters are portrayed in the Canadian-American co-produced series *Queer as Folk* (QAF). While the show was certainly against the grain for its time, Peters (2009) explains that "gay men are explicitly at the center of the QAF universe" and that the jokes used in the program "consistently imply an undercurrent of dislike toward lesbians" (p. 17). After interviewing many Canadian viewers, Peters concludes that "although the representation of lesbians on QAF holds the 'promise of solidarity'" (p. 19), the portrayal of lesbians in the series was ultimately received as a negative one. As the particular television programs discussed above are relatively new, to understand the lifelong educational effects of popular media on individuals we must turn to a different study.

Scholars Wright and Sandlin (2009) have conducted research on the lifelong educational and pedagogical impacts on audiences of the 1960s program *The Avengers*. Of particular interest was the replacement of one of the main male characters in the second season by Dr. Cathy Gale, played by Honor Blackman, who "rocked the existing stereotype of subservient, domesticated TV women" (Richardson, 1996, p. 41, as cited in Wright & Sandlin, 2009). The researchers noted that, among the women who had watched the program when they were younger, many began to examine the more traditional gender roles that their parents had embodied and "they looked to Cathy to provide alternative possibilities" (p. 540). Taking this study further, the research included three trans-women (male-to-female transsexuals) and the impact that Cathy Gale had had on forming their gender identities; the authors say that "all three trans-women indicated Cathy Gale was the only person, in the media or in their lives, they felt comfortable modelling themselves on in terms of performing strength, physical abilities and attitude in confrontational situations" (p. 541).

As demonstrated through the variety of research discussed above, popular media and culture can simultaneously reinforce systems of oppression against women, promote militaristic values among citizens, and create a space for education and resistance to these same values. It is necessary that students both young and old are guided towards a sense of media literacy to help them become or remain critical of the over-whelming amount of content to which they are exposed.

Towards Critical Media Literacy

Encouraging media literacy in Canadian culture and within classrooms will help citizens, viewers, and students to make sense of the ideological and pedagogical implications within popular culture. Broadly, media literacy can be defined by "a set of competencies that enable us to interpret media texts and institutions, to make media of our own, and to recognize and engage with the social and political influence of media in everyday life" (Hoechsmann & Poyntz, 2011, p. 1). Due to the indi-vidual consumer's role in making meaning from popular culture, and the strong potential to unconsciously reinforce the oppressive beliefs of the dominant elites, media literacy is essential in the maintenance of democratic and critical practices in the current age. As Hoechsmann and Poyntz clarify, understanding popular media as educational and pedagogical helps to orient teachers and learners towards a better under-standing of our society and a strengthening of democratic participation (p. 41).

In Canada there are already movements underway to bring popular media into the classroom. Ferguson (2011) sets the scene, explaining that "this openness stems, on the one hand, from the chronic underfunding [of] the neo-liberal era" and, on the other, because "a pedagogy of the 'popular' is on the rise: backed by a multiliteracies approach to learn-ing, teachers are placing great hopes in the potential of nontraditional texts" (p. 138). Without critically minded teachers to guide the negotiation of popular texts, in an argument similar to that of Jarvis (2006), Ferguson claims that ultimately this inclusion of non-traditional texts has thus far failed to displace dominant and oppressive neoliberal ideology. Ferguson claims that this move to include popular media in schools, in the light of the neoliberal emphasis on standardized test performance, can largely be seen as an attempt to solve the "problem of boys' literacy" (p. 142). While boys do tend to have reading literacy levels lower than that of girls (Statistics Canada, 2010a), attempting to address this by dictating what boys and girls are supposedly "into" (Ferguson, 2011) will prove counterintuitive and further limit gender equity in Canada. Regardless, the situation is hopeful, as the Ontario curriculum "offer[s] small openings for more politicized lesson plans that explore the underlying forces of social power and conflict, and that understand the media and culture as potential weapons in the struggle to change the world" (Fergusson, 2011, p. 138). The responsibility, therefore, can be assumed by educators, teacher candidates, and professors of education in order to take advantage of these allowances for critical dissent.

Freire and Giroux (1989) write that critical pedagogy "must incorporate aspects of popular culture as a serious educational discourse into the school curriculum, and it must bring into the discourse of school policy and pedagogical planning the voices who have been marginalized and excluded" (p. ix). It has been shown above that women are often excluded and misrepresented within popular culture, which contributes to the reinforcement of a patriarchal social structure. It is crucial that critically minded women and men play equitable roles in the crafting, teaching, and understanding of media and popular culture as a site of pedagogy. In such a highly militarized era of Canadian (and American) history, during which militaristic values and beliefs about masculinity, femininity, and violence are coming to dominate public discourse (McKay & Swift, 2012; Taber, 2013), the critical analysis and discussion of popular culture and media must be brought to the fore. Doing so will encourage and re-establish a more democratic notion of citizenship among Canadians at home and abroad and hopefully will disentangle militaristic values from the Canadian imaginary.

NOTE

1. My use of Enloe (2007) and her conceptual flashlights was made under the guidance of this book's editor, Nancy Taber, in my graduate-level course work with her in 2013.

REFERENCES

Aronowitz, S. (1989). Working-class identity and celluloid fantasies in the electronic age. In H.A. Giroux & R.I. Simon (Eds.), *Popular culture, schooling, and everyday life*. Granby, MA: Bergin & Garvey.

Bacevich, A.J. (2005). *The new American militarism: How Americans are seduced by war*. New York and Oxford: Oxford University Press.

BBM. (2014). *Weekly top 30 TV programs*. Retrieved on March 27, 2014, from http://assets. numeris.ca/Downloads/March%2017-23,%202014%20(Week%2030).pdf

Ben-Porath, S.R. (2006). *Citizenship under fire: Democratic education in times of conflict*. Princeton, NJ: Princeton University Press.

Cohn, C., & Weber, C. (1999). Missions, men, and masculinities: Carol Cohn discusses *Saving Private Ryan* with Cynthia Weber. *International Feminist Journal of Politics*, 1(3), 460–475.

Cool, J. (2011). Women in Parliament. *Parliamentary Information and Research Service*. Ottawa: Library of Parliament.

CRTC (Canadian Radio-television and Telecommunications Commission). (1999). *Public Notice CRTC 1999-97*. Retrieved from www.crtc.gc.ca

Danesi, M. (2012). *Popular culture: Introductory perspectives*. Lanham, MD: Rowman & Littlefield.

Durkee, C.C. (1982). With beer, back bacon, and banter, SCTV's Bob & Doug mine comedy gold in the Great white North. *People Weekly*, (17), 84–86.

Ellsworth, E. (1989). Educational media, ideology, and the presentation of knowledge through popular cultural forms. In H.A. Giroux & R.I. Simon (Eds.), *Popular culture, schooling, and everyday life*. Granby, MA: Bergin & Garvey.

Enloe, C. (2007). *Globalization and militarism: Feminists make the link*. Lanham, MD: Rowman & Littlefield.

Entertainment Software Association. (2013). *2013 Sales, demographic, and usage data: Essential facts about the computer and videogame industry*. Retrieved from www.theesa.com

Entertainment Software Association of Canada. (2013). *2013 Essential facts about the Canadian video game industry*. Retrieved from http://theesa.ca/wp-content/uploads/2013/10/Essential-Facts-English.pdf

Ferguson, S. (2011). Classroom contradictions: Popular media in Ontario schools' literacy and citizenship education policies. *Education, Citizenship, and Social Justice, 6*(2), 137-151.

Freire, P., & Giroux, H.A. (1989). Foreword to *Popular culture, schooling, and everyday life*, H.A. Giroux & R.I. Simon (Eds.). Granby, MA: Bergin & Garvey.

Giroux, H.A. (2004). Pedagogy, film, and the responsibility of intellectuals: A response. *Cinema Journal, 43*(2), 119-126.

Giroux, H.A. (2008). Militarization, public pedagogy, and the biopolitics of popular culture. In D. Siberman Keller, Z. Bekerman, H. Giroux, and N. Burbules (Eds.), *Mirror Images: Popular Culture and Education* (pp. 39-54). New York: Peter Lang.

Gouthro, P., & Holloway, S. (2013). Reclaiming the radical: Using fiction to explore adult learning connected to citizenship. *Studies in the Education of Adults, 45*(1), 41-56.

Hicks, M. (2013). De-Brogramming the history of computing. *IEEE Annals of the History of Computing, 35*(1), 88.

Hoechsmann, M., & Poyntz, S.R. (2011). *Media literacies: A critical introduction*. Hoboken, NJ: Wiley.

Jarvis, C. (2006). Using fiction for transformation. *New Directions for Adult and Continuing Education, 109*, 69-77. doi: 10.1002/ace.209.

Jarvis, C., & Burr, V. (2011). The transformative potential of popular television: The case of *Buffy the Vampire Slayer*. *Journal of Transformative Education, 9*(3), 165-182.

McCready, A. (2010). Tie a yellow ribbon 'round public discourse, national identity, and the war: Neoliberal militarization and the yellow ribbon campaign in Canada. *Topia: Canadian Journal of Cultural Studies, 23-24*, 28-51.

McKay, I., & Swift, J. (2012). *Warrior nation: Rebranding Canada in an age of anxiety*. Toronto: Between the Lines.

Nielsen Videoscan. (2014). *Top 10 list for DVD and Blu-ray rentals*. Retrieved on March 27, 2014, from www.nielsen.com/ca/en/top10s.html

O'Reilly, J.D. (2005). The Wonder Woman precedent: Female (super)heroism on trial. *Journal of American Culture, 28*(3), 273-283.

Peters, W. (2009). "It feels more like a parody": Canadian *Queer as Folk* viewers and the show they love to complain about. *Journal of Lesbian Studies, 13*(1), 15-24.

Robinson, B. (2011). Canadian military spending, 2010-2011. *Foreign Policy Series*. Ottawa: Canadian Centre for Policy Alternatives. Retrieved from www.policyalternatives.ca

Sarkeesian, A. (2012). Anita Sarkeesian responds to beat up game, online harassment, and death threats on Stephanie Guthrie. *Toronto Standard*. Retrieved from www.torontostandard.com

Sarkeesian, A. (2013a). Damsel in distress: Part 1—Tropes vs women in video games [Video file]. *Feminist Frequency*. Retrieved from www.feministfrequency.com

Sarkeesian, A. (2013b). Damsel in distress: Part 2—Tropes vs women in video games [Video file]. *Feminist Frequency*. Retrieved from www.feministfrequency.com

Siebel Newsom, J. (Producer and Director). (2011). *Miss Representation* [Motion picture]. United States: Girls' Club Entertainment.

Statistics Canada. (2010a). *Measuring up: Canadian results of the OECD PISA study.* (Catalogue number 81-590-XWE). Retrieved from http://www5.statcan.gc.ca

Statistics Canada. (2010b). Women in Canada: A gender-based statistical report. (Catalogue number 89-503-XWE). Retrieved from http://www5.statcan.gc.ca/

Taber, N. (2013). Learning war through gender: Masculinities, femininities, and militarism. In T. Nesbit, S. Brigham, N. Taber, & T. Gibb (Eds.), *Building on critical traditions: Adult education and learning in Canada.* Toronto: Thompson Educational.

Taber, N., Woloshyn, V., & Lane, L. (2013). "She's more like a guy" and "he's more like a teddy bear": Girls' perception of violence and gender in *The Hunger Games. Journal of Youth Studies, 16*(8), 1022–1037.

White, M. (1989). Engendering couples: The subject of daytime television. In H.A. Giroux & R.I. Simon (Eds.), *Popular culture, schooling, and everyday life.* Granby, MA: Bergin & Garvey.

Wright, R.R., & Sandlin, J.A. (2009). Popular culture, public pedagogy and perspective transformation: *The Avengers* and adult learning in living rooms. *International Journal of Lifelong Education, 28*(4), 533–551.

4

OFFICIAL (MASCULINIZED AND MILITARIZED) REPRESENTATIONS OF CANADA

Learning Citizenship

Nancy Taber

THE CANADIAN GOVERNMENT has recently released updated versions of its citizenship study guide, *Discover Canada: The Rights and Responsibilities of Citizenship* (Canada, 2012a), and of Canadian passports. The guide begins with "Rights and Responsibilities of Citizenship" that "reflect our shared traditions, identity and values" (p. 8), while the passports "celebrate our history and our culture" (Passport Canada, 2013, para. 2). These documents perform pedagogically, teaching newcomers, Canadian citizens, and foreign nationals about *who* Canadians are expected to be and *what values* they are supposed to hold and enact. The purpose of this chapter is to explore the ways in which the guide, its associated online educational resources, and passports function as pedagogical instruments of the Canadian government within the current political context. First, I explore literature relating to citizenship, learning, and militarism. Second, I explain my methodology of feminist discourse analysis. Third, I detail my findings, concluding that, although dual discourses of egalitarian and conservative gender relations are present, the latter overrides the former, privileging men, masculinity, and militarism.

Canada, Citizenship, Gender, and Learning

When I received my new Canadian passport in the summer of 2013, I was interested to note that it included images as background on each page. As I flipped through the document, I was (unfortunately) not surprised to note that women and visible minorities were underrepresented, while men and military associations were overrepresented. The passport was yet another example in a long line of recent instances of the Canadian government promoting a national identity that is masculinist and militarized. For instance, the Canadian Museum of History, formerly the Museum of Civilization, has been described as "part of a continued effort by the Conservative government to reshape the country's major symbols with a greater emphasis on the monarchy and past military achievements" (Leblanc, 2012, para. 6). The Canadian military has undergone two name changes in recent years, adding the words *Royal* in 2011 and *Armed* in 2013 (Berthiaume, 2013), resulting in the Canadian Armed Forces, instead of the Canadian Forces, which are made up of the Royal Canadian Air Force, Canadian Army, and Royal Canadian Navy. In August 2013 Canada's prime minister, Stephen Harper, participated in a photo opportunity in which he was prominently featured firing a rifle with the Canadian Rangers (Canadian Press, 2013). The Royal Canadian Mint recently released coins celebrating the War of 1812 and at the time of this writing was promoting the 75th anniversary of Superman, the "Man of Steel" (see http://www.mint.ca). What discourses of citizenship are being promoted, privileged, and taught through these events and artifacts?

Citizenship is too often equated with military service (Enloe, 2000; Feinman, 2000; Woollacott, 1998) that is predicated on a hegemonically masculine ideal of heroic male warriors (Basham, 2009; Lahelma, 2005) as "real fighters" (Taber, 2009). An oft-quoted poem by Charles Province (1970/2005) elevates "the Soldier" above ministers, reporters, poets, campus organizers, lawyers, and politicians, crediting the soldier with the existence of the freedom of religion, press, speech, and protest as well as the right to a fair trial and to vote. This reverence of soldiers above others is reflected in the words of Canadian Defence Minister Peter MacKay, who stated that they "'are the best citizens of our country'" (McKay & Swift, 2012, p. 13). Although there needs to be a "separation of militarism and citizenship" (Feinman, 2000, p. 211), these concepts still seem to be inextricably connected. Furthermore, neoliberal experiences associated with masculinity and the marketplace are typically linked with notions of citizenship, to the exclusion of the caring labour associated with femininity (Gouthro, 2007, 2009). As Ben-Porath (2006) explains, a belligerent citizenship that jingoistically stifles dissent works against efforts to engage in expansive education focused on peace and understanding. If masculine soldiers (whether embodied by men or women) are positioned as protectors, then the feminine protected (whether embodied by men or women) are positioned as subordinate, without the "patriarchal right" (Young, 2003, p. 6) to engage as active citizens.

As described in the introductory chapter to this volume, I was born into a military family and later served in the Canadian military. As such, I am well aware of the supposed dichotomy in that one cannot critique the nation *and* support the troops, the latter of which is the expected path. I often see a bumper sticker stating, "If you don't stand behind our troops, feel free to stand in front of them," insinuating that those who engage in any critique of a nation's military deserve to be cannon fodder. While it may be necessary in certain instances to take military action, it is also necessary to problematize the ways in which the military is idealized and masculinized. Ironically, this may also be the best way to support the troops.

In various ways women and men learn the forms of citizenship that are valued: in classrooms as children (Ben-Porath, 2006; Giroux, 2008) and adults (Giroux, 2008; Y. Guo, 2013) wherein, typically, citizenship is taught at best uncritically and at worst jingoistically; through discourses of lifelong learning in government and educational policies that marginalize immigrants (S. Guo, 2013) and women (Gouthro, 2007); and through the news media where citizens are encouraged to become "foot soldiers" against terrorism (Giroux, 2004). Governments around the world engage in public pedagogies to create ideal citizens (see Ratković, Chapter 8 of this volume, for a discussion of refugee mothers' experiences with immigrating to Canada and struggling to maintain their positions as teachers). For instance, in Guatemala, Martinez-Salazar (2008) argues that the "state terror, as one of the most sophisticated and deadly expressions of violence, is also a teaching-learning process, the main goal of which is to forge a long-term culture of socio-cultural fear and political paralysis" (p. 202). The state terror was intended to teach the Mayans how to be *good* Guatemalans who think and act in ways beneficial to the government. Welton (2003) argues that the September 11, 2001, bombings in the United States were an "appalling and audacious pedagogical act" (p. 637) committed by al Qaeda that should have resulted in a "fantastic learning moment" (p. 638) for the United States. Instead, the American government responded through its military in a gendered war on terror that positioned Western soldiers as saviours of Eastern women (Fluri, 2008).

In a critique of militarized masculinity in the American and Israeli educational systems, Ben-Porath (2006) examines the way in which students are taught a "belligerent citizenship" that demands citizenship allegiance to the nation, suppresses debate, and expects unity. As I have argued in other works, Canadians also interact with a national public pedagogy that is increasingly militarized and masculinized (Taber, 2013). Even Canadian universities, often considered as ideal institutions for progressive thought, are affected by national discourses of militarism that privilege militaristic representations and research funding (Taber, 2014).

Using a feminist anti-militarist theoretical framework (Enloe, 2000, 2004, 2007; Feinman, 2000), I build on the above research to explore the ways in which specific discourses of citizenship in the Canadian citizenship study guide, its educational resources, and the new Canadian passport function pedagogically. Feminist anti-militarism explores the ways in which gender and militarism are societally interrelated. It problematizes the privileging of certain forms of masculinity and femininity that reinforce patriarchal and militarized relations. As such, it critiques the societal valuation (reflected in individual lives) of the use of violence as a way to solve conflict, the heroization of military members, and the demonization of enemy "others." Feminist anti-militarism questions the perceived need for national security to take precedence over human security (i.e., funding for the military eclipsing that for education and health) and the requirement of citizens to patriotically support their national government. Citizenship, therefore, is an integral concept for exploration.

Methodology: Feminist Discourse Analysis

The purpose of this research is to use feminist discourse analysis (Lazar, 2005a, 2005b) to explore the pedagogical implications of representations of Canada in the following documents: *Discover Canada: The Rights and Responsibilities of Citizenship* (Canada, 2012a), *A Look at Canada* (Canada, 2005), Canada Passport (Canada, 2013), and the educational resource web pages of Citizenship and Immigration Canada.

Feminist discourse analysis focuses "on how gender ideology and gendered representations of power are (re)produced, negotiated and contested in representations of social practices, in social relationships between people, and in people's social and personal identities in text and talk" (Lazar, 2005b, p. 11). There are a multitude of ways in which feminist discourse analysis can be conducted, depending on the research context and data types (Lazar, 2005b). In her work examining representations of fatherhood in Singapore, Lazar (2005a) explores how the presence of "two apparently contending discourses, namely the discourse of egalitarian gender relations and the discourse of conservative gender relations" actually "contributes to the remaking of the hegemonic heteronormative gender order to fit in with the changing times" (p. 140). In this research I use Lazar's (2005a) concept of dual discourses to explore the way in which these citizenship documents represent both an open, welcome, multicultural Canada and a masculinist, militarist one. I analyze visual and print data to explore the tensions between an egalitarian pedagogical approach to Canadian citizenship and a conservative approach.

Findings: Dual Discourses?

Although there are varying emphases on each of the dual discourses in each of the Canadian citizenship documents analyzed, as a whole, conservative gender relations privilege men, masculinity, and militarism. In this section I discuss the differences between the two most recent citizenship study guides, explore the associated online educational resources, and examine the new Canadian passport.

A Look at Canada and Discover Canada

The citizenship guides published by Citizenship and Immigration Canada (CIC) aim to assist newcomers in learning about Canada so that they can pass the citizenship test, which is required of all adults between the ages of 18 and 54 (Canada, 2013c). In addition to being able to communicate in English or French (Canada's official languages), one must demonstrate "adequate knowledge of Canada" as relates to

- the right to vote, and right to run for elected office;
- elections procedures;
- the rights and responsibilities of a citizen;
- Canadian social and cultural history and symbols;
- Canadian political history (including the political system and institutions); and
- Canadian physical and political geography (Canada, 2014a).

Interestingly, while *A Look at Canada* mirrors these requirements (pp. 5, 6), the newest guide, *Discover Canada*, referring to the Citizenship Act, specifically adds the phrases *military history* and *constitutional monarchy* (p. 64). There are several other significant changes between the two guides.[1]

There is an interesting backgrounder document (Canada, 2011) that details the main changes between the two citizenship study guides. In so doing, it demonstrates that the guide is an apt example of dual discourses. Arguably, from looking only at the *Backgrounder*, it can be seen that the new guide is both egalitarian and conservative. Sections added include, on the side of egalitarian gender relations: "Equality of Men and Women," "Gay and Lesbian Equality Rights" (see Mizzi, Chapter 6 of this volume, for a critique of the Canadian military's approach to the LGBTQ community), "Aboriginal Peoples," and "Canadian Diversity." The guide also recognizes the historical wrongs (my words, not theirs) of residential schools and Chinese railroad workers. On the side of conservative gender relations are war representations ("Remembrance Day," "WWII," "War of 1812," "1837-38 Rebellions," and the "Canadian Rangers"), "Sports" (football, hockey), and "Heroes" (categories include sports, science, and war). However, in the new guide the dominant presence of conservative gender relations overrides that of egalitarian ones, with a concomitant "remaking of the hegemonic hetero-gender order" (Lazar, 2005a, p. 140). For example, "The Equality of Women and Men" section (Canada, 2012a, p. 9) comprises only two sentences, one of which condemns "cultural" "gender-based violence," and the "Heroes" section on sport and science gets a two-page overleaf (pp. 26, 27), with over 91 per cent of the heroes recognized being male. The "Gay and Lesbian Equality Rights" section has one sentence (p. 13), and the War of 1812 and rebellions of 1837-38 have one page (p. 17), World War I has over half a page (p. 21), and a two-page overleaf is dedicated to the remembrance poppy, the poem *In Flanders Fields*, D-Day, and World War II (pp. 22, 23). Disturbingly, the existence of this backgrounder demonstrates that CIC (and, by extension, the Government of Canada) wants to emphasize these changes, presumably because they are viewed positively, when in actuality the new guide privileges men, masculinity, and war despite some peppering of diversity.

By contrast, *A Look at Canada* (Canada, 2005) names very few people (only Sir John A. Macdonald, Queen Elizabeth II, Jacques Cartier, and John Cabot), does not include any mention of the military or war, and does not include a section on sports. It integrates information about Aboriginal peoples throughout instead of largely isolating it in one section, and includes a discussion of treaty rights (p. 15). Furthermore, it has a two-page overleaf on "Protecting the Environment: Sustainable Development" (pp. 10, 11), while *Discover Canada* includes one line only on this topic (p. 9). Finally, *A Look at Canada* contains 104 study questions (comprising 6 of 47 pages); *Discover Canada* has 32 questions (2 of 66 pages), one of which is about the meaning of the Remembrance Day poppy.

As a result, despite frequent reference in *Discover Canada* to diversity and multiculturalism, such as "diversity enriches Canadians' lives" (p. 25), and some recognition of the ways in which Aboriginal peoples have shaped Canada (e.g., pp. 10-11), people of colour are largely positioned in reference to specific festivals and are dressed in traditional garb (e.g., pp. 12-13), women are largely absent, and Canada is presented as being politically and militarily created by men of European descent. For instance, out of those specifically named in prose or in photograph captions, 102 are men and 18 are women, less than 18 per cent. Just as in the field of adult education, as discussed by Butterwick (1998), women have made societal contributions, but they are eclipsed by those of men.

Furthermore, citizenship is framed by a discourse of "courage," "pride," and "sacrifice" (p. 3) in relation to Canadian pioneers, citizens, and immigrants. Soldiers are "tough, innovative," with a "reputation for valour" (p. 21), with the "brave fallen" making "sacrifices" (p. 22) as they "fought bravely" (p. 23). *Discover Canada* even has a section, "Defending Canada," stating that "serving in the regular Canadian Forces...is a noble way to contribute to Canada and an excellent career choice" (p. 9). Notably, this section is in the "Rights and Responsibilities" chapter. Arguably, the new guide intends to teach newcomers about a very specific discourse of citizenship that is masculinized and militarized, with more focus on Canadian "values" than on specific preparation for passing a multiple-choice citizenship test. The *Discover Canada* guide, and the discourses within it, created for an adult audience, provides a framework for online CIC educational resources, which are created for young children, adolescents, and teachers of students in kindergarten to grade 12 (K–12).

Citizenship Educational Resources

The citizenship online educational resource web pages, *Games: A Fun Path to Learning* (Canada, 2013a) and *Teachers Corner* (Canada, 2014c), also present discourses of egalitarian and conservative gender relations (see Magnusson and Mojab, Chapter 1 of this volume, for an exploration of an alternative reality game as an educational resource that privileges colonial and patriarchal representations of women). The activities for younger children (Canada, 2013a), such as word searches, mazes, and crossword puzzles, recognize multiculturalism and (somewhat) women's experiences. Along with activities focused on voting processes and a Confederation timeline are an "Asian Heritage Month Word Find" and a "Black History Month Crossword Puzzle." The description for the "Prime Ministers of Canada Word Find" is "Do you know who was Canada's first female prime minister?" The "Great Canadian Crossword Puzzle," although still overrepresenting men (13 out of 19 answers), hockey (4 answers), and people of European descent (17 answers), has no military answers and has more named women (6, just over 31 per cent) than does the *Discover Canada* guide. While white men are still privileged, there is at least an increase in women's representations and a decrease in military ones. The existence of activities specifically about minority groups—in ways similar to the site's links to pages on Black History month, Asian Heritage month, and Holocaust remembrance—demonstrates the importance of learning about the experiences of these specific peoples but raises the question of why other groups, such as Aboriginals and women, are not included. Additionally, the isolation of marginalized groups in specific activities marks them as special interest but not central to Canada. The existence of a link promoting the War of 1812 once again highlights military events.

The activities for older children are much more clearly conservative and directly related to *Discover Canada*. (There are also web links to *Discover Canada* and indirect use of the guide's content in the activities for younger children, but the guide is not directly used.) There is a "Discover How Canadians Govern Themselves" link with a "Time Travel" timeline of Canada's government through the years (Parliament of Canada, 2012), based on a 1980 booklet of the same name by Senator Eugene Forsey. This activity is mostly text based, supported by photographs, and as such is likely intended for older children. In 38 entries detailing the time period between 1609 and the present day, white European men are once again represented as prominent in Canada's political history. Women are not mentioned until 1918, when they appear in three entries specific to women's rights (1918, Nelly McClung, women's suffrage; 1919, Agnes MacPhail, first woman Member of Parliament; and 1929, the Famous Five[2] and the Persons Case). Another entry (1982) pictures Queen Elizabeth signing Canada's Constitution Act. Aboriginal peoples are similarly only mentioned in four entries (1870, Louis Riel and the Metis rebellion; 1958, 1960, and 1983 in relation to Aboriginal rights). No other minority groups are mentioned. From the first entry in 1609, Canada is represented as an empty land founded, developed, and governed entirely by European men.

The *Teachers Corner* (Canada, 2014c) explains how K-12 teachers can use CIC citizenship resources as educational curriculum in their classrooms. It contains various links, including all activities from the "Games" (Canada, 2013a) page as discussed above. There is also a link to help teachers conduct citizenship reaffirmation ceremonies. Notably, there is a statement that "all students participating in the ceremony should be Canadian citizens" (Canada, 2013b, "Notice to Teachers"), and *Discover Canada* is listed as a resource. Under "Partner Initiatives" there is a link taking the user to a "Canadian Citizenship Challenge" (CCC, n.d., a) that is being conducted by Historica Canada and sponsored by CIC. It is open to students in grades 7 to 12, with a grand prize that includes a classroom citizenship reaffirmation ceremony. The CCC directly connects Canadian identity and citizenship to the *Discover Canada* guide, by asking young Canadians to "prove" they are Canadian by taking the challenge (CCC, n.d., b); it explains that the questions that students will be asked "are based on the actual guide that Canada's newcomers use to study for their citizenship test. However, you don't have to be a new Canadian to appreciate the Discover Canada Study Guide!" (CCC, n.d., d, para. 1). It is "an excellent reference to learn about all things Canadian" (para. 2).

Under the "Learning Tools" tab, there are links to curriculum lesson plans and worksheets, each with associated pages from the guide to be used as a textbook (CCC, n.d., c). Questions on the worksheets, as in the guide, do mention Aboriginal peoples and women but privilege men, masculinity, and militarism. With the guide as a reference, open-ended questions that ask students to describe historical events and contributions by Canadians will likely result in an overabundance of examples of war and men. Furthermore, several questions privilege military service and presuppose the societal benefit of various wars. For instance:

- "Although military service is not compulsory in Canada, there are other ways to become involved in the Canadian Forces. Give examples." ("Rights and Responsibility of Citizenship, Junior")[3]
- "Although there is no compulsory military service in Canada, the Discover Canada guide describes other ways to contribute to the Canadian Forces. Describe how you or someone you know has been involved with the Canadian Forces." ("Rights and Responsibility of Citizenship, Senior")
- "How does the war of 1812 continue to have an impact on Canada today?" (Pre-Confederation, Junior)
- "The War of 1812 is called 'The Fight for Canada.' Why do you think it is given that title? Go beyond a literal meaning and consider the impact of the war on Canada as a nation." (Pre-Confederation, Junior and Senior)
- "How are both the First and Second World War still historically significant to Canadians today?" (Post-Confederation, Junior)

Out of six links to other Historica projects co-sponsored by the Government of Canada (both on the site as a URL and in the lesson plans that suggest specific class activities), two are specifically about war: "The Memory Project" (which aims for current and retired military members to visit classrooms) and the "War of 1812 Educational Programming" (one element of which encourages citizens to attend citizenship ceremonies at War of 1812 sites).

The introduction of Ben-Porath's (2006) book about the links between citizenship and military service in both Israel and the United States begins with an example of a civic studies exam question that asks students to "'Explain why conscientious objection is subversive.'" In her exploration of this question, Ben-Porath states that "with a stroke of a pen, the exam writers had abandoned decades of democratic deliberation on the balance between conscience and compliance, between majority rule and minority dissent" (p. 1). While the Canadian questions above may not be quite so leading, the educational resources as a whole shape the course of learning in ways that privilege military history and military service over other historical events and other ways to demonstrate citizenship. The positive aspects of warfare are highlighted while alternative perspectives are sidelined. As the creator of these resources, the Canadian government has the power to promote a masculinized and militarized ideal of citizenship, not only for newcomers who are required to read the guide but for students in the K–12 system as well as anyone using the online resources.

Passport

The new Canadian passport also fits into a discourse of conservative gender relations that privileges militarized masculinity. Although the first overleaf of images forefronts Canada's Aboriginal peoples, it does so through the exclusive use of symbols; no people are pictured. The majority of the 31 pages with images depict males (12), transportation vehicles such as ships and trains as well as a warship and a warplane (8), infrastructure such as Parliament Buildings and Pier 21 (4), scenic locations such as Niagara Falls and Cape Spear (3), or war memorials (3). Hockey and football have their own pages, with associated Stanley and Grey Cups, as do the North West Mounted Police and the Royal Canadian Mounted Police (upon close inspection, it is possible that one of the RCMP officers may be a woman). All told, there are actually over 65 males in various images. The only place women are clearly represented is on a page celebrating the Famous Five, with one rather unflattering statue and four photographs from a newspaper article. Additionally, the fact that women are solely represented in direct relationship to women's rights situates women as only important with respect to issues that relate to women. All else is men's domain. Furthermore, there are no people of colour depicted. Canada as a whole is presented as masculinized and militarized, with white European men represented as founders and heroes. There are no dual discourses here. The content in the passport is very much connected to that of the guide. In a few cases, the same photographs are used in both documents.

Implications

The new citizenship study guide, as the "only official study guide for the citizenship test" (*Discover Canada*, p. 2) is positioned as a powerful pedagogy that teaches newcomers about privileged forms of Canadian citizenship. The discourses in the guide align with those in the online educational activities and the new Canadian passport, demonstrating the ways in which the government is promoting a masculinized and militarized discourse of citizenship.

As I was completing this chapter, the Canadian government tabled changes to citizenship laws in the form of Bill C-24. Three are of note: a longer waiting period with more stringent residency requirements, a broader age range for demonstration of language abilities and knowledge of Canada (increasing from ages 18-55 to 14-64), and "a faster track to citizenship for those who are a permanent resident who enlists with, or a foreign national on exchange with, the Canadian Forces" (Wingrove, 2014, para. 5). In a news release the government explains that the fast track for military members is "a way of recognizing the important contributions for those who serve Canada in uniform" (Canada, 2014b, para. 6). Once again military members are deemed to be more valued citizens, above those who make other contributions to Canada. If Bill C-24 passes, it will be enshrined in the Canadian Citizenship Act that, to use Province's (1970/2005) comparison, "the Soldier" is more worthy than ministers, reporters, poets, campus organizers, lawyers, and politicians. One might also add educators, community workers, artists, and all others who make important contributions to Canada to the list of those who are perceived as less important than military members. The claim by Defence Minister MacKay that military members "'are the best citizens of our country'" (McKay & Swift, 2012, p. 13) will be upheld. In her discussion about American citizenship rights as relates to gender, masculinity, and the military, Feinman (2000) argues for the need to "separate martial service from first class citizenship rights" (p. 212). Fourteen years later

Canada has done the opposite; "the military is [continues to be] too important to citizenship" (Feinman, 2000, p. 89).

When I began my analysis, I was looking at the CIC documents as connected yet discrete texts. However, as I continued, it became clear that *Discover Canada* is a "boss text" (a term discussed by Smith at a postgraduate workshop, May 16, 2006; see also Taber, 2009) in an "intertextual hierarchy" (Smith, 2006) wherein "higher-order texts regulate and standardize texts that enter directly into the organization of work in multiple local settings" (p. 79). In other words, certain texts dictate the contents of other texts; in this case, the CIC citizenship educational documents derive from the content of *Discover Canada*. Just as military boss texts are intended to codify the values of military members (Taber, 2009), the CIC documents "limi[t]...the sayable" (Butler, 2004, p. xvii), working to codify the values of Canadian citizens in ways that promote a militarized discourse. As Lazar (2005a) argues, while dual discourses of conservative and egalitarian gender relations may exist, the tensions between them result in conservative ones. The CIC documents teach a "sentimental history" that "enhance[s] the endorsement of the war culture" (Ben-Porath, 2006, p. 53) by advancing a very specific masculinized and militarized national identity.

CIC, as a department of the Government of Canada, is responsible for "promot[ing] the unique ideals all Canadians share" (Canada, 2012b, para. 1). Certainly, very specific ideals (discourses) are promoted in *Discover Canada*, the online educational resources, and the Canadian passport. From the representations therein, it appears that, despite a few exceptions, the ideals that *all* Canadians supposedly share are militaristic and masculinist, with *Discover Canada* functioning as a boss text. Prospective citizens have to demonstrate that they have learned these valued Canadian discourses in a test that determines their suitability for citizenship; students are asked to do the same when they learn about and reaffirm their citizenship; citizens prove their uniquely Canadian identity with their passport when travelling internationally. *Discover*

Canada and the discourses it promotes are not isolated. The guide is connected to pedagogical attempts by the Canadian government to teach citizens about accepted forms of national identity through the media, the passage of particular laws, and the celebration of military historical events. This lifelong learning for the state occurs in various contexts such as schools, in citizenship preparation, in affirming or re-affirming citizenship, and in daily life as children and adults interact with the media and government decisions. As the government appears to be focusing so much of its attention on creating a very particular education of the Canadian public, so must educators work to problematize these discourses of citizenship, offering alternative understandings and ways to learn about Canadian "ideals" that are pluralistic, critical, and complex.

NOTES

1. *A Look at Canada* was published by a Liberal government with copyright held by the Minister of Public Works and Government Services. *Discover Canada* was published by a Conservative government with copyright held by Her Majesty the Queen in Right of Canada, represented by the Minister of Citizenship and Immigration Canada.
2. A group that argued that women should be considered "persons" under Canadian law.
3. Junior refers to grades 7, 8, and 9, and Senior refers to grades 10, 11, and 12, corresponding to approximate ages of 13 to 18. In some provinces, Junior is grades 7 and 8, and Senior is grades 9, 10, 11, and 12.

REFERENCES

Basham, V. (2009). Effecting discrimination: Operational effectiveness and harassment in the British Armed Forces. *Armed Forces & Society, 35*(4), 728–744.

Ben-Porath, S.R. (2006). *Citizenship under fire: Democratic education in times of conflict.* Princeton, NJ: Princeton University Press.

Berthiaume, L. (2013, March 12). Canada's military is getting a new name—again. *National Post.* Retrieved from http://news.nationalpost.com

Butler, J. (2004). *Precarious life: The powers of mourning and violence.* London: Verso.

Butterwick, S. (1998). Lest we forget: Uncovering women's leadership in adult education. In G. Selman, M. Selman, M. Cooke, & P. Dampier (Eds.), *The foundations of adult education in Canada* (2nd. ed., pp. 103-116). Toronto: Thompson Educational.

Canada. Citizenship and Immigration Canada. (2005). *A look at Canada.* Minister of Public Works and Government Services Canada.

Canada. Citizenship and Immigration Canada. (2011). *Backgrounder—Substantial changes to the citizenship study guide: How* Discover Canada *differs from* A Look at Canada. Retrieved from www.cic.gc.ca/english/department/media/backgrounders/2009/2009-11-12a.asp

Canada. Citizenship and Immigration Canada. (2012a). *Discover Canada: The rights and responsibilities of citizenship.* Her Majesty the Queen in Right of Canada, represented by the Minister of Citizenship and Immigration Canada.

Canada. Citizenship and Immigration Canada. (2012b). Our mandate. Retrieved from www.cic.gc.ca/english/department/mission.asp

Canada. Citizenship and Immigration Canada. (2013a). Games: A fun path to learning. Retrieved from www.cic.gc.ca/english/games/index.asp

Canada. Citizenship and Immigration Canada. (2013b). Reaffirmation ceremony. Retrieved from www.cic.gc.ca/english/games/reaffirmation/index.asp

Canada. Citizenship and Immigration Canada. (2013c). Who has to take the citizenship test? Retrieved from www.cic.gc.ca/english/helpcentre/answer.asp?q=374&t=5

Canada. Citizenship and Immigration Canada. (2014a). Glossary: Adequate knowledge of Canada. Retrieved from www.cic.gc.ca/english/helpcentre/glossary. asp#adequate_knowledge_canada

Canada. Citizenship and Immigration Canada. (2014b). Strengthening and modernizing the Citizenship Act. Retrieved from www.cic.gc.ca/english/department/media/ releases/2014/2014-02-06.asp

Canada. Citizenship and Immigration Canada. (2014c). Teachers Corner. Retrieved from www.cic.gc.ca/english/games/teachers-corner.asp

Canada. Parliament of Canada. (2012). *Discover how Canadians govern themselves: Time travel.* Retrieved from www.parl.gc.ca/About/Parliament/SenatorEugeneForsey/time_travel/ index-e.html

Canada. Passport Canada. (2013). *Canada's new ePassport is here!* [Flyer included with new passport.]

The Canadian Press. (2013, August 21). Harper goes target shooting with Canadian Rangers in Arctic: PM tries out vintage rifles used by Northern reservists. *CBC News.* Retrieved from www.cbc.ca

CCC (Canadian Citizenship Challenge). (n.d., a). Citizenship challenge. Retrieved in February 2014 from http://canadiancitizenshipchallenge.ca/hdi.php

CCC. (n.d., b). Citizenship challenge: "I am Canadian" Prove it! Take the challenge. Retrieved from http://canadiancitizenshipchallenge.ca/index.php

CCC. (n.d., c). Citizenship challenge: Learning tools. Retrieved from http:// canadiancitizenshipchallenge.ca/index.php

CCC. (n.d., d). Citizenship challenge: Study guide. Retrieved in February 2014 from http:// canadiancitizenshipchallenge.ca/study_guide.php

Enloe, C. (2000). *Maneuvers: The international politics of militarizing women's lives*. Berkeley: University of California Press.

Enloe, C. (2004). *The curious feminist: Searching for women in a new age of empire*. Berkeley: University of California Press.

Enloe, C. (2007). *Globalization and militarism: Feminists make the link*. Lanham, MD: Rowman & Littlefield.

Feinman, I.R. (2000). *Citizenship rites: Feminist soldiers and feminist antimilitarists*. New York: New York University Press.

Fluri, J. (2008). "Rallying public opinion" and other misuses of feminism. In R. Riley, C. Mohanty, & M. Pratt (Eds.), *Feminism and war: Confronting US imperialism* (pp. 143-157). London: Zed Books.

Giroux, H.A. (2004). War on terror: The militarising of public space and culture in the United States. *Third Text, 18*(4), 211-221.

Giroux, H.A. (2008). Education and the crisis of youth: Schooling and the promise of democracy. *Educational Forum, 73*(1), 8-18.

Gouthro, P. (2007). Active and inclusive citizenship for women: Democratic considerations for fostering lifelong education. *International Journal of Lifelong Education, 26*(2), 143-154.

Gouthro, P. (2009). Life histories of Canadian women as active citizens: Implications for policies and practices in adult education. *Canadian Journal for the Study of Adult Education, 21*(2), 19-35.

Guo, S. (2013). Citizenship, immigration, and lifelong learning: Towards recognitive justice. In T. Nesbit, S. Brigham, N. Taber, & T. Gibb (Eds.), *Building on critical traditions: Adult education and learning in Canada* (pp. 319-329). Toronto: Thompson Publishing.

Guo, Y. (2013). English as a second language (ESL) programs for adult immigrants in Canada: Critical issues and perspectives. In T. Nesbit, S. Brigham, N. Taber, & T. Gibb (Eds.), *Building on critical traditions: Adult education and learning in Canada* (pp. 330-341). Toronto: Thompson Publishing.

Lahelma, E. (2005). Finding communalities, making differences, performing masculinities: Reflections of young men on military service. *Gender and Education, 17*(3), 305-317.

Lazar, M. (2005a). Performing state fatherhood: The remaking of hegemony. In M. Lazar (Ed.), *Feminist critical discourse analysis: Gender, power, and ideology in discourse* (pp. 139-163). New York: Palgrave Macmillan.

Lazar, M. (2005b). Politicizing gender in discourse: Feminist critical discourse analysis as political perspective and praxis. In M. Lazar (Ed.), *Feminist critical discourse analysis: Gender, power, and ideology in discourse* (pp. 1-28). New York: Palgrave Macmillan.

Leblanc, D. (2012, October 15). Museum of Civilization to change name, focus only on Canadian history. *Globe and Mail.* Retrieved from http://theglobeandmail.com

Martinez-Salazar, E. (2008). State terror and violence as a process of lifelong teaching-learning: The case of Guatemala. *International Journal of Lifelong Education, 27*(2), 201-216.

McKay, I., & Swift, J. (2012). *Warrior nation: Rebranding Canada in an age of anxiety.* Toronto: Between the Lines.

Province, C. (1970/2005). *It is the Soldier.* International War Veterans' Poetry Archives, 2013. Retrieved from www.iwvpa.net/provincecm/

Smith, D. (2006). Incorporating texts into ethnographic practice. In D. Smith (Ed.), *Institutional ethnography as practice* (pp. 65-88). Lanham, MD: Rowman & Littlefield.

Taber, N. (2009). The profession of arms: Ideological codes and dominant narratives of gender in the Canadian military. *Atlantis: A Women's Studies Journal, 34*(1), 27-36.

Taber, N. (2013). Learning war through gender: Masculinities, femininities, and militarism. In T. Nesbit, S. Brigham, N. Taber, & T. Gibb (Eds.), *Building on critical traditions: Adult education and learning in Canada* (pp. 139-148). Toronto: Thompson Publishing.

Taber, N. (2014). Generals, colonels, and captains: Discourses of militarism, higher education, and learning in the Canadian university context. *Canadian Journal of Higher Education, 44*(2), 105-117.

Welton, M.R. (2003). "No escape from the hard things of the world": Learning the lessons of empire. *International Journal of Lifelong Education, 22*(6), 635-651.

Wingrove, J. (2014, February 6). Ten ways Ottawa is changing how to become a Canadian citizen. *Globe and Mail.* Retrieved from www.theglobeandmail.com

Woollacott, A. (1998). Women munitions makers, war, and citizenship. In L.A. Lorentzen & J. Turpin (Eds.), *The women and war reader* (pp. 126-131). New York: New York University Press.

Young, I.M. (2003). The logic of masculinist protection: Reflection on the current security state. *Signs: Journal of Women in Culture and Society, 29*(1), 1-25.

5

A CRITICAL DISCUSSION ON DISABLED SUBJECTS

Examining Ableist and Militarist Discourses in Education

Mark Anthony Castrodale

IN THIS CHAPTER I DISCUSS militarization as it relates to the constitution of gendered and disabled subjects. According to Enloe (2007), militarization refers to a set of militaristic beliefs and values such as hierarchy, obedience, and use of force. Peterson and Runyan (1999) note that "militarization refers to processes by which characteristically military practices are extended into the civilian arena" (p. 258). As such, militarization represents a set of values and related regimes of practices. Militarized discourses support the representation and constitution of disabled bodies as lacking, deficient bodies, in contrast to those represented as ideal, normal, able bodies (Goodley, 2013; Titchkosky, 2007). I argue that dominant militarist ideologies materially and discursively produce disability.

First, I discuss the field of critical disability studies (CDS). CDS allows for increasingly nuanced ways of thinking about disabled bodies and *all* bodies as sites of possibilities (Titchkosky, 2003a, 2007, 2011) for considering what human bodies are, signify, and come to represent in new ways. I adopt a Foucauldian theoretical analytic framework to examine how militarization, gender, and disability are interconnected through discourses framing certain bodies and minds as valued and devalued in various times, places, and contexts. Lastly, I critically discuss disability as a pedagogical site of opportunity in Canadian educational contexts. I argue that considering the ways in which gendered and disabled bodies are constituted through knowledge-power relations and militarized discourses opens up pedagogical possibilities to counter dominant educational militarized norms and values and reimagine gendered and disabled subjectivities.

I identify as a temporarily able bodied (TAB) (Marks, 1999, p. 18), heterosexual, white, middle-class, male, and CDS university instructor (see also Castrodale & Zingaro, 2015). I identify as TAB to acknowledge that my embodied lived experience as an able-bodied person is likely temporary and may change, and perhaps through aging and life processes I may experience impairment and processes of disablement and forgo my able-bodied status. In my personal and professional life I actively engage in disability-related teaching and advocacy. I became involved in disability-related research, motivated by curiosity and the desire to understand better the lived experiences and socio-cultural meanings of disability in society (Castrodale & Crooks, 2010). I also wanted to challenge the oppression experienced by disabled persons including my mother, Lorraine, a special education teacher who passed away from breast cancer, and my lifelong friend Daniel Zingaro, who is blind (Castrodale & Zingaro, 2015). I developed and instruct a course titled "Critical Disability Studies in Education" at the Faculty of Education, University of Western Ontario. I would like to identify as a disability ally but do not feel that this is a designation I can give myself; rather, it is a title that I would gladly accept if it came from persons with disabilities. I reject the notion that disability exists as a problem, and instead posit that disability represents an educational site of the possibility to challenge the conventional, taken-for-granted ableist ways of being and knowing in the world. The problem then becomes the dominant societal norms and values inherent in education, whereby disability is constructed and understood as a problem by its very socio-cultural essence and appearance. This influences my pedagogical decisions at various junctures in my critical teaching praxis, which entails "reflection and action upon the world in order to transform it" (Freire, 2009, p. 51) and challenge the complex realities of oppression often experienced by disabled persons.

Critical Disability Studies: Unpacking Intersections of Disability and Gender

CDS is an interdisciplinary field in which scholars draw from a number of theoretical, methodological, and onto-epistemological frameworks to critically examine the construction of disability (Meekosha & Shuttleworth, 2009). Canadian CDS scholars often examine normalization, inclusion, accessibility, movement, mobility, knowledge-power relations, identity politics, and intersectionality; researcher and subject positionality; and ableism and privilege, among other interests (Michalko, 2008; Reaume, 2008; Titchkosky, 2011). The Canadian Disability Studies Association, founded in 2004, meets annually as part of the Congress of Humanities and Social Sciences connecting scholarship and activist work. Disability has emerged as a field of study at some Canadian universities (Reaume, 2008).

CDS-informed perspectives counter the prevailing historically informed tendency "to view people with disabilities as in need of fixing and control through treatment, cure or regulation" (Meekosha & Dowse, 2007, p. 169). A CDS framework thereby rejects the premise that disability is a problem that resides in individuals (Magasi, 2008; Michalko, 2008; Titchkosky, 2009, 2011). CDS scholars are often critical of the pathologization, individualization, and medicalization of disabled subjects.

According to Shildrick (2012), CDS may challenge existing knowledges and understandings of the nature of disability and raise "questions of embodiment, identity and agency as they affect all living beings" (p. 30). CDS draws on disabled persons' knowledges and interrogates able-bodied norms. Goodley (2011) asserts that disability represents a site of investigation "from which to think through a host of political, theoretical and practical issues that are relevant to all" (p. 157). CDS represents a lens through which to consider the entire human condition.

CDS offers ways to consider normalized functions and aesthetics ascribed to bodies and the socio-cultural values attached to being human (Titchkosky, 2011). Linton (1998) asserts that disability studies can inform thinking about "issues such as autonomy, competence, wholeness, independence/dependence, physical appearance, aesthetics, community, and notions of progress and perfection" (p. 118). Thus, CDS represents an effective lens for examining the discursive ways in which human bodies are constituted, the blending of bodies and new technologies, and various societal representations of disability.

Some CDS scholars have theorized and discussed the intersection of gender- and disability-related issues (see Begum, 1992; Ghai, 2002; Meekosha, 1998; Price, 2007; Thomas, 1999; Thompson 2004; Wendell, 1996, 2006). Feminist scholars have attested to the privileging of masculinity and patriarchal systems and to structures of power that characterize disabled individuals as feminine (Garland-Thomson, 1997). According to Sjoberg (2006), feminizing "something or someone is to directly subordinate that person, political entity or idea, because values perceived as feminine are lower on the social hierarchy than values perceived as neutral or masculine" (p. 34).

Feminist disability scholars have noted that intersections of disability and gender need to be examined because women with disabilities often encounter issues that are different from those encountered by disabled men (Garland-Thomson, 2005, 2006). Feminist disability studies extend scholarship beyond that which explores women with disabilities to interrogate and challenge the ways in which broader socio-cultural-political systems uphold dominant conceptualizations about gender and disability. To do so, feminist disability studies assert human rights, think critically about identity politics, make central the experiences of gendered and disabled persons, and reimagine disability (Garland-Thomson, 2005, p. 1557). Garland-Thomson (1997) argues that disability is a site that holds transgressive potential because it may challenge and disrupt able-bodied norms of movement, thought, and action, and open new ways to conceptualize or reconceptualize human bodies.

Parallels exist between feminism and disability studies as academic and activist pursuits that examine existing social relations and problematize universalizing norms (Garland-Thomson, 1997). Titchkosky (2012) notes that both feminist research and disability studies examine how exclusion is normalized and question "how certain people are regarded as on the edge of all that counts as human" (p. 82). The fields of CDS and feminist studies examine the human body as a bio-political site of contention and possibility. CDS and feminist disability-related inquiry thus converge in political interests in interrogating how the human body-mind is constituted through various knowledge-power relations and in examining the ways in which people are represented.

Both gendered and disabled subjects are constituted through knowledge-power relations where disability and femininity are often associated with deficiency and weakness in comparison with able-bodiedness and masculinity (Sjoberg & Via, 2010). According to Sjoberg and Via (2010), "characteristics traditionally associated with masculinity include strength, protection, rationality, aggression, public life, domination, and leadership. On the other hand, weakness, vulnerability, emotion, passivity, privacy, submission, and care have been traditionally associated with femininity....Manliness is prized whereas femininity is undesirable" (p. 3). Feminist disability scholar Wendell (1996) has noted that disciplinary and normalizing practices of femininity encourage women to meet physical standards linked to control and objectification of their bodies.

In "Examined Life," Butler and Taylor (2008) "take a walk" together to discuss "normalizing standards of movements" and the roles and functions of bodies. Importantly, they discuss techniques of walking, and Butler suggests that perhaps "we have a false idea that the able-bodied person is radically self-sufficient," asserting the need for interdependence and help. This counters individualistic ways of thinking and asserts collective connectivity in the meaning making of bodies. Butler argues for a rethinking of "what a body can do," in challenging normalized bodily functions. Gendered and disabled subjects are discursively constituted in relation to gendered and able-bodied norms. Extending Butler's point, orienting towards appreciating different modes of presentation, movement and thought destabilize the normative ways of presenting oneself, functioning, and being in the world. Asking what a body can do necessarily focuses attention on how human beings are discursively constituted through knowledge-power relations as disabled and gendered subjects.

Theorizing Militarism and Disability

Drawing on the works of Foucault (1984, 1994, 1995, 2003), one sees that gendered and disabled bodies are constituted discursively through webs of knowledge-power relations, and subjects may also work to constitute themselves. Examination of the intersection of gender and disability may shed new light on the ways in which bodies are constituted in various educational sites in potentially disempowering and empowering ways. In *Discipline and Punish* Foucault (1995) discusses disciplinary tactics and the "vast science of war" (p. 168) that applies to "the general foundation of all military practice, from the control and exercise of individual bodies to the use of forces specific to the most complex multiplicities" (p. 167). Military knowledges represent a body of knowledge of how to know, move, coerce, discipline, and govern people (Foucault, 1995). Foucault demonstrates military knowledge as a foundation of tactics, procedures, manoeuvres, exercises, and functions, which may be used to regulate and shape entire societies, thereby extending into educational realms.

According to Foucault (1995), discipline entails a series of calculated measures, methods, and techniques aimed at observing, knowing, ranking, and rendering bodies useful and *docile*. For Foucault, a disciplined *docile body* may be corrected, controlled, and regulated as an "object and target of power," where in every society individuals are subjected to "constraints, prohibitions, or obligations" (p. 136). Discipline increases the forces of the body in terms of socio-economic utility and decreases forces of resistance to encourage obedience (Foucault, 1995). *All* bodies may be enhanced. The perfect body, in military terms, is mouldable, moveable, and trainable (Foucault, 1995).

Militarization entails seeking advantages, advancing a position, finding tactical opportunities, and developing new technologies. Coordinating bodies that are unpredictable and unruly becomes troublesome. Militaries have been interested and invested in bodies, in making bodies perform certain spatio-temporally coordinated tasks (Foucault, 1995). For militaristic purposes bodies are trained, observed, organized, located, fixed, coordinated together or independently, and moved in rhythmic timings and particular places. Foucault describes this ideal soldier as a male

> who could be recognized from afar; he bore certain signs: the natural signs of his strength and his courage, the marks, too, of his pride; his body was the blazon of his strength and valour...the soldier has become something that can be made; out of a formless clay, an inapt body, the machine required can be constructed; posture is gradually corrected; a calculated constraint runs slowly through each part of the body, mastering it, making it pliable, ready at all times, turning silently into the automatism of habit. (p. 135)

Soldiers' bodies thus represent mouldable bodies that can be trained in the service of their country; they are paradoxically disposable and indispensable citizens (see Taber, Chapter 4 of this volume, for a discussion of the latter).

Disabled bodies are often characterized as deviant, labelled and sorted according to biomedical, psychological disciplinary fields of knowledges (Murray, 2007), understood as imperfect, faulty, fat, weak, penetrable, and leaky (Shildrick, 1997). The disabled body is seen as deficient, abnormal, and in need of fixing. Disability is associated with dependence, and the disabled body often represents an "entity to be conquered" (Batts & Andrews, 2011, p. 558). Urla and Terry (1995) assert that "scientific and popular modes of representing bodies are never innocent but always tie bodies to larger systems of knowledge production and, indeed, to social and material inequality" (p. 3).

Unpacking the constitution of all bodies entails critically thinking about the biomedical gaze (Foucault, 2003), dividing practices, hierarchical rankings, and normalizing judgements (Foucault, 1995), the materiality of bodies (Butler, 1993), the carnal politics of embodiment, and theorizing relating to the intersection of disability, gender, sexuality, race, and class. According to Goodley (2011), "a body or mind that is disabled is also one that is raced, gendered, trans/nationally sited, aged, sexualised and classed" (p. 33). Seeking to improve bodies deemed to be weak and fragile, military operations have developed bio-robotic, technological inventions such as the exoskeleton, which may enhance balance, speed, agility, and efficiency of movement and increase load-carrying capacity (Bogue, 2009). Not only do these technologies support direct military objectives, but they extend into the civilian arena, improving and rehabilitating disabled bodies often to move further and function faster in accordance with able-bodied norms. All bodies may be blended with biomedical, militarized technologies to render them more useful and productive.

CDS offers avenues to critically examine military technologies in relation to how they shape the mattering of bodies. Technologies relating to augmentation and enhancement are of particular military interest. The ways in which bodies are moulded to fit and function with new technologies create hybrid bodies and perhaps new cyborg-body identities (Haraway, 1991). As an example, the prosthetic limbs of the model and athlete Aimee Mullins are imbued with aesthetic form and function. Thompson (2004) comments on how she "counters the insistent narrative that one must overcome impairment rather than incorporating it into one's life and self, even perhaps as a benefit....Mullins uses her conformity with beauty standards to assert her disability's violation of those very standards. As legless and beautiful, she is an embodied paradox, asserting an inherently disruptive potential" (p. 97).

Thus, socio-cultural standards of beauty and ability are tied to norms of gendered performativity, connected in a nexus of function and form, aesthetic norms and norms surrounding movement, and ability in various spaces and contexts. To transgress these norms is to violate the "ideal" of "able-bodied" and the "ways of being, or moving, that...approximate more closely to the bodily actions and practices of 'able-bodied' people" (Price & Shildrick, 2002, p. 67).

As militarized technologies, ideals, standards, and values enter educational realms and inform pedagogical practices, it is essential to critically evaluate new educational technologies, examining how they relate to the ways in which teachers and learners are constituted. Such technologies may reflect normalized, gendered, and able-bodied ideals and reinforce dominant ways of thinking and being in the world. For Falk (2008), all pedagogies may represent military pedagogies because education is a strategic weapon that shapes individuals' subjectivities as nation-states vie for power. As such, "education doesn't win hearts and minds. Education makes them" (p. 2).

How Does Militarism Materially and Discursively Produce Disability?

Unpacking the ways in which disability is understood in relation to militarized discourses entails examining the ways in which disability as individual impairment is often thought of as a consequence of war. Batts and Andrews (2011) note, in reference to the American wars in Iraq and Afghanistan, that "improvements in protective gear and medical technology have reduced the occurrence of battlefield deaths, but the soldiers who survive often come home with missing limbs, traumatic brain injuries and permanent paralysis" (p. 556). Disability is thus viewed as an outcome of conflict and war, and not as a related discursive theme of militarism that is embedded into the very fabric of dominant educational paradigms and related pedagogies on disability.

Images and representations of soldiers often display young, fit, brave or heroic, able-bodied, male individuals (see Lane, Chapter 2 of this volume, for an exploration of such images and representations on the Canadian Armed Forces' Facebook pages). Thinking about the norms of function, aesthetics, ability, movement, body capacities and capabilities highlights the complex intersection of gender and disability. Fitness is another similar normative concept (see Saul, Chapter 10 of this volume, for an examination of militaristic influences in sport). In the nexus of military, state, citizen, and education, disability is something undesirable, thought of only as an unfortunate outcome of war. Bodies are measured as fit or unfit in relation to other bodies and are targeted to be trained to meet the expectations of what is deemed fit. Pedagogical methods of training are perpetually refined to fashion the correct types of persons suited to meet militarized needs.

How do war and militarism create disability? According to Garland-Thomson and Bailey (2010), "war creates disability in two ways. It makes disabled populations, often specific to the technologies of particular wars, through wounding; at the same time, it sustains populations of disabled people by producing new medical treatments applied to soldiers and civilians alike" (p. 409). Furthermore, "mutilation, dismemberment and disability are expected, and intentional, outcomes of warfare" (p. 557). Disability is thereby thought of as an unfortunate outcome for injured soldiers, *brave warriors* maimed in the service of their country.

Notable recent Canadian examples of the devaluation of disability include the experiences of soldiers with post-traumatic stress disorder such as Leona MacEachern who died on Christmas Day, having committed suicide (Stone, 2014), and Bruce Moncur who "lost part of his brain for Canada" (Maloney, 2013). Justin Stark's mother was mailed a cheque for one cent from the Canadian military, presumably for owed military pay because it had been concluded that the suicide of her son while he was on service was not related to his tour in Afghanistan (Carter, 2014). There were 13 military suicides 2013, and 8 suspected suicides in 2014 as of April (Canadian Press, 2014). Quoting veterans ombudsman Guy Parent, "as of March 2013, there were 38,380 veterans in receipt of the disability award, with that number expected to increase by 5,000 over the next five years" (Maloney, 2013). The overall absurd response is not to re-examine the Canadian military expansion that perpetuates disability and post-traumatic stress disorder in soldiers, but to call for the hiring of more mental-health professionals. According to Erevelles (2011), there is a notable absence of scholarship on disability and war in both disability studies and feminism. Erevelles states that "war is one of the largest producers of disability in a world that is still inhospitable to disabled people" (p. 132). Thus, wars impair bodies and minds to materially produce disabled subjects.

Able-bodied soldiers come back from war less able, shell shocked, maimed, incapacitated, or struck down. Military strikes involve surgical precision and smart bombs (Gross, 2010), operatives, military intelligence, shock-and-awe tactics, and disarmament. Westernized war rhetoric employs biomedical discourses that camouflage the constitutively and materially violent nature of war. Biomedical, psychological, and neuro-scientific knowledge is embedded in military discourses and in the fabric of weapon design and military strikes (Gross, 2010). Non-lethal weapons are designed to inflict damage in ways that "incapacitate targets," causing physical distress and disorientation (Gross, 2010, p. 34). As such, weapons from their very fruition are conceived and designed to quite literally impair individuals. Wars are thus testing grounds for such bio-medical technologies in which human beings are the research subjects.

The United Nations report "Enable Development of Human Rights for All" (2008) notes that rises in disability and the marginality of disabled persons are linked to wars and the consequences of wars, destruction, and violence, among other factors. Canadian Armed Forces members have reported 3,424 disability claims—most often the psychiatric disabilities of depression, post-traumatic stress disorder, and substance abuse, relating to the war in Afghanistan of 40,000 troops—and 158 of the claimants have died (Terry, 2014). Other "gravely injured," disabled veterans are being dismissed before the minimum 10 years of service that is required for a pension (Brewster, 2013). Wars materially produce disability through violence that renders bodies and minds impaired. Wehbi (2011) notes that disabled people are not merely in need of care in times of war; many also engage in disability rights and anti-war-related protests and activism. Yet unpacking the implications of militarized discourses in the very constitution of disabled subjects is a different endeavour. This form of critique entails being attentive to the military complex, institutions, technologies, knowledges, regimes of truth, practices, and discourses that support, maintain, and further reproduce militarized consciousness. It is this militarized, discursive, knowledge-power web that acts like shrapnel deeply embedded in the material bodies and minds of members of society. Disability is thus conceptually formed as a militarized discursive product. As an example, Remembrance Day, which is typically observed in Canadian schools with lesson plans—some of which are developed and available online on the Veterans Affairs (Canada, 2014) website—and moments of silence, is a day that heroically acknowledges soldiers' war efforts while espousing messages of peace.

Sjoberg and Via (2010) attest: "Though war is an essential condition of militarism—the apex, the climax, the peak experience, the point of all the investments, training, and preparation—militarism is much, much broader than war, comprising an underlying system of institutions, practices, values, and cultures. Militarism is the extension of war-related, war-preparatory, and war-based meanings and activities outside of 'war proper' and into social and political life more generally" (p. 7). Militarism extends conceptually to pervade the very ways in which social actors may think and act to cultivate a readiness to engage members of a given society in war. In this sense, war is not an end point; rather it is a constellation of technologies and tactics inscribed onto the fabric of societies that is woven through individuals' bodies and minds. Thus, challenging militaristic discourse entails thinking critically about the historical, socio-economic, and political relations involved in constituting individuals and categorizing, training, normalizing, and rendering people useful as implicated in support of a broadly cast military-complex net. Challenging militarism entails examining the educational tools of teaching and training and the ways that gendered and disabled subjects are discursively constituted in educational settings.

Pedagogies of Possibility: Examining Militarism, Gender, and Ability or Disability

In Canadian post-secondary education, disabled students encounter barriers to education (Hutcheon & Wolbring, 2012; Low, 2009) where female students may experience greater obstacles than do male students (Erten, 2011). Now at the beginning of my journey as a university instructor developing CDS-informed pedagogical frameworks, I engage with a CDS-informed pedagogy as a set of fundamental teaching principles that entail building positive relationships; valuing the voices and knowledges of persons with disabilities; thinking critically about representation, power, and privilege; and questioning able-bodied norms and values. Enacting a CDS-informed pedagogy entails viewing education as a site of struggle, and teaching and learning as dynamic processes without end points. Developing a CDS pedagogy also entails operationalizing a set of onto-epistemological tools to counter the dominant ableist and sanist values perpetuating the societal oppression of disabled and mad persons (Castrodale, 2014). I often start with issues of physical access in order to demonstrate that an absence of accessible ramps excludes persons with mobility impairments; I then relate this to forms of information and teaching practices that limit the engagement and full participation of all learners. I espouse that in Canadian contexts there is a need to conceptually draw on CDS in ways that promote full inclusion: being flexible in teaching approaches, drawing on multiple perspectives, acknowledging educational social actors as having agency, treating knowledge as socially constructed, providing options for assessments and opportunities for students' success, modifying teaching practices and pedagogies in response to diverse learning styles and needs, building rapport, providing materials in multiple accessible formats, and considering the classroom as a dynamic socio-spatial place as a site with meaning and value.

Why turn to critical pedagogy? Judith Butler (1993) asks, "Which bodies matter, and which bodies are yet to emerge as critical matters of concern?" (p. 4). Educational systems struggle to deal with different bodies and minds. In educational contexts schools may represent places where students with disabilities can be categorized as "other" and subsequently treated in harmful ways (Kumashiro, 2000). Critical pedagogies are needed to appreciate and acknowledge different voices, bodies, experiences, abilities, sentiments, and knowledges in classrooms.

Barton and Slee (1999) note that conceptions of *ability* and *failure* are reflected in policies and practices of schooling as part of a broader regulatory discourse involving power and control. Davis (1995) states, "To understand the disabled body, one must return to the concept of the norm, the normal body...the 'problem' is not the person with disabilities; the problem is the way that normalcy is constructed to create the 'problem' of the disabled person" (pp. 23-24). Educational systems and regimes of practices classify and categorize individuals on the basis of cognitive and physical ability in relation to gendered and able-bodied dominant norms. Despite Canadian provincial and territorial legislation promoting inclusion of disabled students in regular classrooms, students with disabilities continue to be marginalized and segregated in relation to non-disabled students in elementary and secondary educational settings (Canadian Council on Learning, 2007). Education policies such as the British Columbia Ministry of Education's Policy Framework on Special Education, Alberta's Special Education Policy, and Ontario's Education Act on Special Education, and practices informed by medicine, rehabilitation, special education, and social work have focused on cure, care, and rehabilitation of disability, in contrast to critical pedagogies informed by disability studies that are often characterized by reflection, empowerment, and transgression (Ware, 2009). Special education represents a culture that believes that disabled students are less than non-disabled students and thereby more deserving of an education based on their ability (Slee, 2011). Within the cultural politics of Canadian education, when students with disabilities are characterized and subsequently treated as special or exceptional, disability is individualized, thereby removing the onus on teachers to question their own attitudes, ableist educational values, and normalizing pedagogical practices.

How can the field of CDS inform pedagogy? Titchkosky (2012) notes the importance of understanding and discussing disability that is "lived as something other than a negative add-on to personhood" as a way to appreciate "disability and person, human and body," which may open "pedagogic possibility" (p. 84). Importantly, Titchkosky asserts that "the meaning of bodies, minds and senses [is] formed from our relations—from the in-betweens of histories, politics, and cultures....Once recognized as limit and at the end of what counts as human, disability is emptied of life" (p. 92). Considering the meanings of bodies in educational settings opens the possibilities of reconsidering what bodies do. Bodies become learning and teaching sites of pedagogic possibility for thinking critically about human knowledges and experiences. This rejects the notion that disability represents a problem; "disability is often regarded as a problem not only for individuals but also for the state" (Titchkosky, 2003b, p. 521). All bodies thus become sites of possibility for learning about the social relations formed in those socio-spatially negotiated places that exist between material bodies. McLaren (2009) notes that critical pedagogy "asks how and why knowledge gets constructed the way it does, and how and why some constructions of reality are legitimated and celebrated by the dominant culture while others clearly are not" (p. 63). Pedagogies informed by CDS appreciate complex socio-political, knowledge-power relations in which disability is perpetually made, or remade, and understood. CDS opens pedagogical possibilities for examining disability as a site of socio-cultural meaning, joy, struggle, and contestation and as a place to learn about humanity.

CDS-informed pedagogies recognize systemic violence against human bodies; they ponder what it means to be human and how all humans might live with freedom. Such pedagogies reflect a radical commitment to challenge oppressive knowledges, norms, and structures in ways that break from "stifled humanity" and promote empowerment and freedom in hopes of a "fuller humanity" (Freire, 2009, p. 47). Critical pedagogies informed by CDS may unpack the marginalizing militarized discourses and the related regimes of practices that are embedded in educational systems. According to Freire, in attending to oppression it is necessary to counter dehumanizing pedagogies and epistemic violence inherent in society and education. A possible avenue of resistance is the posing of critical, reflexive questions about what it means to be a student, learner, teacher, or citizen in society. Educational sites represent paradigmatic battlegrounds. How might educational technologies, knowledges, and practices be potentially co-opted in support of militarism and a militaristic society? Posing such questions is part of a critical pedagogy that is attentive to gender, disability, and militarism. How might the constellation of converging educational and military technologies and regimes of practices be mapped? Questions such as these critically examine knowledge-power relations and social constructions of disability and gender—not solely as important concepts to think about but as onto-epistemological concepts with which to think.

When disability is understood solely in reductionist biomedical terms as an individual problem, educational attitudes and related regimes of practices stemming from this paradigm of a disabled subject as a problem person perpetuate the oppression of disabled persons (Baglieri & Shapiro, 2012). This entails understanding the socio-political nature of disability, that meanings ascribed to disability are socio-cultural constructs (Ware, 2009), and that educational contexts and pedagogical decisions may enable and disable particular students to demonstrate particular skills and abilities. This fits within a Freirian (2009) notion that "knowledge emerges through invention and re-invention, through the restless, impatient, continuing, hopeful inquiry human beings pursue in the world, with the world, and with each other" (p. 72). CDS-informed pedagogies may critically question the militarized values of individualism, independence, competition, efficiency, and productivity. Instead, collective action, social relationships, communication, modes of expression, respect for difference, and complex understandings of various lived and embodied experiences might hold greater value. Teaching and learning may draw upon the voices of disabled persons, and the field of CDS represents a platform for dialogic encounters (Freire, 2009). CDS disrupts militaristic ideals and offers moments to pause and ask not what education is, but what education can do.

CDS pedagogies would necessarily draw on the subjugated knowledges and voices of disabled persons in ways that inform increasingly inclusionary educational policies and practices. People who wish to paradigmatically wage *war against war* need to consider CDS as a theoretical, tactical toolbox that holds possibility on these discursive battlegrounds.

Non-conclusion: New Game Openings

Disability is rarely conceived as a critical lens through which militarism and related concepts may be examined and discussed in new ways. Militaristic discourses evoke numerous connected concepts such as performativity, strength, fitness, individualism, othering, progress, technological innovation, strategies, and tactics; security, surveillance, spying, and defence; border policing and crossings; invasion and infiltration; violence, torture, and disciplining of bodies and minds. Moreover, Westernized war-related rhetoric, such as *friendly fire, collateral damage, military intelligence,* and *smart bombs,* subtly disguises and disregards the truly abhorrent destructive consequences of militaristic forces on bodies and minds. Such language effectively camouflages the militaristic discourses and knowledges used to placate the destructive, violent procedures, tactics, and ethics and the murderous politics-enacted consequences of war.

CDS disrupts the taken-for-granted notion that disability exists as an individual problem, as a personal calamity, deficiency, lack, absence of full function, or naturally foreseeable outcome of war. A CDS lens reveals the thoughts and actions in support of militarism as inherently ableist. CDS challenges the underlying beliefs and attitudes that deem non-disabled bodies and minds as worthy while devaluing others that do not function in able-bodied, masculine, normalized ways; as such CDS is a field that is inherently anti-military. It is anti-militaristic in the following ways: it offers critical spaces to think about individualization and collective human experiences while still appreciating, valuing, and understanding difference (Titchkosky, 2011); it problematizes and questions the notions of progress and technological interventions aimed at making bodies and minds better, more productive, stronger, faster, and functionally and aesthetically beautiful and desirable according to normative societal values; it critically examines the temporal norms that make bodies and minds work and do things at particular paces and within certain organized, orchestrated timings; it problematizes the spatial norms that categorize, sort, divide, move, and arrange or rearrange bodies and minds in particular places and contexts. Problematizing and rejecting the desire to perpetually make disabled and gendered bodies perform in normalized ways asserts that people can act and think at their own pace, in their own ways, differently, individually and collectively, and with personal-political agency.

There is a need for research that examines the ways in which militarized technologies, systems, practices, knowledges, and regimes of truth relate to the societal constitution of gendered and disabled subjects. Why is disability often understood as a foreseeable, logical, and accepted outcome of war and not as a conceptual basis and rich theoretical site for critiquing militarism? CDS provides such a platform for launching criticisms that take aim at the militarized ways of thinking and being in the world. As a field of inquiry, scholarship, and knowledge, CDS offers onto-epistemologic vantages and strategic counter-ethics to think, act, and live differently. Teaching about disability-related social justice in Canadian contexts necessarily means critically examining the marginalization experienced by disabled persons. Critical pedagogy becomes a means to counter the societal values, norms, attitudes, policies, and practices that oppress disabled persons.

REFERENCES

Baglieri, S., & Shapiro, A. (2012). *Disability studies and the inclusive classroom: Critical practices for creating least restrictive attitudes.* New York: Routledge.

Barton, L., & Slee, R. (1999). Competition, selection and inclusive education: Some observations. *International Journal of Inclusive Education, 3*(1), 3-12.

Batts, C., & Andrews, D.L. (2011). "Tactical athletes": The United States Paralympic Military Program and the mobilization of the disabled soldier/athlete. *Sport in Society: Cultures, Commerce, Media, Politics, 14*(5), 553-568.

Begum, N. (1992). Disabled women and the feminist agenda. *Feminist Review, 40,* 70-84.

Bogue, R. (2009). Exoskeletons and robotic prosthetics: A review of recent developments. *Industrial robot: An international journal, 36*(5), 421-427.

Brewster, M. (2013, October 29). Injured Canadian troops booted from military before qualifying for pension. *Toronto Star.* Retrieved from www.thestar.com

Butler, J. (1993). *Bodies that matter: On the discursive limits of "sex."* New York: Routledge.

Butler, J., & Taylor, S. (2008). *Examined life* [Motion picture]. United States: Zeitgeist Films.

Canada. Veterans Affairs. (2014, March 24). *Veterans Affairs: Government of Canada.* Retrieved from www.veterans.gc.ca

Canadian Council on Learning (2007). *Equality in the classroom: The educational placement of children with disabilities.* Retrieved from www.ccl-cca.ca

The Canadian Press. (2014, April 8). Depression, suicide among Canadian soldiers concerns military surgeon general. Retrieved from www.cbc.ca

Carter, A. (2014, March 4). Dead soldier gets 1-cent cheque from federal government. *CBC News*. Retrieved from www.cbc.ca

Castrodale, M.A. (2014). Mad matters: A critical reader in Canadian mad studies. *Scandinavian Journal of Disability Research*. doi: 10.1080/15017419.2014.895415.

Castrodale, M., & Crooks, V.A. (2010). The production of disability research in Human Geography: An introspective examination. *Disability & Society, 25*, 89-102.

Castrodale, M.A., & Zingaro, D. (2015). "You're such a good friend": A woven autoethnographic narrative discussion of disability and friendship in higher education. *Disability Studies Quarterly, 35*(1).

Davis, L.J. (1995). *Enforcing normalcy: Disability, deafness, and the body*. London: Verso.

Enloe, C. (2007). *Globalization and militarism: Feminists make the link*. Lanham, MD: Rowman & Littlefield.

Erevelles, N. (2011). *Disability and difference in global contexts: Enabling a transformative body politics*. New York: Palgrave Macmillan.

Erten, O. (2011). Facing challenges: Experiences of young women with disabilities attending a Canadian university. *Journal of Postsecondary Education and Disability, 24*(2), 101-114.

Falk, C. (2008). All pedagogy is military. In T. Kvernbekk, H. Simpson, & M.A. Peters (Eds.), *Military Pedagogies: And why they matter* (pp. 1-16). Rotterdam: Sense Publisher.

Foucault, M. (1984). Space, knowledge, and power. In P. Rabinow (Ed.), *The Foucault Reader* (pp. 239-256). New York: Pantheon.

Foucault, M. (1994). *The order of things: An archeology of the human sciences*. New York: Vintage Books.

Foucault, M. (1995). *Discipline and punish: The birth of the prison*. New York: Vintage Books.

Foucault, M. (2003). *Birth of the clinic: An archaeology of medical perception*. London: Routledge.

Freire, P. (2009). *Pedagogy of the oppressed*. New York: Continuum.

Garland-Thomson, R. (1997). *Extraordinary bodies: Figuring physical disability in American culture and literature*. New York: Columbia University Press.

Garland-Thomson, R. (2005). Feminist disability studies. *Signs: Journal of Women in Culture and Society, 30*(2), 1557-1587.

Garland-Thomson, R. (2006). Integrating disability, transforming feminist theory. In L.J. Davis (Ed.), *The Disability Studies Reader* (2nd ed., pp. 257-275). New York: Routledge.

Garland-Thomson, R., & Bailey, M. (2010). Never fixed: Modernity and disabled identities. In M. Wetherell & C.T. Mohanty (Eds.), *The Sage handbook of identities* (pp. 403-436). Thousand Oaks, CA: Sage.

Ghai, A. (2002). Disabled women: An excluded agenda for Indian feminism. *Hypatia: A Journal of Feminist Philosophy, 17*(3), 49-66.

Goodley, D. (2011). *Disability studies: An interdisciplinary introduction*. London: Sage Publications.

Goodley, D. (2013). Dis/entangling critical disability studies. *Disability & Society, 28*(5), 631-644.

Gross, M.L. (2010). Medicalized weapons and modern war. *Hastings Center Report, 40*(1), 34-43.

Haraway, D. (1991). A cyborg manifesto. In *Simians, cyborgs and women: The reinvention of nature* (pp. 149-183). London: Free Association Books.

Hutcheon, E.J., & Wolbring, G. (2012). Voices of "disabled" post secondary students: Examining higher education "disability" policy using an ableism lens. *Journal of Diversity in Higher Education, 5*(1), 39-49.

Kumashiro, K.K. (2000). Toward a theory of anti-oppressive education. *Review of Educational Research, 70*(1), 25-53.

Linton, S. (1998). *Claiming disability: Knowledge and identity*. New York: New York University Press.

Low, J. (2009) Negotiating identities, negotiating environments: An interpretation of the experiences of students with disabilities. In T. Titchkosky & R. Michalko (Eds.), *Rethinking normalcy: A disability studies reader* (pp. 236-250). Toronto: Canadian Scholars' Press.

Magasi, S. (2008). Disability studies in practice: A work in progress. *Topics in Stroke Rehabilitation, 15*(6), 611-617.

Maloney, R. (2013, October 11). Former soldier who lost part of his brain for Canada says sacrifice being demeaned. *Huffington Post*. Retrieved from huffingtonpost.ca

Marks, D. (1999). *Disability: Controversial debates and psychosocial perspectives*. London: Routledge.

McLaren, P. (2009). Critical pedagogy: A look at the major concepts. In A. Darder, M.P. Baltodano, & R.D. Torres (Eds.), *The critical pedagogy reader* (2nd ed., pp. 61-83). New York: Taylor & Francis.

Meekosha, H. (1998). Body, battles: Bodies, gender and disability. In T. Shakespeare (Ed.), *The disability reader: Social science perspectives* (pp. 163-180). London: Continuum.

Meekosha, H., & Dowse, L. (2007). Integrating critical disability studies into social work education and practice: An Australian perspective. *Practice: Social Work in Action, 19*(3), 169-183.

Meekosha, H., & Shuttleworth, R. (2009). What's so "critical" about Critical Disability Studies? *Australian Journal of Human Rights, 15*(1), 47-75.

Michalko, R. (2008). Double trouble: Disability and disability studies in education. In
S. Gabel & S. Danforth (Eds.), *Disability and the politics of education: An international reader* (pp. 401-416). New York: Peter Lang.

Murray, S. (2007). Corporeal knowledges and deviant bodies: Perceiving the fat body. *Social Semiotics, 17*(3), 361-373.

Peterson, V.S., & Runyan, A.S. (1999). *Global gender issues: Dilemmas in world politics.* Boulder, CO: Westview Press.

Price, J. (2007). Engaging disability. *Feminist Theory, 8*(1), 77-89.

Price, J., & Shildrick, M. (2002). Bodies together: Touch, ethics and disability. In M. Corker & T. Shakespeare (Eds.), *Disability/postmodernity: Embodying disability theory* (pp. 62-75). London: Continuum.

Reaume, G. (2008). Introduction to DSQ theme issue on disability in Canada. *Disability Studies Quarterly, 28*(1).

Shildrick, M. (1997). *Leaky bodies and boundaries: Feminism, postmodernism and (bio)ethics.* New York and London: Routledge.

Shildrick, M. (2012). Critical Disability Studies: Rethinking the conventions for the age of postmodernity. In N. Watson, A. Roulstone, & C. Thomas (Eds.), *Routledge handbook of disability studies* (pp. 30-41). London: Routledge.

Sjoberg, L. (2006). *Gender, justice, and the wars in Iraq: A feminist reformulation of just war theory.* Lanham, MD: Lexington Books.

Sjoberg, L., & Via, S. (2010). Introduction to C. Enloe, L. Sjoberg, & S. Via (Eds.), *Gender, war, and militarism: Feminist perspectives* (pp. 1-16). California: Praeger.

Slee, R. (2011). *The irregular school: Exclusion, schooling, and inclusive education.* London: Routledge.

Stone, L. (2014, April 15). Invisible wounds: Is the new veterans charter working? *Global News.* Retrieved from www.globalnews.ca

Terry, A. (2014, April 15). Crisis in the military. *Global News.* Retrieved from www.globalnews.ca

Thomas, C. (1999). *Female forms: Experiencing and understanding disability.* Buckingham, UK: Open University Press.

Thompson, R.G. (2004). Integrating disability, transforming feminist theory. In B.G. Smith & B. Hutchison (Eds.), *Gendering disability* (pp. 73-103). New Brunswick, NJ: Rutgers University Press.

Titchkosky, T. (2003a). *Disability, self and society.* Toronto: University of Toronto Press.

Titchkosky, T. (2003b). Governing embodiment: Technologies of constituting citizens with disabilities. *Canadian Journal of Sociology, 24*(4), 517-542.

Titchkosky, T. (2007). *Reading and writing disability differently: The textured life of embodiment.* Toronto: University of Toronto Press.

Titchkosky, T. (2009). Disability images and the art of theorizing normality. *International Journal of Qualitative Studies in Education, 22*(1), 75-84.

Titchkosky, T. (2011). *The question of access: Disability, space, meaning.* Toronto: University of Toronto Press.

Titchkosky, T. (2012). The ends of the body as pedagogic possibility. *Review of Education, Pedagogy, and Cultural Studies, 34*, 82-93.

United Nations. (2008). Enable development of human rights for all: World programme of action concerning disabled persons. Retrieved from www.un.org/disabilities/default. asp?id=23

Urla, J., & Terry, J. (1995). Introduction: Mapping embodied deviance. In J. Terry & J. Urla (Eds.), *Deviant bodies: Critical perspectives on difference in science and popular culture* (pp. 1-18). Bloomington: Indiana University Press.

Ware, L. (2009). Writing, identity, and the other: Dare we do disability studies? In A. Darder, M.P. Baltodano, & R.D. Torres (Eds.), *The critical pedagogy reader* (2nd ed., pp. 397-416). New York: Taylor & Francis.

Wehbi, S. (2011). Advancing a disability rights agenda in a context of war: Challenges and opportunities. *International Social Work, 55*(4), 522-537.

Wendell, S. (1996). *The rejected body: Feminist philosophical reflections on disability.* New York: Routledge.

Wendell, S. (2006). Toward a feminist theory of disability. In L.J. Davis (Ed.), *The disability studies reader* (pp. 243-257). New York: Routledge.

6

UNCOVERING RAINBOW
(DIS)CONNECTIONS

Sexual Diversity and Adult Education
in the Canadian Armed Forces

Robert C. Mizzi

THERE ARE CERTAIN PLACES, such as sports arenas and fraterni-
ties, that are undoubtedly marked as heteromasculine. Anderson
(2009) describes heteromasculinity as being a form of masculinity that
suppresses women and lesbian, gay, bisexual, transgender, and queer
(LGBTQ) people through terminologies, codes, behaviours, understandings, or practices that privilege heterosexual men. I include in this
concept of heteromasculinity the notion of "hegemonic masculinity,"
which asserts that masculinity of men is made dominant by way of
culture, institution, and persuasion and that femininity and subordinated masculinity are inferior (Connell & Messerschmidt, 2005). As a
gay man, I was acutely aware of and navigated through encounters of
heteromasculinity in these specific places. When I approached recruiters of the Canadian Reserves at the University of Windsor in 1997, I was
aware that I was entering another heteromasculine space in the context

of Canadian military environments (Kinsmen & Gentile, 2010). My non-normative gender role (that is, I am considered to be not a "real man" or a "normal man" because of my sexuality and effeminate mannerisms) may be an unwelcomed feature to these military personnel. As it turns out, I did not receive my invitation to an information night that was promised to me by the recruiters. When faced with questionable and senseless encounters of rejection, bias, and marginalization, LGBTQ people could assume, with good reason, that the roots of such encounters are based on homophobic or transphobic beliefs and practices and sexual stigma, as Herek (2004) and Pharr (1997) note in general.

As I have said elsewhere (Mizzi, 2013), there needs to be more explorative work to probe the covert forms of marginalization that target LGBTQ people, now that there has been a policy change to include sexual orientation (and, in some parts, gender identity) in anti-discrimination frameworks such as provincial human rights legislation. This chapter traces such covert forms of marginalization and has two functions: (1) to suggest how the Canadian Armed Forces (CAF) could make a better effort to confront the systemic and social marginalization of LGBTQ people through their associations and practices, and (2) to argue that education can act as a useful space in which to explore and discuss the topic of sexual and gender diversity in military contexts. Based on my research and on the literature, I suggest that, although Canada and the CAF have made significant progress towards inclusion, more work is needed towards eradicating structural and social homophobia and transphobia in all aspects of military life. If a homophobic culture indeed exists in the CAF, as identified by Poulin, Gouliquer, and Moore (2009), then this culture can conceivably go beyond affecting LGBTQ members; it also shapes the ways that service members and leaders view and interact with military and civilian others, nationally and internationally. My research into two international agencies acts as one such example for consideration, in which Canada aligned itself with, and communicated, questionable information through training discourses. Although this is one small study, and I do not argue for generalizability of CAF practices, this chapter does provide a glimpse into some of the possible realities facing LGBTQ people in peacebuilding and peacekeeping training contexts, which may be helpful to the CAF as they continue to explore and practice LGBTQ inclusion. In this chapter I use LGBTQ persons and issues as my lens, but the dismantling of a homophobic culture has much greater implications for gaining mutual respect, insights into human diversity, and new ways of interaction.

This chapter begins with a chronicle of the uneasy, historical relationship between Canadian LGBTQ citizens and the CAF, based on the literature. Very little research had been done from the time of the CAF's creation to the present day on what it means to be LGBTQ in the CAF. Despite this limitation, bringing to light some of the socio-historical context illustrates how the past can affect the current conditions in which teaching and learning take place (Butterwick & Egan, 2010). As my study examines the teaching practices of adults, I then describe some of the literature around being LGBTQ in adult education settings. I illustrate a study (Mizzi, 2011) conducted in a foreign mission (Kosovo) and share how I stumbled across a Canadian military connection to teaching practices there. In that study I noted how Canada funded two agencies that drew on the military expertise of the CAF to train aid workers for their missions in conflict situations. Although some of this study has been reported elsewhere (Mizzi, 2013, 2014, in press), this chapter offers a secondary analysis of the research project and explores the unexpected Canadian connection (e.g., some CAF personnel's designing curriculum for, and Canada's financial assistance to, third-party agencies) to a study of adult education and sexuality in a post-conflict situation. I then summarize the chapter with a series of recommendations for administrative consideration that include enhanced attention to the way in which gender and sexual diversity are considered in military life. A summary is also provided at the conclusion of the chapter.

Historical Context

Before 1992: Heteromasculine Obstinacy in the Canadian Armed Forces

Sexual regulation has been part of military life since the creation of the Canadian Armed Forces (Kinsman & Gentile, 2010). From the outset, military leadership required male military personnel to be financially stable and to have female partners who were of "good moral character" prior to marriage (Jackson, 2010). Otherwise, as Jackson describes, the perception was that the soldier might not be willing to engage in dangerous combat because his attention would be focused on the activities back home. Generally speaking, in these marriages the constant movement of military personnel had a negative impact on the family, disrupting social lives, which over time drew attention to the need for benefit plans for families, pensions for wives, crisis counselling, and family life enrichment programs (Harrison & Laliberté, 1997). The emphasis on "good moral character" as a fundamental value is significant to LGBTQ people because of the medical, legal, and social discourse that casts LGBTQ people as perverted, sick, and immoral (Janoff, 2005; Terry, 1999), all of which compromise "good moral character."

The history of gay and lesbian personnel working in the Canadian military is marked by controversy and exclusion.[1] Until 1992, for instance, openly gay and lesbian personnel were not allowed to participate or serve in the Canadian military (Belkin & McNichol, 2001; Jackson, 2010; Kinsman & Gentile, 2010). In their analysis of the Canadian military, Kinsman and Gentile explain that "women and homosexuals were perceived as disruptive of these relations of bureaucratic rationality in that they introduced a 'subjective' eroticism and emotionality into these allegedly non-erotic institutional settings, thus subverting hierarchical relations between superiors and subordinates" (p. 60). Heteromasculinity, then, becomes threatened by the presence of openly gay and lesbian people and of women, which has led to the suppression of these two groups over time. Whitworth (2004) explains that militaries have been resistant to this inclusion because "the presence of the 'other' makes the strategies of recruitment, basic training, and the inculcation of an appropriate militarized masculinity all the more difficult to accomplish, and those involved in recruiting and training have long understood this" (p. 162).

Harsh humiliation and persecution of homosexuality in the CAF has traumatized some, perhaps all, gay and lesbian military personnel. As a result of living secret lives, they have experienced high stress, exhaustion, depression, addictions, and isolation (Jackson, 2010; Kinsman & Gentile, 2010; Osborne, 2007; Poulin et al., 2009). This is largely in response to the Canadian Forces Administrative Order 19-20, which states that "service policy does not allow homosexual members or members with a sexual abnormality to be retained in the CF" (Canada, 1992, n.p.). In a lesbian context, Kinsman and Gentile (2010) write that "as part of the military's sexist gender organization, anti-lesbian policies have worked to keep all women in line" (p. 63). Poulin et al.'s study (2009) on these policies and their impact on lesbian health suggests that the surveillance, persecution, and the overall witch hunt of lesbians qualify as torture under Canada's Criminal Code. Although no women in Canada were investigated and court-martialled for homosexuality during the war years (Kinsman & Gentile, 2010), Poulin et al.'s study suggests that persecution can be detrimental to a person's well-being, even without that person experiencing judicial tribunals that determine fate and consequence (see also Osborne's study for a similar gay male perspective, 2007). Poulin et al. argue that, owing to this persecution, support agencies (e.g., psychologists) may need to treat lesbian military personnel (as well as gay men in many respects) as "torture victims" when it comes to determining the kinds of assistance that need to be made available. What did work for lesbians and gay men was the military provision of some respite through the offer of a career that eluded the social expectation of entering a cross-sex marriage. Women, in particular, were often expected to become housewives and mothers, but when they decided to enter the military, this expectation was not as significant. Lesbians were then able to enjoy same-gender intimate relationships to some degree while being in the military, as long as the relationships remained secret (Kinsman & Gentile, 2010).

The secret lives of lesbians and gay men prompted investigative practices in the CAF in order to uncover same-sex sexual and emotional activities. Jackson (2010) points out that military psychiatrists played the role of investigator to determine homosexuality in an individual during "routine examinations" of military personnel. During this time, homosexuality was a criminal offence in Canadian law, repealed in 1969. A so-called "fruit machine" was approved in 1962 as a mechanism by which a series of psychological tests was forced onto suspected gay or lesbian military personnel in order to identify and remove them from the CAF and from the civil service broadly (Jackson, 2010; Kinsman & Gentile, 2010; Smith, 2012). According to Smith (2012), the "fruit machine" incited gay and lesbian military personnel, as well as other civil service personnel, to "socialize with each other in private networks, meeting only in each other's homes for fear of discovery; hiding their relation-ships and sexual lives from their families, co-workers, and communities; and living a veritable double life, in some cases, for all of their lives" (p. 121).

Besides these measures there was also generally a forced visibility of gay or lesbian military personnel as well as other civil servant workers. Tactics such as (a) observing and analyzing dress, mannerisms (such as effeminate mannerisms), or places visited, (b) using postal and military censors to sift through and read private mail of military personnel, and (c) engaging training exercises, such as those in Brandon, Manitoba, to communicate homophobic slurs (e.g., "queers," "fruits"), kept homosexu-ality firmly in the closet (Jackson, 2010; Kinsman & Gentile, 2010). The literature explains that when suspected gay or lesbian military person-nel were identified, rightly or wrongly, commanding officers typically ignored the situation until other military personnel vocalized their discomfort, in which case the uncovered gay or lesbian personnel would often be transferred elsewhere (Kinsman & Gentile, 2010; Osborne, 2007).

Court martials took place whenever sexual behaviours disgusted the commanding officers or comrades, proof of homosexual relationships was given to military police (who would then choose whether or not to pursue the matter), and/or the homosexual activity was considered an embarrassment to the unit. A guilty verdict of indecent conduct would likely result in a dishonourable discharge and imprisonment (Osborne, 2007). Clearly, there was no consistency in the way that the military addressed same-sex sexual activity (Jackson, 2010), and the "fruit machine" never really accomplished its goal of eradicating lesbians and gay men from the military or civil service (Kinsman & Gentile, 2010). Although there are reports of "thousands of Canadian women and men" being discharged for homosexuality (Kinsman & Gentile, 2010), to date there has been no effort to recant dishonourable discharges, offer an apology, or provide compensation for personal traumas caused by the CAF to their gay and lesbian military personnel (Simcoe, 2015; Smith, 2009).

Higate and Henry (2009) argue that the military is undoubtedly a gendered space, one that privileges masculine or heteromasculine self-interest. They argue for a critical awareness of this gendered space and male privilege, and create opportunities to re-conceptualize masculinity. Included in this critical awareness is an exploration of the various forms of "performances" that express masculinity in military contexts. An analysis of homosocial bonding in the CAF prior to 1992 may provide one avenue by which to explore the notion of performances. In particular, Jackson (2010) and Halladay (2004) highlight how homosocial bonding was a part of life in the CAF. There were incidences during World War II of male-to-male "marriages" among Canadian prisoners of war and/or active-service military personnel (Jackson, 2010), and "marriages" of males to "campy," cross-dressing female impersonators as part of entertainment units (Halladay, 2004). What generally made this an acceptable practice was that the military personnel who were engaged in male-to-male marriages and female-impersonator performances performed well as soldiers, and they remained as men after the performance finished. Put differently, using the Australian military as a case study, Flood (2008) describes how homosocial behaviour is a result of "highly organized relations *between men*" (p. 341, original italics), whereby performance of manhood is granted as a way for men to seek and obtain approval and improve their position in a social hierarchy (wealth, power, achievement, and so forth). According to Flood, homosocial bonds tend to perpetuate gender inequality by privileging male-male relationships over male-female relationships, engaging in cross-sex sexual activities towards elevating social status, using heterosexuality as the basis for bonding, and shaping sexual storytelling through homosocial masculine cultures, such as military cultures. These marriages and female-impersonator performances in the CAF allowed men to express homosocial behaviour in heteromasculine culture and were in no way indications of a military culture that accepted sexual and gender diversity.

The literature reported in this section is based on pre-1992 activities and provides a glimpse into the socio-historical contexts and conditions for gay and lesbian military personnel in that time period. The next section chronicles events after 1992, the year that the Canadian ban on openly gay and lesbian military personnel was removed.

Post-1992: Visualizing Practices and Their "Problems"

The legal and social situation for LGBTQ military personnel started to positively change after the subsequent removal of the ban on gay and lesbian military personnel in 1992. One of the key activists for the policy change to remove the ban was Michelle Douglas, a lesbian serving in the military who, with four other service members, successfully challenged the constitutionality of the ban (Enloe, 1993). Douglas (2009) comments that when the policy changed to allow openly lesbian and gay citizens to serve in the military, its administrators budgeted for the creation of separate washrooms for lesbian and gay male military personnel as a means to *protect* heterosexual soldiers from the perception of homosexual deviance, if not advances. The issue for top leaders of the CAF was the fact that they wanted to maintain military effectiveness and minimize conflict within the forces (Belkin & McNichol, 2001). Although separate washrooms were never built, and there was "no impact on military performance, readiness, cohesion or morale" (Belkin & McNichol, 2001, p. 74) as a result of the removal of the ban, the presence of these discussions indicates an uphill battle for LGBTQ acceptance and inclusion.

An uphill battle may mean the way the notion of homosexuality is broadly considered in military culture. For example, in the case of Somalia, Canadian peacekeepers used the term *homosexual* in a pejorative way to cast Somalians as the "enemy." Whitworth (2004) explains that "the Canadians, indeed, had already decided that Somalis—in particular Somali men—could not be trusted. They were black; they were the enemy; they had no respect for their women; they were liars and thieves; they were not grateful for Canadian efforts; and they were even, in the opinion of many Airborne soldiers, homosexuals. Marked in this way, the violence perpetuated on them seems almost evitable" (p. 101).

This example is an indication of how notions of heteromasculinity and manliness subverted the "enemy" and created an "other" group of unwanted people. Representing the enemy as homosexual is not entirely a new phenomenon in military culture (see Arsić, 2002). In an earlier study (Mizzi, 2002), a Canadian Reservist explained to me the notion of "blanket parties," in which a blanket is thrown over a presumably LGBTQ person before they are beaten in order to hide evidence of bruising from violent homophobic or transphobic attacks. What is troublesome here is that it is a war practice that repositions the homosexual "other" as an enemy of the Canadian state at a time after the removal of the ban and after other legal changes, such as the inclusion of sexual orientation as prohibited grounds of discrimination in the Canadian Human Rights Act in 1996 (Canada, 2013). Events such as those in Somalia act as useful benchmarks in the way that language and practices are being exercised, now that the CAF are becoming more concentrated on LGBTQ inclusion.

Recently, the CAF have made an intentional outreach to signal their inclusion of the LGBTQ community. This outreach is evidenced by public participation in LGBTQ spaces such as Canadian gay pride events. For example, during the 2013 Edmonton pride festival the rainbow flag (an international symbol of LGBTQ pride and equality) was flown at Canadian Forces Base Edmonton, which was the first time in Canadian history that this flag had been raised on an army base (Canadian Broadcasting Corporation, 2013). On the one hand, these efforts should be applauded; recruitment efforts at pride festivals, facilitation of same-sex marriages at military chapels, and support for sex-reassignment surgery for transgender military personnel communicate that the CAF can be a safe and meaningful career option for LGBTQ citizens. On the other hand, as with other Canadian institutions such as schools and hospitals, more work can be done towards inclusion of sexual and gender diversity. What may be of use in this inclusion-building effort is a close examination of the relationships and interactions that shape the CAF's activities and draw attention to the spaces in which homophobia and transphobia continue to exist. Training curriculum and program planning provide one avenue for exploration, given that education provides opportunity for critical discussions to take place and ask difficult questions.

Teaching Practice, Sexuality, and Silence

Scholars in queer studies have long argued that there has been a pattern of LGBTQ exclusion in the teaching of adults (Brooks & Edwards, 1999; Grace, 2001; Grace & Hill, 2001). Heterosexism shapes the language, decisions, and symbols used in teaching practice, which neglects and eradicates LGBTQ persons from curriculum and pedagogy (Grace, 2001). Queer knowledge becomes, then, "fugitive," in that "knowledge...is constructed by individuals and groups outside of officially recognized knowledge-makers or canonists of a field" (Hill, 2006, p. 8). Fugitive knowledge means that queer knowledge is locked out of education discourse; it is not welcomed or appreciated in an educational setting. Teaching adults in a non-heterosexist way and welcoming queer knowledge mean that, according to Grace and Hill (2001), "adult educators can investigate and expose institutional and structural aspects of adult education that support and maintain heterosexualizing discourses and heteronormative learning climates to the detriment of the queer educators and learners it disenfranchises. On a micro-level, adult educators can strategize and develop policies, programs, courses, and activities that problematize anti-queer perspectives, initiatives, symbols, and language in a heterosexualizing culture-power-nexus" (p. 4).

Grace and Hill's work has implication for teaching mechanisms, such as training seminars and curriculum, and for educators working in the CAF. Investigating and exposing heterosexualizing discourses, and then taking steps to ensure that sexuality and gender difference are discussed through education, may build on the CAF's position towards LGBTQ inclusion. My research project, as described in the next section, offers one such example that exposes various degrees of heterosexism, and may provide some direction for a next stage of LGBTQ inclusion.

Research Project

I conducted research with gay male, adult educators who had crossed borders into Kosovo after the 1999 conflict[2] to work with Kosovars on different subject matters, such as democracy, media ethics, and civic participation. In addition to in-depth interviews with staff personnel, and similar to Taber's methods (Chapter 4 in this book), I analyzed relevant official documents. In my situation, training curricula, websites, and policies from two international aid agencies ("Agency 1" and "Agency 2") in Kosovo were analyzed to further understand how these agencies included certain identities while marginalizing "others." Access to both agencies was facilitated by the fact that I am a Canadian citizen and that Canada provides financial support and guidance to these two agencies. In addition, I was able to enrol in two online courses on the topics of ethics (Agency 1) and security (Agency 2), which provided me with an indication of the kinds of content that was being introduced to aid workers prior to their departure to their placements. Computer-based instruction was used to deliver the curriculum. Through this work I uncovered how CAF personnel have become involved in the training of aid workers and how they have transplanted their value systems, understandings, and practices—some of which I found to be problematic—into a civilian workforce. This military involvement is problematic in that there are negative effects, such as a racial and gendered "other," that peacekeepers create in the name of "peace" (Duncanson, 2009; MacKay, 2003; Whitworth, 2004). Although this may not be general practice of the CAF, nonetheless it is present in this study, and further discussion that strengthens an approach to LGBTQ inclusion may be of value.

Although both agencies are not directly part of the Canadian Ministry of Defence, Canada remains accountable in this project when it (1) forms professional relationships with agencies that work to serve the needs of Canadians and (2) allows some of its military personnel to be hired by such agencies for the purposes of writing curriculum and training new hires, which was the situation for Agency 2. Below are two perspectives on the data-collection process and what was revealed with respect to sexual and gender diversity. Since I view my role as a researcher as being multifaceted, which includes being a student, teacher, learner, collaborator, inquirer, and social critic, I separated out two of these perspectives for consideration. The first perspective is my own experience as a student in the computer-based, pre-departure orientations. The second perspective is the data that was uncovered from analysis of the training content. I reveal the data below and follow with my analysis.

Researcher as Student

During my experience as a student in the online course for Agency 2, I noticed that sexual orientation issues surfaced within HIV/AIDS pedagogy. In the curriculum it states that "most men who have sex with men have no characteristics that distinguish them from other men. Some may have adapted certain *looks* or *mannerisms* which identify them as being gay" (p. 85, emphasis added). Further explanation is not provided about the meaning of these two sentences in the course (e.g., how do effeminate, heterosexual men fit into this code?), and there is no adult educator, or other learners, present to discuss them. Noteworthy about the program of Agency 2 is that it expects respect "regardless of rank, ethnic or national origin, race, or gender" and outlines in a very detailed module on culture the importance of being inclusive towards members of specific social groups. LGBTQ people are not listed as one of these groups. Further, no information is provided about the meaning of *rank* for a civilian population.

Besides the learning through pre-departure orientations, my research suggests that informal learning became necessary for agencies to teach *acceptable* and *correct* professional behaviours. In the online course for Agency 1, I observed in the curriculum that informal learning was encouraged as a form of professional development:

> There are many places to go for information, such as: (1) Personnel who have experienced similar difficulties to you can give you *good advice* not only on the local culture and customs, but also on methods that they have found effective in coping with the differences, and (2) Local staff who understand your culture will be well placed to advise you on the differences and how to avoid the *"classic" mistakes* that they often see made. ("Culture and Influence," para. 6, emphasis added)

No other explanation was offered about the incidences that comprised these "classic mistakes" or the sort of "good advice" that would be passed on to me from colleagues.

Researcher as Inquirer

Information gathered from the analysis of training programs reveals that sexual orientation was considered a low priority in the training material. The emphasis was more on organizational structure, systems, performance measures, and competences and on safeguarding the organization's image. For example, in Agency 1, the training took place in room called "The Square of Heroes" and featured lecturers from mixed military and civilian backgrounds. An exploration into social differences and the implications for human interaction and development was allowed two to three hours in both training sessions, which lasted for three to four days.

In addition, despite my having had a lengthy conversation about sexuality with the training director for Agency 2, he still identified "more driving time" as a much-needed resource in the training of aid workers. He redirected to the staff psychologist questions regarding sexual orientation. My follow-up conversation with the psychologist confirmed that homophobic assaults, such as verbal attacks, would be grounds for the person who had experienced the assault to be transferred elsewhere, and little emotional support would be provided because, unlike issues relating to racial or religious oppression, issues relating to homosexuality and homophobia were, as the staff psychologist said, "not in the curriculum, not what is requested and not in our terms of reference."

Discussion

Although it was not my goal to research, examine, and analyze the CAF in my study, it indirectly filtered into my data collection by way of the associating and supporting training organizations that draw on CAF expertise and Canada's financial resources. In the two agencies considered, an implicit curriculum reinforces silence around homosexuality when sexuality issues are excluded from or awkwardly referred to during training sessions. I interpret the training director's decision to ignore my comments on sexual orientation as a form of ignorance and lack of understanding towards the inclusion of sexuality matters. Coupling this discussion with my own experience in the online courses informed me that sexuality is considered to be a low priority for course development and that sexuality topics are seemingly silenced in military culture.

Yet, when curricula do mention sexuality, it becomes a form of otherness that is marked by "looks" and "mannerisms," as described through one of the online courses, whereas there are no "looks" or "mannerisms" to be watchful of heterosexual people. Such implicit curricula act as a form of surveillance, in which people learn about gay men as containing a standard set of attributes and that these attributes are to be treated as suspect—given that this information was shared during a module on HIV/AIDS risks. It also ignores the possibility of some gay men being very masculine and passing as "straight," and some heterosexual men being very effeminate. Further, there is no guarantee, given the controversial history of homosexuality, that LGBTQ people will be able to safely find the information and the support needed from their local or international counterparts without making some form of "classic mistake" that may cause them to be ostracized from their workplaces.

The actions of Agency 2 to transfer persons who experienced homophobic violence is similar to the way in which pre-1992 gay men and lesbians were transferred elsewhere if their homosexuality was perceived to be a nuisance. I noticed that staff psychologists followed the curriculum written by Canadian military personnel and/or supported by Canada, which suggests that the practice of transferring away the "problem" of homosexuality has not yet disappeared. Following Belkin and McNichol (2001), higher-ranking officers can be of assistance by minimizing discriminatory and disruptive conduct based on sexual-orientation differences.

With this point in mind, there may be some staunch opposition to addressing homophobia in any military setting, given that the state once supported such oppression. There was no clear direction evident during this study for the appropriate handling of sexual and gender diversity. The knowledge and inclusion gaps cause me to question the sincerity and comprehensive nature of facilitating sexual and gender diversity in international settings (similar to Hanson, in Chapter 7 of this volume). These gaps may very well remain until there is sufficient and adequate attention given to policy and social change. This means that military

personnel of any Western nation may be expected to accept openly
LGBTQ recruits and to participate in pride events, but heteromasculinity
remains steadfast in other aspects of military culture.

Recommendations and Concluding Thoughts

More research is clearly needed in the areas of teaching practices and
relationships identified in this chapter. Yet, despite the gap, the data in
this research study suggests that an implicit curriculum may reinforce
silence and that this form of curriculum goes against the diversity and
equity goals of any agency. I suggest an open discussion concerning
all teaching and learning practices so that sexual and gender diversity
becomes part of mainstream interactions and relationships in the activities of the CAF, both inside and outside of Canada. This would assist in
the widespread identification and removal of activities that maintain an
uneven balance between heterosexual and LGBTQ persons.

In line with Poulin et al. (2009), Schwartz (2012), and others, in
addition to instrumental strides towards LGBTQ inclusion, the CAF
may want to review their current activities and examine the ways that
heteromasculinity infiltrates their training systems, from new recruits
to top leadership. This initiative means a frequent revision of curriculum
because queer knowledge is constantly changing as new insights are
garnered about human diversity. Hanson (in Chapter 7 of this volume)
comments that education has the potential for the radical change of
social norms. That said, this pedagogical approach functions as an
informational source for everyone, including those involved in procur-
ing services. Embedded in this sensitivity training should be an acute
awareness of the socio-historical contexts and conditions that have
challenged LGBTQ military personnel; the different kinds of indirect
and direct homophobia and transphobia, and strategies to confront
them; an awareness of the struggles facing LGBTQ children of military
personnel and children with same-sex parents in the military; and the

ways in which militarized situations (e.g., reserves and peacekeepers) may experience sexual and gender diversity. Discussions of this nature position sexuality as a source of insight into the way world cultures function, and thus reshape understanding about human relationships. Tools such as critical media literacy, which Haddow describes in this book (Chapter 3), can help critique the ways in which sexuality and militarism are depicted in popular culture.

There are two goals to this educational approach: (1) sexual and gender diversity becomes an ongoing, thoughtful exploration about human difference, and (2) military personnel can respectfully discuss and tackle difficult encounters that may stem from sexual and gender differences. Higate and Henry (2009) identify the military as being a gendered space that privileges masculinity; therefore, these recommended goals invite an open dialogue about the history of homosexuality in the CAF and an exploration into the ways in which the military can further realize the impact of a heteromasculinist culture in its operations and among its members and stakeholder groups. Leaders will have to acknowledge that such a culture exists and take further steps towards sexual and gender inclusivity. One foreseeable challenge to this approach is the dependence on a politic of visibility, that is, LGBTQ service members being willing to disclose themselves to describe their situations (Poulin, 2001). Sometimes this is easier said than done. Such a challenge then implicates heterosexual allies to become aware of, and speak up against, homophobia, transphobia, and heteromasculinity in their day-to-day activities and associations.

Furthermore, and in alignment with Magnusson and Mojab and in this book (Chapter 1), it is important to continue to make strides towards rendering *invisible* social relations *visible*. This means a comprehensive review of existing systems and relationships to ensure that they align with LGBTQ inclusiveness, respect, and safety. It became clear in the data that some members of the CAF incited homophobic behaviours through training discourses. A "rainbow audit" is one way to inform the Canadian military about demonstrating inclusiveness (e.g., the Halifax

Rainbow Health Project's Inclusion Program, 2006). While community work such as participation in pride parades is important towards communicating an open military, a rainbow audit is a type of systemic analysis that identifies queer-exclusion practices among organizations. A rainbow audit can then (a) develop the possibility of new understandings that can be integrated in educational programs, (b) unlearn the values and information that create silence, (c) problematize initiatives that stifle LGBTQ inclusion, (d) promote an atmosphere that proffers and welcomes queer knowledge, and (e) compensate for past damages as an effort to build credibility. With this audit comes a commitment to changing the heteromasculinization of military systems so that LGBTQ Canadians do indeed experience comprehensive inclusion and respect when it comes to engaging with all levels of the CAF.

To summarize, in this chapter I have provided a snapshot of the historical patterns of LGBTQ exclusion in the CAF and then have profiled recent LGBTQ efforts. I illustrated two cases of training curricula abroad, and their Canadian connections, and suggested how the behaviours of associated personnel (curriculum designers, human resource developers) may lead to silence and exclude LGBTQ realities. Without a doubt, the CAF need to continue their efforts towards LGBTQ inclusion by better identifying and addressing issues relating to heteromasculinity. A review of training mechanisms and the creation of rainbow audits may assist the CAF in their inclusion efforts.

NOTES

1. There is scant literature on the lives of transgender and bisexual military personnel.
2. At the time of writing this chapter, Kosovo remained a contested state. Although it declared independence on February 17, 2008, it was still considered a province by Serbian authorities (Judah, 2008).

REFERENCES

Anderson, E. (2009). *Inclusive masculinity: The changing nature of masculinities.* New York: Routledge.

Arsić, B. (2002). Queer serbs. In D. Bjelić & O. Savić (Eds). *Balkan as metaphor: Between globalization and fragmentation* (pp. 253-277). Cambridge, MA: MIT Press.

Belkin, A., & McNichol, J. (2001). Homosexual personnel policy in the Canadian Forces: Did lifting the gay ban undermine military performance? *International Journal, 56*, 73-88.

Brooks, A., & Edwards, K. (1999). *For adults only: Queer theory meets the self and identity in adult education.* Paper presented at the Annual Adult Education Research Conference, University of Minnesota, Minneapolis, MN.

Butterwick, S., & Egan, J. (2010). Sociology of adult and continuing education: Some key understandings for the field of practice. In C. Kasworm, A. Rose, & J. Ross-Gordon (Eds.), *Handbook of adult and continuing education* (pp. 113-122). Los Angeles: Sage.

Canada. Canadian Heritage. (2013). Sexual orientation and human rights. Retrieved from www.pch.gc.ca

Canada. Office of the Commissioner for Federal Judicial Affairs Canada. (1992). *Douglas v. Canada (T.D.), [1993] 1 F.C. 264.* Retrieved from http://reports.fja.gc.ca/eng/1993/1993fca0430.html

Canadian Broadcasting Corporation. (2013). *CFB Edmonton 1st base to raise gay-pride flag.* Retrieved from www.cbc.ca

Connell, R.W., & Messerschmidt, J.W. (2005). Hegemonic masculinity: Rethinking the concept. *Gender and Society, 19*(6), 829-859.

Douglas, M. (2009). [untitled]. Keynote address at the 2009 Outgames Human Rights Conference, Copenhagen, Denmark.

Duncanson, C. (2009). Forces for good? Narratives of military masculinity in peacekeeping operations. *International Feminist Journal of Politics, 11*(1), 63-80.

Enloe, C. (1993). *Sexual politics at the end of the Cold War: The morning after.* Berkeley: University of California Press.

Flood, M. (2008). Men, sex, and homosociality: How bonds between men shape their sexual relations with women. *Men and Masculinities, 10*(3), 339-359.

Grace, A. (2001). Using queer cultural studies to transgress adult educational space. In V. Sheared & P. Sissel (Eds.). *Making space: Merging theory and practice in adult education* (pp. 257-270). Westport, CT: Bergin & Garvey.

Grace, A,. & Hill, R. (2001). *Using queer knowledge to build inclusionary pedagogy in adult education.* Paper presented at the Annual Adult Education Research Conference, Michigan State University, Lansing, MI.

Halifax Rainbow Health Project. (2006). *Inclusion program.* Retrieved from www.rainbowhealth.ca

Halladay, M. (2004). A lovely war. *Journal of Homosexuality, 46*(3-4), 19-34.

Harrison, D., & Laliberté, L. (1997). Gender, the military, and military family support. In
L. Weinstein & C. White (Eds.), *Wives and warriors: Women and the military in the United States and Canada* (pp. 35-53). Westport, CT: Bergin & Garvey.

Herek, G. (2004). Beyond "homophobia": Thinking about sexual prejudice and stigma in the twenty-first century. *Sexuality Research & Social Policy, 1*(2), 6-24.

Higate, P., & Henry, M. (2009). *Insecure spaces: Peacekeeping in Liberia, Kosovo and Haiti.* London: Zed Books.

Hill, R. (2006). What's it like to be queer here? *New Directions for Adult and Continuing Education, 112,* 7-16.

Jackson, P. (2010). *One of the boys: Homosexuality in the military during World War II.* Montreal and Kingston: McGill-Queen's University Press.

Janoff, D. (2005). *Pink blood: Homophobic violence in Canada.* Toronto: University of Toronto Press.

Judah, T. (2008). *Kosovo: What everyone needs to know.* New York: Oxford University Press.

Kinsman, G., & Gentile, P. (2010). *The Canadian war on queers: National security as sexual regulation.* Vancouver: University of British Columbia Press.

MacKay, A. (2003). Training the uniforms: Gender and peacekeeping operations. *Development in Practice, 13*(2-3), 217-222.

Mizzi, R. (2002). *Peace OUT! Visualising the invisible in peace education* (Unpublished master's research project). University of Alberta, Edmonton.

Mizzi, R. (2011). *Disturbing boundaries: How professionalism (mis)manages adult educators working in international development* (Unpublished doctoral dissertation). York University, Toronto.

Mizzi, R. (2013). "There aren't any gays here": Encountering heteroprofessionalism in an international development workplace. *Journal of Homosexuality, 60*(11), 1602-1624.

Mizzi, R. (2014). Troubling preparedness: Investigating the (in)visibility of LGBT concerns within pre-departure orientations. *Development in Practice, 24*(2), 286-297.

Mizzi, R. (in press). Tackling cultural blinders: Towards an understanding of a sexuality, adult education, and intercultural dynamic. In G. Strohschen (Ed.), *Metagogy: Toward a praxis for adult education in intercultural contexts.* Marietta, GA: American Scholars Press.

Osborne, Z. (2007). *Queer consequence: Homosexuality and its penalties in the Canadian military, 1939-1945* (Unpublished master's thesis). Acadia University, Wolfville, NS.

Pharr, S. (1997). *Homophobia: A weapon of sexism.* Berkeley, CA: Chardon Press.

Poulin, C. (2001). "The military is the wife and I am the mistress": Partners of lesbians in the Canadian military. *Atlantis, 26*(1), 65-76.

Poulin, C., Gouliquer, L., & Moore, J. (2009). Discharged for homosexuality from the Canadian military: Health implications for lesbians. *Feminism & Psychology, 19*(4), 496-516.

Schwartz, A. (2012, February 22). Gay in the army. *Daily Xtra*. Retrieved from www.dailyxtra.com

Simcoe, L. (2015, June 1). Group demands apology for Canadian government's gay "purges." *Metro News*. Retrieved from www.metronews.ca

Smith, D. (2009, December 9). Peter MacKay retreats on gay veterans issue. *Daily Xtra*. Retrieved from www.dailyxtra.com

Smith, M. (2012). Identity and opportunity: The lesbian and gay rights movement. In M. Fitzgerald & S. Rayter (Eds.), *Queerly Canadian: An introductory reader in sexuality studies* (pp. 121-137). Toronto: Canadian Scholars' Press.

Terry, J. (1999). *An American obsession: Science, medicine and homosexuality in modern society.* Chicago: University of Chicago Press.

Whitworth, S. (2004). *Men, militarism, and UN peacekeeping: A gendered analysis.* London: Lynne Rienner Publishers.

7 ✖ ✖ ✖ ✚ ✖

THE COMPLEXITIES OF GENDER TRAINING IN CONTEXTS OF CONFLICT AND PEACEBUILDING

Cindy Hanson

GENDER TRAINING, which is typically delivered in non-formal, adult learning workshops, is frequently seen as a way to increase the capacity of individuals and organizations to respond to structural inequities in relation to gender. Within the context of peacebuilding, for example, a gender training workshop might assist in building awareness of the ways in which women and men are affected differently by violence, so that care can be taken to ensure that opportunities such as education for girls and leadership roles for women are built into post-conflict community operations. In order to create possibilities for community rebuilding that embraces gender equity issues, however, gender training workshops need to be structured and presented in ways that also facilitate transformational learning. Additional attention to ideas such as masculinity as a form of dominance or violence, multiple and diverse conceptualizations of women and girls, and critical pedagogies of intervention may contribute to transformational learning and increased gender equality within a region's rebuilding process. Frequently, gender training does not adequately address these issues, largely because it is facilitated using gender-specific applications that present women as a homogenous group (Kanji, 2004), and, consequently, it does not recognize multiple forms of diversity and inequality. Such a perspective, particularly in the context of conflict and militarism, presents a dilemma for activists concerned with taking a more liberatory or transformative approach that goes beyond techno-rational[1] responses to gender training.

A feminist lens might offer a window of inquiry through which to explore the diversity that exists among groups of women (and men), and the multiple ways in which power and dominance are structured into dynamic and diverse contexts of conflict. In an attempt to suggest critical points and critical pedagogies of intervention in this context, this chapter braids anecdotes from the field of gender training with related literature. The anecdotes, most of which were shared by facilitators of women's rights and gender equality who participated in my doctoral study (Hanson, 2009),[2] provide testimonies that illustrate how the practices of dominant and critical conceptualizations of gender training in the context of militarism are experienced, and how Canada, as a nation with wide international commitments to gender equality in fragile states,[3] falters in its domestic and international practices. Finally, the chapter offers insights and suggestions for transforming practices of gender training.

Canada's Commitment and Practice

Violence against women is a multi-dimensional global issue that is tied to concepts of masculinity, femininity, and sexual discrimination. According to the Canadian Research Institute for the Advancement of Women (CRIAW, 2013), gender roles are enacted in various ways depending upon context: "toughness and aggression are part of the socially-supported normative constructions[s] of dominant forms of masculinity" (p. 10). Issues surrounding violence against women are linked to historical and political relationships. Many international treaties and policies, for example, have been put in place to identify how gender rights are human rights. Canada is a signatory to many of these international agreements.

According to the Government of Canada's Department of Foreign Affairs, Trade and Development (2014), "Canada is a world leader in the promotion and protection of women's rights and gender equality. These issues are central to Canada's foreign and domestic policies. Canada is committed to the view that gender equality is not only a human rights issue, but is also an essential component of sustainable development, social justice, peace, and security" (para. 1). Ironically, however, Canada's recent Standing Committee on the Status of Women has indicated that legislation and accountability mechanisms in relation to gender equality, within Canada itself, are urgently required. According to a presenter at the Canadian Parliamentary Standing Committee on Gender Equality (Canada, 2005), "while some departments have well-established gender equality or GBA [gender-based-analysis] units, others have none in place. Moreover, Status of Women Canada reports that the lack of binding obligations to conduct gender-based analysis, internal resistance and the lack of shared responsibility have led, over time, to a decreased interdepartmental capacity to ensure gender equality." Canada has been widely criticized for its domestic practices in relation to gender equality, including federal government funding cuts to the Status of Women Canada, which forced the closure of 12 of 16 regional offices. Furthermore, Canada has met with international criticism for its systemic failure to address the hundreds of cases of murdered and missing Canadian Aboriginal women (Oppal, 2012, p. 26).

While the aforementioned points illustrate the inadequacy of Canada's domestic practices and policies in relation to gender equality and gender-based analysis, Canada's strategies, policies, and practices for addressing international gender inequality are also weak. This is particularly true in conflict-affected or fragile states, despite commitments by the Canadian government to support international initiatives that promote gender equality and the empowerment of women. The Government of Canada has, for example, made international commitments to support the United Nations Security Council Resolution (UNSCR) 1325,[4] the Convention on the Elimination of All Forms of Discrimination against Women, the Beijing Declaration and Platform for Action, and the UN Millennium Development Goals. The third of the Millennium Development goals is to "promote gender equality and empower women" (United Nations, 2013). The UNSCR 1325, among other things, calls for the participation of women in peace processes at all levels, the implementation of gender training in peacekeeping operations, and gender mainstreaming[5] in the reporting of the conflict, security, and peace implementation systems of the United Nations (Mechanic, 2004). As UNSCR 1325 has been ratified by member states, it is an important instrument to hold governments accountable; however, it is also problematic because governments all too often view gender as *women-centred*, which eliminates the need to address the role of men and masculinities in peace processes (Mechanic, 2004).

Although such international commitments offer the potential for formal, systemic change, they are also associated with high levels of investment and require a systematic review of how Canada integrates gender equality at home as well as abroad. Internationally, gender training is frequently delivered as a way to satisfy policy obligations, such as gender mainstreaming, and although resources appear to be available for gender training as a techno-rational intervention, ongoing systemic resources that might open possibilities for sustained transformation are not evident. Gender training solely as a techno-rational intervention lacks analysis in relation to race, class, and gender. Consequently, such analyses are virtually absent from the public discourse, and white, Western, heteronormative values continue to be privileged in government practices.

Canada's role in gender training and peace processes in Afghanistan provides a specific case in point. The Canadian government has equated training for gender equality with the achievement of peace and security in Afghanistan when, of course, the complexities of achieving peace are more nuanced and complex. Based upon statements made by Senator Jaffer (2010), the Canadian government assumes that peace in Afghanistan will only follow if there is gender-sensitivity training that will integrate Afghani women into the peace and security frameworks of national machineries. The assumption that gender-sensitivity training can have such a powerful and comprehensive impact is problematic, given that the conditions leading to inequality have not occurred overnight. Jaffer states, "If Canada is going to help create a more stable and secure Afghanistan then it will need to ensure that women are part of the equation. In addition, they will also have to adapt their training so that it is gender sensitive. If this is not done then Afghanistan, a country that has experienced over 23 years of war, will never see peace" (p. 1).

This example, like many other projects or plans in Afghanistan that are premised on gender-based inequalities, presents gender training as a panacea for a long, historic, militarily constructed condition. Domestically, however, gender-sensitivity training is not a high priority for members of the Canadian military (Harrison, 2002), despite a report by the Canadian Armed Forces Military Police that "tracked an increase in the incidence of marital violence, from 33 incidents in 2005 to 103 in 2008. The increase was especially acute at CFB Petawawa and coincided with the return of soldiers from Afghanistan" (CRIAW, 2013, pp. 63–64). Violence against women in the context of conflict, the military, and peacebuilding is part of a more complex discourse that requires commitment and the integration of a much deeper gender analysis than is offered in typical gender training workshops. The concept of *training for gender equality* that is used by UN Women introduces this shift in emphasis.

Training for Gender Equality

According to the United Nations organization that oversees gender equality and the empowerment of women, UN Women, the complexities of educating towards a goal of gender equality include a range of considerations—from context to political will. For this reason, UN Women advocates using the phrase *training for gender equality* (TGE) and emphasizing that the process of providing training and support must be continuous and maintained by the commitment of all the parties involved. At the UN Women Training Centre, TGE is described as a transformative process that aims to enhance "knowledge and skills, while providing techniques and resources to improve the performance and quality of our actions to bring about positive change for all and create an equitable and peaceful society" (UN Women, 2014, para. 1). Although agencies at the United Nations and governments in the European Union have recently used TGE as a strategy to attain gender equality (European Institute for Gender Equality, 2012), few countries, including Canada, have designated the appropriate financial resources towards achieving the broader goals of gender equality.

According to the Organisation for Economic Co-operation and Development (OECD, 2010), only 20 per cent of the foreign aid designated for fragile states includes a gender analysis in its application. The following story illustrates the potentially life-saving impacts that training for gender equality can have on operationalizing culturally appropriate, gendered perspectives. Michele, a Canadian, was working in Pakistan as a gender adviser at the time that this incident took place. She explains:

> Immediately after the 2005 earthquake in Pakistan, the Pakistani army very efficiently mobilized helicopters to fly into the remote mountain communities to fly the wounded down for medical care. Unfortunately, the copter crews were all male. As many of the devastated communities were conservative and Muslim, there are anecdotal reports of critically injured women refusing help, some screaming at the team not to touch them. Gender analysis [training] would have alerted the rescuers to the need of having

a woman in each copter crew: one who spoke the local language and whose presence could protect the honour of injured girls and women. We didn't need a female doctor, we didn't need a nurse, we needed one local woman who could speak the language and knew her ability and had permission to be there or maybe two local women to be on the 'copter, to give support and to protect the honour and dignity of women and their right to healthcare. So we can save lives. (Michele in Hanson, 2009, p. 142)

As this story illustrates, there is a critical need for gendered perspectives, but often a theoretical shift is also needed to effect the deep changes that can move training for gender equality beyond a techno-rational response.

Problematizing Gender and Gender Training

True (2013) stated that a gender perspective in the context of peacebuilding and post-conflict requires addressing "physical/political/military and economic/livelihood/societal insecurities" (p. 2). This statement helps to illustrate the breadth of gender inequality in the context of peacebuilding and post-conflict and, subsequently, also the depth of educational interventions needed to address it. The typical structure of gender training, which is often facilitated as a single workshop, offers little to address such complexities. This is, in part, because gender training faces significant hurdles, including a lack of resources allocated to this work, the absence of accountability mechanisms, and a limited structured or situated analysis of gendered relations. Addressing the complexities of gender inequality is also problematic because gender training, as it is often practised, diverts attention away from the more ethical or political questions that require critical reflection, such as the role of emotions or an analysis of power relations in the situation (Hanson, 2009). Moreover, from the perspective of feminist anti-militarism, a military approach such as that in a region of conflict is contrary to the objectives of gender equality because it "privileges hegemonic masculinity and traditional forms of femininity" (Taber, 2013, p. 139). In the context of conflict and militarism, questions abound in relation to how gender training as solely a technical intervention can contribute to gender equality, because there are no common or clear understandings of what gender equality is (Hendricks & Hutton, 2008). Gender equality is too often associated only with women and women's groups, which means that violence and masculinities are not challenged (Bent & Lau, 2013; Mechanic, 2004). When gender training is delivered as a technical intervention, attention is focused on the stated goals of the workshop, which may include informing or analyzing how social roles are gendered, understanding how gender is socially rather than biologically constructed, and recognizing what gender discrimination might look like in practice. These goals, however, are often predetermined by funders and are not necessarily shared by all the participants. Consequently, the focus of the gender training becomes the techniques and activities that help to achieve the goals of the workshop, and not on what is important to the participants or what will create social changes. This focus is in sharp contrast to that of transformative education, such as that inspired by Brazilian educator Paulo Freire (1970), and which is described here by O'Sullivan (2002):

> Transformative learning involves experiencing a deep, structural shift in the basic premises of thought, feeling, and actions....Such a shift involves our understanding of ourselves and our self-locations; our relationships with other humans and with the natural world; our understanding of relations of power in interlocking structures of class, race, and gender; our body-awareness; our visions of alternative approaches to living; and our sense of the possibilities for social justice and peace and personal joy. (p. 11)

Transformative learning as a form of critical adult education can be a way to envision changes to current manifestations of gender training.

Conceptions of Gender Training

In an assessment of gender training, Mukhopadhyay and Appel (1998) argued that it is important to consider how the gender learning process itself is conceptualized. Feminism suggests that analyses or ways of understanding should be built on acknowledgements of the interconnections and intersections between, among, and within representations of identities; in this way, it acknowledges complex categorizations of difference and diversity. Intersectional links draw attention to the ways in which gender is experienced in relation to other aspects of identity—for example, race, class, ability, and sexuality—and offer a situated understanding of these representations of identity in relation to privilege, oppression, and inequality (Weber, 2010). These complexities, however, are seldom considered by facilitators in the field of gender training, which has implications in the ways that the practice is understood.

White (2003), for example, states that "activists with a background in feminist politics are perplexed by calls for 'gender training' as a purely technical intervention" (p. 2), which is uncritical of Western values and depoliticizes gender and gender work (Kerr, 2004). Often a techno-rational approach is requested by intervening bodies, which creates a conundrum for facilitators with a critical consciousness about what this means in practice. Jennifer, a Canadian gender adviser, working internationally, was often perplexed by the inconsistencies between what she was being asked to do and how she really felt. The following example illustrates her dilemma:

> I think there is a naivety in some of the approaches we propose or put forward....I constantly reflect critically on the "gender training" I do in terms of, "Am I really getting people to question the *status quo* or is this just a blip on the screen that won't make a difference a week from now?" There is the donor (or other agency) requirements for a workshop, and then there is what I really feel. (Jennifer in Hanson, 2009, p. 125)

According to Wilson and Hayes (2000), the inability of critical educators and facilitators to engage in transformative processes is a function of institutionalized structures of power. They explained that "the lack of time and rewards allocated for such [critical] reflection are symptomatic of a broader institutional culture that continues to be enmeshed in technical rationality. A critically reflective approach to practice threatens to challenge the status quo in such institutions, by opening up opportunities for practitioners to question the very values and assumptions that underlie and legitimatize institutional culture and customs" (p. 669).

Although it is the transformation of gender and power relations that can most likely create a significant resource for peace and safety in the world (Cockburn, 2013), transforming social norms around masculinity, violence, and gender continues to be a challenge, in part because the norms are historically and politically linked to dominant ideologies about gender and consequently are not considered in the design and delivery of gender training.

Shifting the Design and Delivery of Training

Literature suggests that gender training models would benefit greatly from increased dialogue with those working in the fields of adult education and participatory development (Ferguson & Forest, 2011; Hanson, 2009). Guijt and Shah (1998), for example, concluded that there is a lack of training in participatory methodologies used by gender trainers in the field. Bridging some of the pedagogical gaps that exist in gender training, however, requires not just knowledge of participatory methodologies but also a commitment to theories behind participation and transformation. For example, addressing the multifaceted ways in which participation takes place and can create meanings may greatly assist gender trainers who are accustomed to implementing only a techno-rational approach. Linked to transformative and participatory approaches is a body of literature that suggests that inquiries into the different and intersecting ways in which individuals develop meaning through experience are required in gender training and analysis (Ferguson & Forest, 2011; Hanson, 2009). Ferguson and Forest (2011), for example, suggested that gender training needs to be more mindful of the interconnections between, and intersectionalities among, issues and identities so that the dynamic and complex ways that difference and diversity are experienced can be incorporated into pedagogical decisions. Mindry (2001) used the term *moral politic of engagement* (p. 1207) to describe a reflective practice whereby relationships are scrutinized as historical, social, and political and, in all likelihood, in need of transformation and democratization. Such negotiations of position and power and how they affect the politics of engagement and relationships are not well documented (Hanson, 2009). The adult education mantra of "learning from experience," however, can shift attention on multiple and diverse sites, understandings, and relationships that are integral to the process of gender training, as the following story from Alicia, an activist-facilitator working with local and global experience, illustrates:

In working with a team of women from South America and Central America on the issue of violence against women, there were strong tensions due to differences in race, class, politics and whether or not each woman considered herself a feminist or not. In order to resolve the tensions, we spent a lot of time sitting together around the table listening to each other. In the end, our shared understanding of what we were to cover in the workshop broadened. Violence against women had to be defined in broader terms. It had to be defined by the women. The women from South America, who had lived more years in Canada, were more focused on domestic violence; while the Central American women, who were recent refugees, were focused on the violence women experience in war and at the hands of repressive governments. In the end, the analysis for both groups shifted as they listened to each other. If we were to address violence against women, we needed to address all their experiences of violence as experienced in war, torture, human rights abuse, extreme poverty, rape, as well as domestic violence....The trick is to keep it broad enough to be inclusive of different realities. In my work in Canada, when you talk about crime prevention with Somali women, their main concern

is the risk of their youth getting into gangs and committing crimes. So to work across
difference it is necessary to keep the basket big enough to include different realities and
perspectives, so as to then find a shared focus of action. (Alicia in Hanson, 2009, p. 155)

Alicia's story offers insights into the multiple perspectives and attention
that are demanded in the design and facilitation of training for gender
equality in order to create spaces where meaningful and potentially
transformational learning can occur. Among other things, this focus
involves examining how different participants represent lived experiences and how critically reflective facilitation requires paying heed to
the multiple ways in which seemingly similar aspects of women's lives
are understood and represented. Ideas from feminist practices of elimi-
nating conflict in society by working with different people influenced
by violence can therefore be an important point of integration (Bent &
Lau, 2013). The use of case studies and matrices of identity (personal and
social) can be a pedagogical starting point for "consciencitizing" participants of training for gender equality to understand how these dynamics
are situated and can shift.

According to the report *Gender Training in Fragile States*, the internal
dynamics of participants' relationships to each other, to the organization, to the community, and to the trainer all need to be considered
in the design and delivery of gender training (Hanson & McInturff,
2008). Hearing stories from training participants is one way to build
understanding, relationships, and sites of hope and transformation
(Hanson, 2009). The following example, which illustrates the ways in
which participants' stories became important pedagogical tools during
a workshop, demonstrates that attention to difference can also offer
possibilities for personal healing and validation:

The group was very diverse. They started to do these dyad interviews....
Afterwards, they presented their stories of the [military] checkpoint and what became
really clear, when they debriefed the whole thing, was that everybody was affected by

this violence, by the militarization, by the threats and intimidation that took place when you stop at a checkpoint. (Kate in Hanson, 2009, p. 110)

Kate's story illustrates the need for analysis that includes experiences of diverse groups of both men and women. Men and concepts of masculinity need to be more widely addressed in discussions about gender equality. Often, the efforts to include masculinity as a topic in training for gender equality, particularly in post-conflict environments and fragile states with peculiarities of gender-based violence, are rejected and not seen as relevant. This is consistent with male gender norms being so "given" that they go unnoticed. Sometimes training in gender equality can involve being an ally and exposing other elements at play. In this example, violence is understood as something that affects everyone:

> It didn't matter whether it was Kosovo, or Timor Este, or the RCMP, the women, mostly women, or a couple of men who were speaking from their own experience as police officers—who are genuinely committed to this—they can't even get a toehold in their own hierarchical structures. What they need most are allies that encourage them, who are coming from their own national context. (Carmin in Hanson, 2009, p. 136)

This kind of information, however, is not always available in advance, and much of it is never articulated at all. Consequently, the use of local case studies and narratives of experience can be particularly helpful in facilitating gender training (Hanson, 2007), as the above quotation reveals.

Although meaningful gender training must be context specific, there are some general considerations that might address concerns in relation to gender training in diverse locations. These include the need for time to build relationships both inside and outside of the training environment, and both inside government as well as within civil society; a knowledge of local examples and history; a co-facilitation or co-training role that considers diverse perspectives and the multiplicity of identities represented in the conflict; the adaptation or development of locally derived models; and a meaningful role for civil society in the process (Hanson & McInturff, 2008). Additionally, the development of training programs that are resourced and informed by a theory of transformation would go a long way in addressing (pedagogical) gaps (Ferguson & Forest, 2011). A feminist-inspired intersectional analysis built on a premise of social and political transformation may assist in framing the training for gender equality in the contexts of conflict or fragile states as a longer-term project. Although much is written about the explicit connections between military service and citizenship, this literature primarily serves to perpetuate the ideological links between hegemonic masculinity and militarism (Cockburn, 2013; Enloe, 1988; Taber, 2013). These are the relationships, therefore, that a critical practice of training for gender equality needs to interrogate. A starting place might be educating learners about the constructions of masculinity and femininity and how these are played out in society, in particular in contexts of violence. While most academic work related to gender theory and war has emerged from sociology and international relations (Cockburn, 2013), in the context of training or non-formal education, pedagogical intervention from the field of critical adult education may additionally offer insights and techniques to disrupt the power relationships that are inherent in conflict situations. The process of applying such an approach, however, cannot take place through a single training event but must be part of a larger analytical and systematic effort at disrupting the hierarchies that sustain gender inequities and hegemonic masculinities in the context of militarism and beyond.

NOTES

1. By *techno-rational*, I am referring to a focus on techniques and activities that might increase effectiveness or help meet the stated goals of an activity, not on the role of emotions or an analysis of power relations in a learning situation. A techno-rational response can be differentiated from a perspective of praxis in its attention to techniques rather than ethical or political questions.

2. My doctoral thesis explored the ways in which participatory and feminist pedagogies are experienced by activist-facilitators of women's rights and gender equality in transnational contexts.

3. *Fragile states* is used to describe the contexts of conflict, war, and peacebuilding, or even the seemingly peaceful contexts wherein specific groups of people, such as indigenous people, are living with high levels of violence.

4. The UN Security Council Resolution 1325 on women, peace, and security is described as "a groundbreaking international law that has become a vital rallying point for organizations and individuals across the world. It calls for full and equal participation of women in all peace and security initiatives" (UN-INSTRAW, 2006).

5. Following the Fourth World Conference on Women in Beijing, Canada along with many countries worldwide commited to supporting the practice of mainstreaming gender equality into all aspects of development.

REFERENCES

Bent, G. & Lau, S. (2013, October 21). War and peace: Still a man's world. *The Guardian*.

Canada. Foreign Affairs, Trade and Development Canada. (2014). Canada's commitment to gender equality and the advancement of women's rights internationally. Retrieved from www.international.gc.ca

Canada. Parliament of Canada. Standing Committee on Gender Equality. (2005, April). *Gender-based analysis: Building blocks for success*. Ottawa: Government of Canada. Retrieved from www.parl.gc.ca

Canadian Research Institute for the Advancement of Women. (2013, September). *Violence against women in Canada* (Fact sheet). Retrieved on January 30, 2014, from www.criaw-icref.ca

Cockburn, C. (2013). War and security, women and gender: An overview of the issues. *Gender & Development, 21*(3), 433-452.

Enloe, C. (1988). *Does khaki become you? The militarization of women's lives*. London: Pandora.

European Institute for Gender Equality. (2012). Good practices in gender training. Retrieved from http://eige.europa.eu

Ferguson, L., and Forest, M. (Eds.). (2011, May). *OPERA final report: Advancing gender+ training in theory and practice* (Technical report). EU: Quality in Gender+ Equality Policies Integrated Project. Retrieved from www.quing.eu/files/results/final_opera_report.pdf

Freire, P. (1970). *Pedagogy of the oppressed*. New York: Continuum.

Guijt, I., & Shah, M.K. (1998). *The myth of community: Gender issues in participatory development*. London: Intermediate Technology Publications.

Hanson, C. (2007). Gender-based analysis training in South Africa: Daily dynamics and development dilemmas. *International Feminist Journal of Politics, 9*(2), 198-278.

Hanson, C. (2009). *Toward transformative learning and a transnational feminist pedagogy: Experiences of activist-facilitators working in development* (Doctoral dissertation). University of British Columbia, Vancouver. https://circle.ubc.ca/

Hanson, C., & McInturff, K. (2008). *Gender training in fragile states: What works?* (Technical workshop report). Ottawa: Peacebuild. Retrieved on March 10, 2013, from www. peacebuild.ca

Harrison, D. (2002). *First casualty: Violence against women in Canadian military communities.* Toronto: James Lorimer.

Hendricks, C., and Hutton, L. (2008). Defence reform and gender (Tool 3). Published by UN-INSTRAW and Centre for the Democratic Control of Armed Forces. Retrieved from www.dcaf.ch

Jaffer, S.B. (2010, December 17). Canada's role in Afghanistan: The importance of gender sensitivity training. *Vancouver Sun.* Retrieved on March 14, 2014, from http://mobinajaffer.ca/women/afghanistan/ canadas-role-in-afghanistan-the-importance-of-gender-sensitivity-training/

Kanji, N. (2004). Reflections on gender and participatory development. *Participatory Learning and action, 50,* 53-62.

Kerr, J. (2004). From "opposing" to "proposing": Finding proactive global strategies for feminist futures. In J. Kerr, E. Sprenger, & A. Symington (Eds.), *The future of women's rights: Global visions and strategies* (pp. 14-37). London: Zed Books.

Mechanic, E. (2004). *Why gender still matters: Sexual violence and the need to confront militarized masculinity; A case study of the conflict in the Democratic Republic of the Congo* (Technical report). Plan Africa Canada. Retrieved on March 20, 2014, from http://dspace. cigilibrary.org/

Mindry, D. (2001). Nongovernmental organization, "Grassroots," and the politics of virtue. *Signs, 26*(4), 1187-1211.

Mukhopadhyay, M., and Appel, M. (1998). Gender training and social transformation: An agenda for change. In S. Cummings, H. van Dam, & M. Valk (Eds.), *Gender training: The source book* (pp. 13-25). Amsterdam: Royal Tropical Institute and Oxfam GB.

Oppal, W.T. (2012, November 15). *Forsaken: The report of the Missing Women Commission of Inquiry, volume III.* [Electronic resource]. Victoria, BC. Retrieved from www.ag.gov. bc.ca

Organisation for Economic Co-operation and Development. (2010, October 9). *Aid in support of gender equality in fragile and conflict-affected states.* Retrieved from www.oecd.org

O'Sullivan, E. (2002). The project and vision of transformative education: Integral transformative learning. In E. O'Sullivan, A. Morrell, & M.A. O'Connor (Eds.), *Expanding the boundaries of transformative learning: Essays on theory and praxis* (pp. 1-12). New York: Palgrave.

Taber, N. (2013). Learning war through gender: Masculinities, femininities, and militarism. In T. Nesbit, S.M. Brigham, N. Taber, and T. Gibb (Eds.), *Building on critical traditions: Adult education and learning in Canada* (pp. 139-148). Toronto: Thompson Educational.

True, J. (2013). *Women, peace and security in post-conflict and peacebuilding contexts* (Policy brief). Norwegian Peacebuilding Resource Centre. Retrieved from www.peacebuilding.no

UN International Research and Training Institute for the Advancement of Women (INSTRAW). (2006). *Securing equality, engendering peace: A guide to policy on women, peace and security (UN SCR 1325)*. Santo Domingo: INSTRAW. Retrieved from http://www.responsibilitytoprotect.org/files/1325guide-finalen.pdf

United Nations. (2013). Millennium Development Goals. Retrieved on March 28, 2013, from www.un.org/millenniumgoals/gender.shtml

UN Women. (2014). Training for gender equality and women's empowerment. Retrieved from www.unwomen.org

Weber, L. (2010). *Understanding race, class, gender, and sexuality*. Oxford: Oxford University Press.

White, S. (2003). *The "gender lens": A racial blinder?* Paper presented at the international workshop Feminist Fables and Gender Myths: Positioning Gender in Development Policy and Practice. Institute of Development Studies, Sussex, UK.

Wilson, A.L., & Hayes, E.R. (2000). *Handbook of adult and continuing education*. San Francisco: Jossey-Bass.

8 ✖ ✖ ✖ ✚ ✖

MILITARISM, MOTHERHOOD, AND TEACHING

A Yugoslav-Canadian Case

Snežana Ratković

Više moja djeca gladovati neće	**My Children Will Never Go**
Nase diplome ne priznaju ovdje,	**Hungry Again**
a ja 53,	Our credentials are denied here,
da idem u školu većje kasno bilo,	and I was already 53,
djecu treba školovati.	my children needed education,
Više moja djeca gladovati neće	It was too late for me.
ma šta ja radila,	My children will never go hungry again
i ulice čistila,	no matter what it takes,
i deset poslova imala,	cleaning streets,
al' više moja djeca gladovati neće.	or ten jobs,
	my children will never go hungry again.

(Mira, transcript poem, as cited in Ratković, 2014, pp. 141-142)

IN THE LAST FEW DECADES American popular culture has "propelled increasing numbers of images of motherhood, as well as mothers' voices, into the public sphere" (Hewett, 2009, p. 121). Some of the literature written about and by mothers has reflected the complexities of mothers' lives, challenging traditional narratives of being a "good" or "sacrificial" mother (Hewett, 2006; Hill Collins, 2000; O'Reilly, 2004, 2006, 2010). Despite this growing body of literature on mothering, few writings reflect refugee mothers' experiences of war and militarism. Militarism is an ideological script by which societies and individuals "adopt militaristic values (e.g., a belief in hierarchy, obedience, and the use of force) and priorities as one's own, to see military solutions as particularly effective, to see the world as a dangerous place best approached with militaristic attitudes" (Enloe, 2007, p. 4). This script promotes correct behaviours, attitudes, and identities of "good mothers." Good mothers provide soldiers (i.e., their sons and daughters), raise funds, and offer advocacy in order to support the nation's military agenda. The main goal of such motherhood ideologies is to perpetuate othering, patriarchy, and imperialism. In such a context, war is often viewed as a suitable national response; white men as heroic soldiers; and women as dependent mothers, sisters, and wives in need of protection (Enloe, 2007).

This chapter emerges from my doctoral research that explored experiences, transitions, and identities of 10 refugee women teachers from Yugoslavia who immigrated to Canada during and after the war in the country (Ratković, 2014). I conducted two in-depth, open-ended individual interviews with each woman and two focus group interviews (one focus group in Ontario and one in Quebec). Owing to my limitations in French language, I interviewed the refugee women residing in Quebec in the Serbo-Croatian language and then translated all their excerpts and transcript poems from Serbo-Croatian to English. Borrowing from narrative inquiry into teaching and teacher knowledge (Clandinin & Connelly, 2000; Connelly & Clandinin, 1990, 1999), I engaged with alternative methods of data analysis and representation. I employed the storying stories model (McCormack, 2000a, 2000b, 2001, 2004), poetic transcription (Furman, Lietz, & Langer, 2006; Glesne, 1997; Richardson, 1992, 1994), and concentric storying (Elliott & Drake, 1999) to unpack the complexities, contradictions, and meanings of the women's stories.

In this chapter I draw on feminist anti-militarist theories (Cockburn, 2007; Eisenstein, 2007; Enloe, 2004; hooks, 2004; Mohanty, 2006), motherhood myths and ideologies (Bolton, 2000; Hart, 2001; Hunter, 2000; Rothman, 1994; Ruddick, 1989; Scheper-Hughes, 1996; Trebilcot, 1983), and Foucault's (1995) theory of surveillance to discuss militarism, motherhood, and teaching through the lens of Jagoda and Mira, refugee women teachers from Yugoslavia who brought their families to Canada despite their husbands' disagreement. I explore how Jagoda's and Mira's experiences of war and militarism have shaped their understandings of mothering and teaching at the dawn of the 21st century.

Militarism, Patriarchy, and Surveillance

Whether or not armed conflict is present, militarism distorts the everyday life of women in many countries, affecting their societal participation (Cockburn, 2007; Eisenstein, 2007; Enloe, 2004). Cockburn (2007) speaks about othering, about the historical and current creation of "others" who are exploited by the powerful elite: "Men and the masculine principle are empowered, women and the feminine principle disempowered. It is the moment historians like to call the rise of 'civilization'—although I prefer to distance myself with quote marks out of respect for the many alternative cultures it has destroyed" (p. 254). She argues that civilization is a synonym for militarization and colonization. Cultural scripts of masculinity in many societies are not only celebrating men as soldiers but also cherishing women as "mothers-of-soldiering-sons" (Enloe, 2004, p. 107), ordering women to make sacrifices not only for their families but also for the nation.

Patriarchy promotes the global expansion of capitalism and imperialism (Ebert, 1993). The US patriarchal society has emerged as
"the lead bully on the block" (Mohanty, 2006, p. 8), with Canada as an
unconditional partner in foreign policy (Arat-Koc, 2005). This military
alliance was demonstrated in the 1999 NATO bombing of Yugoslavia
when NATO forces (including US and Canadian military) bombed
Serbia and Montenegro (then Yugoslavia) for 78 days, destroying not
only military targets but also civilian bridges, residential buildings,
television stations, and hospitals. While NATO leaders and Western
media justified the bombing campaign as the best course of action for
resolving the ethnic conflict between Serbs and Albanians in Serbia's
Kosovo province, the motive behind this intervention was rooted in
the desire to put Yugoslavia under the rule of free-market globalization
(see Magnusson and Mojab, Chapter 1 of this volume, for a discussion
of colonialism and imperialism). Parenti (2002) explains, "They [NATO
leaders] hail self-determination while exercising coercive colonial rule
over other peoples...to transform the world into a global economy under
the tutelage of the transnational corporations, backed by the unanswer-
able imperial might of the United States and its allies. A key component
of the global strategy, of course, entails capitalist restorations within the
former communist countries" (pp. 2–3). In the aftermath of the Yugoslav
wars and the NATO bombing of Yugoslavia, four million people were
displaced or became refugees.

Militarism, war, and othering are rooted in, shaped by, achieved
through, and perpetuated by patriarchy (Eisenstein, 2007; Reardon,
1996). Patriarchy is a social system that positions men as "inherently
dominating, superior to everything and everyone deemed weak,
especially females" (hooks, 2004, p. 18). Patriarchal ideologies shape
educational institutions, knowledge systems, and social relations,
such as "work, citizenship, reproduction, ownership, pleasure, and
identity" (Hennessy, 2000, p. 23). Subtler expressions of patriarchy lie
in symbolism through cultural stories and legends highlighting the
self-sacrificing image of women and the dominant role of the woman

as faithful wife and devoted mother (Desai & Krishnaraj, 2004, p. 299). Postmodern feminist theory has replaced such unitary notions of female identity with plural and complex conceptions of social identity, "treating gender as one relevant strand among others, attending also to class, race, ethnicity, age, and sexual orientation" (Nicholson, 1999, p. 114).

Patriarchy feeds on surveillance and discipline. Foucault (1995) writes about the notion of surveillance in Western societies and uses the concept of the panopticon to describe the workings of this disciplinary power. The panopticon was a watch tower surrounded by a ring of cells, from within which a single supervisor was able to see inside each cell. In the panopticon, Foucault (1995) states, "visibility is a trap" (p. 100). He explains: "Power has its principles not so much in a person as on a certain concerted distribution of bodies, surfaces, lights, gazes" (p. 202). The panopticon controls human behaviour through the fear of being watched, resulting in the establishment of a "disciplinary society" (Foucault, 1995, p. 209).

Schools are often understood as panoptic spaces (Foucault, 1995; Gallagher, 2010), where power is exercised through constant monitoring. The panoptic design of schools allows for ongoing surveillance and the feeling of visibility or vulnerability. A school is an "enclosed, segmented space, observed at every point, in which individuals are inserted in a fixed place, in which the slightest movements are supervised, in which all events are recorded...in which power is exercised without division, according to a continuous hierarchical figure, in which each individual is constantly located, examined" (Foucault, 1995, p. 197).

Power is continuously visible as the teacher monitors and manages student behaviour in the classroom. Although the teacher's power is obvious, invisible forms of surveillance also exist, altering the teacher's role as the surveillance agent to a self-regulating inmate. Students and teachers are "controlled through dominant 'official discourses' of institutions that determine conduct through the regulation of space, time, and capacities (Foucault, 1972, 1973, 1977)" (Jabal & Rivière, 2007, p. 207). Educational authorities create a regime of power by defining what is "normal," as well as what is "abnormal" and "deviant." Schools discipline students and teachers by making them individualized and constantly visible.

Feminist scholars have explored the concept of discipline, extending Foucault's analysis of disciplinary practices to the creation of feminine docile bodies in all areas of life (Bartky, 1998). In a patriarchal society men control production, reproduction, and mothering. According to Rothman (1994), mothering is "what mothers and babies signify to men. For women this can mean too many pregnancies or too few; 'trying again' for a son; covering up male infertility with donor insemination treated as the deepest darkest secret; have some of our children called 'illegitimate'; not having access to abortion we do want; being pressured into abortions we may not want" (p. 140). In such a context women might be rendered as "nurturers of men's seed, the soil in which seeds grew" (p. 142). Men's seeds might be viewed as being irreplaceable, the mothering as being substitutable. At the same time, the female body might be viewed as a site of domination and resistance: "These bodies are not passive which have only a space, but they also make space. They negotiate their desire and feelings, and their place in the world" (Ayuttacorn, 2012, p. 10).

While contemporary Canada praises itself for promoting democracy and women's rights agendas, gender equality remains an issue of political and philosophical concern for educators, employers, and policy-makers (see Magnusson and Mojab, Chapter 1 of this volume, for a discussion of women's rights in a heteronormative, colonial, and militarized world). Women are usually expected to prioritize their identities as wives and mothers, regardless of their professional identity (Fenwick, 2004; Gouthro, 2009). They are held responsible for their children's behaviour and success in life (Crittenden, 2001; Hill Collins, 2000). Minority women are particularly blamed if their children are perceived as being culturally deficient (Hill Collins, 2000). To maintain patriarchy, militarism, and imperialism men tend to control mothering.

Maternal Thinking and the Politics of Exile

Motherhood is a complex social and historical construction (Glenn, 1994; Risman, 1998). Culture prescribes motherhood ideologies, as well as correct maternal behaviours, attitudes, and identities. Motherhood ideologies often perpetuate patriarchy (Rothman, 1994), economic dependency of middle-class women, and economic exploitation of working-class and migrant women (Chang, 1994). Culture defines and rewards "good mothers" and disciplines "bad mothers." A number of scholars have noted, for example, that teenage mothers (Bailey, Brown, & Wilson, 2002), older mothers, single mothers, and lesbian mothers (Lewin, 1994) fall outside of the "good mothers" club. Motherhood ideologies evolve from the myths that are not only compiled into coherent philosophies but also politically authorized by the dominant culture (Johnston & Swanson, 2003). Myths of employed and at-home mothers continue to flourish. On the one hand, employed mothers are portrayed as tired, busy, and guilty (Bolton, 2000); they neglect their children or have difficulty in providing them with appropriate food, clothing, protection, and supervision. On the other hand, at-home mothers are often described as living in a state of happiness (Hunter, 2000). While society may praise middle- and upper-class women who stay at home to raise their children, working-class mothers living on welfare are often portrayed as lazy and living off the state (Hart, 2001). Motherhood positions women in the domestic sphere and "creates a basis for the structural differentiation of domestic and public spheres" (Trebilcot, 1983, p. 132). These spheres are organized in a hierarchical order, perpetuating the public-sphere domination. The primary purpose of these maternal myths is the maintenance of patriarchy (Hays, 1996; Johnston & Swanson, 2003).

When children are endangered by war and/or poverty, mothering becomes "cruel and bitter work....It [war or poverty] defines maternal work as a consuming identity, requiring sacrifices of health, pleasure, and ambitions unnecessary for the well-being of children" (Ruddick, 1989, p. 29). In particular, refugee mothers are a highly vulnerable population. Many refugee women desert their homes to save their lives and the lives of their children, leaving behind their property and most of their support networks. Some refugee mothers lose family members to war, and many have been the victims of violence themselves. Mothers are often considered as tending to value life, human growth, and a politics of peace (Ruddick, 1989). However, motherhood ideologies in times of conflict, war, and political upheaval can "allow women to readily surrender their sons (and their husbands) to war, violence, and death" (Scheper-Hughes, 1996, p. 353).

In pre-war Yugoslavia many mothers worked outside the home, shared parenting and domestic responsibilities, and involved family, community, and support services in raising their children. The loss of employment, property, and family members during the war produced "not only suffering, but also a change of women's social status or even a crisis or loss of identity" (Mrvić-Petrović, 2000a, pp. 135-136). Even when refugee women succeed in finding employment, their jobs are usually short term, low wage, and without social benefits. Women are often exposed to discrimination and exploitation in order for them to secure survival. The host country's society (i.e., the society that welcomes refugees from other countries in order to protect them from prosecution) habitually looks down on refugee women while pressuring them to "be discreet, to renounce their religious or ethnic identity and to humbly accept their changed social status" (Mrvić-Petrović, 2000b, p. 175). When refugees come knocking at First World doors, "we are able to view them as supplicants asking to be relieved of the disorder of their world and to be admitted to the rational calm of ours" (Razack, 1998, p. 91), under any conditions. Lack of acceptance and respect in the new country might lead to apathy or bitterness. For example, some refugee mothers might fall ill or lose interest in their children (Kaličanin, Lečić-Toševski, Bukelić, & Ispanović-Radojković, 1994).

Although skilled refugee and immigrant mothers (e.g., physicians, engineers, and teachers) are viewed as desirable immigrants and citizens, international education and work experiences do not provide access to employment (Teelucksingh & Galabuzi, 2005). The main barriers to obtaining employment in Canada include a lack of language proficiency (Phillion, 2003; Walsh & Brigham, 2007; Walsh, Brigham, & Wang, 2011), attitudinal barriers among employers (Teelucksingh & Galabuzi, 2005), non-recognition of international credentials (Medic, 2007; Mojab, 1999), and non-recognition of international work experience (Aydemir & Skuterud, 2005), as well as "the costs of examinations or certification and limited internship positions through which to gain employment experience" (Dlamini, Anucha, & Wolfe, 2012, p. 3). For example, refugee mothers who are teachers and desire to teach in Ontario and Quebec experience tensions and conflicts as they navigate the workplace and re-certification in their new country. On the one hand, they are required to submit an application to the Ontario College of Teachers (OCT) or the Ministère de l'Éducation, du Loisir et du Sport / Ministry of Education, Recreation and Sports (MELS), or to complete a teacher education program in the province. On the other hand, the women are often unable to return to their home countries or connect with their home universities owing to a well-founded fear of persecution. As a result, they are often incapable of providing the documentation required by OCT or MELS. Additionally, many women struggle with continuing their education because of unsupportive partners, child care, and domestic responsibilities, which, in turn, hinders their academic aspirations and confidence (Gouthro, 2005).

Refugee women teachers' credentials and work experiences are often "mediated by the unequal distribution of power along lines of gender, class, race, language, ethnicity, national origin and the state of economy" (Mojab, 2000, p. 33). Such a deficit model in assessing international credentials and work experiences challenges the notion of diversity, multiculturalism, and social justice in Canadian society (see Taber, Chapter 4 of this volume, for a discussion of Canadian ideals). Internationally educated women teachers tend to internalize this deficit approach to assessing their knowledge and skills; they often believe that their teaching styles and practices must be modified to meet Canadian standards (Myles, Cheng, & Wang, 2006). Dlamini and Martinovic (2007) and Ratković (2011, 2013, 2014) urge educators and educational authorities to challenge the deficit approach to assessing international teaching credentials and work experiences, as well as to recognize the value and the potential of a diverse student-teacher population in Canada.

In the section below I present Mira's and Jagoda's narratives of mothering and teaching in Yugoslavia and Canada. Next, I discuss the women's experiences, transitions, and identities in relation to war, militarism, mothering, and teaching. Finally, I challenge the image of Canada as a compassionate and caring nation (Dauvergne, 2005) and reimagine the Canadian educational landscape as a terrain of trans-national education.

Mira's Narrative: My Children Will Never Go Hungry Again

Mira is an elementary-school mathematics teacher from Bosnia and Herzegovina, formerly part of Yugoslavia. During the war she faced violence, starvation, and fear daily. In 1994 Mira escaped from Bosnia and Herzegovina to Serbia (then also part of Yugoslavia) to join her family. She wanted to immigrate to Canada, but her husband disagreed. Mira insisted: "We are leaving. My children will never go hungry again" (Interview transcript). She was 53 years old when she brought her family to Ontario. Her husband fell ill and was unable to work. To feed her family Mira worked as a chambermaid at a Canadian hotel. She did not pursue teacher re-certification in the province, owing to financial difficulties, limited language skills, pressing family obligations, and her belief that she was too old to study. Additionally, Mira believed that

Canadian educational authorities would never welcome her mastery-of-mathematics pedagogy: "Canadian teachers teach children how to play. I taught my students mathematics" (Interview transcript).

Mira's narrative reveals the multiple effects of war on her teaching, learning, and professional identity. In the war-torn Yugoslavia Mira taught in underground shelters:

U Podrumima	Underground
Zima.	It's winter.
Podrumi.	Underground.
Nigdje grijanja,	No heat,
Ni struje, ni vode, ništa.	No electricity, no water, nothing.
Obučem čarape, pa debele čarape, pa još jedne.	I put on my socks, another pair, and then another one.
A bila sam smršala, bila ko moj Goran od 15 godina.	I lost weight, I looked like my son, looked 15 again.
Obučem njegovu trenerku, pa sve njegovo, pa onda obučem moje.	I wear his clothes, first his, and then mine to keep warm, to endure, to survive.
Rukavice na ruke, i kapa, i šal, pa onda na nastavu.	I put on my gloves, my hat, my scarf, and then I teach again.
Djeca isto tako. Pišu u rukavicama.	My children do just the same; they write in gloves, hats, and scarves.
Ispada je bilo, tu I tamo.	Troubles come and go;
Poneki hoće na silu ocjenu,	Some children demand better marks,
pa prijeti malo, i tako,	they even threaten me if I resist,
ali ja sam luda glava.	but stubborn and fearless I am.
Nastava trajala oko tri sata, ne više,	Classes last for three hours a day, that's all,
A nekad ne bude ni sat, zavisi od granata.	sometimes even less, because of the bombs.
Zimi u podrumima,	In the winter, underground,
a kad dođe proljeće izađemo napolje,	In the spring, back to light,
pa na sunce kao gušteri,	Like lizards in the sun,
I onda opet granate,	and then bombs chase us again,
I opet u podrume.	back to darkness, back to shade.

After dropping down to the weight of her 15-year-old son, seeing her daughter starve, and recognizing that her husband was seriously ill, Mira chose downward mobility over education, obedience over resistance, and cleaning over teaching. She promised herself that her children would never go hungry again. Mira concluded that the biggest barrier to teaching in Canada was her age: "Da sam bila samo malo mlađa, gdje bi mi bio kraj!?" (If I were just a little younger, nothing would have stopped me!) (Interview transcript).

Jagoda's Narrative: Caught in the Light

Jagoda is a French- and Latin-language teacher from Bosnia and Herzegovina. As refugees in Serbia, Jagoda's family lived in poverty, and she suggested immigration to Canada. Her husband was initially opposed to her suggestion, but Jagoda stood her ground: "We are submitting our application in two days. You have two days to change your mind" (Interview transcript). Jagoda's husband changed his mind. Jagoda was 40 years old when she brought her family to Quebec. Her husband did not speak French and was unable to find employment. Jagoda wanted to pursue teacher re-certification in the province and discussed the matter with the principal of a local school. He told her that after she had obtained a teacher certificate, her chance of teaching would be fifty-fifty. Jagoda found this probability to be too slim and too risky; she gave up teaching.

Jagoda recognized that refugeehood was a transnational phenomenon and that refugees across cultures, countries, and continents shared some common experiences of othering and discrimination. Jagoda first had escaped from Bosnia and Herzegovina to Serbia. She was unable to obtain citizenship papers in Serbia and failed to keep the teaching job that she initially acquired. In Canada she obtained citizenship papers (see Taber, Chapter 4 of this volume, for a discussion of valued forms of

Canadian citizenship) but was forced to give up teaching. Abandoned by her "Mother Serbia" (Interview transcript), Jagoda greeted Canada as *Maćehu* (Stepmother) and accepted her *Orphan* (read "marginalized") identity with stoicism.

In pre-war Yugoslavia Jagoda was a strict teacher with high expectations for her students. After escaping to Serbia she was warned by some of her students' parents that she was a refugee and did not have the authority to give low marks to their children. Initially, Jagoda resisted these attacks:

I nastavnica i izbjeglica	**Refugee Woman Teacher**
Bila sam izbjeglica,	I was a refugee woman,
predavala sam,	I taught,
i mnogo problema,	a lot of problems,
mnogo stresa imala.	a lot of stress I had.
Moja komšinica mi govorila,	A neighbour of mine even said,
"Daj im dvojke. Majke će te tući."	"Give them Ds. The mothers will beat you bad."
Neka tuku.	
Ja ne dajem dvojku učeniku koji se ne trudi;	So be it. I never give Ds for not even trying;
moja struka je moj zivot,	my teaching is my life,
moja snaga.	my integrity.

As time went by, Jagoda felt even more pressured to lower her assessment criteria. She was told that all the refugee teachers coming from Croatia and Bosnia to Serbia had unacceptable learning-assessment criteria. As a result she stopped caring about teaching other people's children and cared only about feeding her own.

Education authorities in Quebec did not recognize Jagoda's teaching credentials. An elementary-school principal, however, sent her to teach in a primary classroom. A parent of one of her students doubted the value of her Yugoslav degree:

Kad sam počela da radim, onda je jedan roditelj došao I pitao me da li ja imam diplomu iz Kanade. Ja sam rekla, "Ne, imam univerzitetsku diplomu ali nije iz Kanade." Da bi on sutradan otišao I ispisao svoje dijete I prebacio ga u drugu školu, što je za mene bio hladan tuš, mislim, nije to bilo iznenađenje, ali do tad nisam bila doživjela [diskriminaciju] tako direktno...I poslije, mada su to bila mala djeca i mi smo sjeckali, ljepili, bojili, ja sam se toliko iscrpljivala na tom poslu zato što sam znala da moram da radim pet puta bolje nego drugi [kanadski nastavnici] samo da me ostave na miru.

When I started teaching, a parent came into the classroom and asked me if I had a Canadian degree. I replied, "No, I have a university degree, but it is not a Canadian degree." The next day he transferred his child to another school. For me, it was a slap in the face; it was not a surprise by any means, but such overt discrimination I had never experienced before....And later, although they were little kids, and we were cutting, gluing, colouring most of the time, I was exhausted; I knew I had to work five times harder than others [Canadian-born teachers] so they would leave me alone.

Jagoda had difficulties in grasping the teaching methods and the learning objectives of the Canadian classroom. She did not understand why elementary-school students were treated as learners who were incapable of learning:

Ne smiješ ni na šta da ga [učenika] tjeraš; ni da uči jer on ne smije da se umori. To dijete ne smije da se umori, ne smije, ako je propterećeno to je stres, ne smije....što da radiš? Pa zašto onda ide u školu? Osnovna škola jeste jedna vrsta obdaništa da bi se rešio problem čuvanja djece roditelja koji rade.

You are not allowed to push your student to do anything, not even to learn, because the student is not supposed to get tired. That child is not supposed to get tired, no way, if the child is overwhelmed, that's stress....What can you do? Well, why is this child going to school then? Elementary school is a kindergarten. Children are taken care of while their parents are at work.

Jagoda's teacher identity shifted from being that of a strict teacher in Yugoslavia to being that of a caring grandmother or a lunch supervisor in Canada. She believes that if she had re-established a teaching career in Canada, it would have taken her away from her children, and "who knows what evil would have happened to them" (Interview transcript). Moreover, Jagoda grew to believe that teaching in the Canadian classroom would send her to the hospital or to the psychiatric institution. When reflecting on the Canadian government's commitment to the integration of refugee women teachers into the Canadian education system, Jagoda concluded, "We don't count; they want our children" (Focus group transcript).

Discussion

Jagoda and Mira insisted on immigrating to Canada despite their husbands' disagreement; they brought their families to this country, secured the basic conditions for life, and provided their children with a good education. Jagoda's and Mira's narratives challenge the patriarchal notion of men as family providers. By making their choices to immigrate to Canada and provide for their family, these women exercised social agency (Mahler & Pessar, 2001).

Mira came to Canada for her children's sake; she would clean streets, pursue ten jobs, and do whatever it took to protect, feed, and educate her children. Mira's refugee journey from the underground classrooms in war-torn Yugoslavia to underground laundry rooms in Canada revealed the price she had to pay to protect her family from war, fear, and hunger; acceptance, discipline, and love for her family became Mira's best allies in navigating the margins of Canadian society. In this foreign space Mira learned how to feed her family, how to humbly accept her impoverished social status (Mrvić-Petrović, 2000b), and how to find her peace under the Canadian sun.

Jagoda's narrative reflects her experiences of the panopticons of a Yugoslav and a Canadian school in which Jagoda learned how closely she was watched not only by her colleagues and her students' parents but also by her own timid eye. As a refugee woman in Serbia and Canada (a woman of different origin, education, and/or accent), Jagoda became visible and vulnerable in the classroom. Similar to Foucault's (1995) notion of visibility as a trap, Jagoda found herself trapped in her teaching position, caught in the light of the panopticon, watched and controlled by others, and eventually by her own suspicious eye. Jagoda's narrative confirmed that schools are panoptic spaces (Foucault, 1995; Gallagher, 2010), and Canadian society a "disciplinary society" (Foucault, 1995. p. 209). She was so intensively watched, judged, and disciplined in her classroom that she internalized this gaze: "I was not myself. I was exhausted all the time" (Interview transcript). Jagoda could not bear this panoptic gaze any longer; she left teaching primary grades and became a lunch supervisor in a kindergarten. She, however, made peace with this decision for the sake of her children. Jagoda was afraid that pursuing teacher re-certification in Canada would force her to neglect her children and become a tired, busy, and guilty mother (Bolton, 2000). According to Jagoda, the Canadian government did not need refugee women teachers but their children. This comment reflects disciplinary practices that work to create feminine docile bodies in all areas of life (Ayuttacorn, 2012; Bartky, 1998; Rothman, 1994), especially in the processes of forced migration and settlement. In Canada, the participants felt that refugee mothers were what they and their children signified to the government; the government used refugee women to get to their children and grandchildren, to educate their offspring, and turn them into *real* Canadians. Refugee women are viewed as the nurturers of the Canadian future, the soil in which the seeds of Canada grow. Refugee children are precious; refugee mothers are expendable (Rothman, 1994).

Once in Canada, Jagoda and Mira learned that teaching was a luxury that remained out of their reach. Non-Canadian teaching credentials, financial difficulties, and multiple family responsibilities (including their motherhood ideology re-moulded by the pressures of war and militarism) forced the women to give up teaching and retreat to the domestic sphere (Enloe, 2007). They left their professional careers for domestic, low-paid jobs and mothering. Jagoda, for example, gave up teaching because of the Canadian gaze; a parent doubted Jagoda's international teaching expertise and transferred his child to another school. This parent viewed Jagoda's classroom as a "dangerous place best approached with militaristic attitudes" (Enloe, 2007, p. 4) such as othering and control.

Mira grew to believe that her mastery-of-mathematics pedagogy would be unacceptable in the Canadian, playful classroom. In the same vein, Jagoda referred to the Canadian elementary classroom as a kindergarten playground. Interestingly enough, these responses are in congruence with the current debates about mathematics education in Canada: "Formal math training and rote learning were jettisoned, victims of a creeping fear that children would be turned off math because they found drills stifling. As it turns out, for kids learning math, there's something even more off-putting than boredom: a lack of knowledge, and struggling to solve real-world problems because they lack a strong grounding in math fundamentals" (Editorial, 2014, para. 2).

In light of the above, Alberta and Ontario have announced significant changes to mathematics instruction that show the shift from discovery learning to basic mathematical facts and functions. While recognizing the value of both teaching methods (i.e., play or discovery learning, and subject mastery), it is fair to conclude that Canadian educators might benefit from gaining a deeper understanding of Mira's and Jagoda's teaching philosophy.

Although Mira and Jagoda encountered external barriers in the processes of settlement such as othering, distrust, and surveillance, the love for their children overpowered their love for teaching. This was evident in the motherly narratives and metaphors used by the women when they were talking about war, exile, and teaching. Mira referred to her students in the underground shelters as "my children" (Interview transcript) and noted that her only priorities in Canada were being a courageous mother and a caring grandmother. Jagoda also argued that protecting her children remained her priority. To escape war and poverty, Mira and Jagoda immigrated to Canada. To escape othering (Cockburn, 2007; Eisenstein, 2007), surveillance, financial difficulties, and the fear of neglecting their children, the women retreated to their motherhood. Mira's and Jagoda's motherhood became "a consuming identity, requiring sacrifices of health, pleasure, and ambitions unnecessary for the well-being" (Ruddick, 1989, p. 29) of their children. This shift was a response to war, as well as to the financial difficulties, othering, and surveillance that they encountered in the process of becoming Canadian. Extreme forms of patriarchy (e.g., war, violence, militarism, and imperialism) were salient in shaping Jagoda's and Mira's lives; they forced the refugee women teachers to migrate from a space of professional expertise to a space of survival.

Conclusion

This chapter explored the effects of war and militarism on the mothering ideologies and professional identities of Mira and Jagoda as they transitioned from pre-war Yugoslavia to war-torn Yugoslavia and finally to the landscapes of militarism in Canada. The women shared their experiences of war, refugeehood, othering, and teaching (or not teaching) within these three distinct spaces. Jagoda's and Mira's narratives remind educators that patriarchy and militarism operate across cultures, ideologies, and societies (Cockburn, 2007; Eisenstein, 2007; Enloe, 2004). The women described their world as a panoptic world, a "place for experiments on men [sic]" (Foucault, 1995, p. 204), and even more often on women (Bartky, 1998). Through the workings of war, militarism, and NATO-driven imperialist agendas, Mira and Jagoda were deprived of their home country, social networks, and material belongings. Through the workings of immigration, settlement, and teacher re-certification processes or discourses in Canada, the women were deprived of their teaching careers; Mira's and Jagoda's international teaching credentials and work experiences were rendered as subjugated knowledges, dangerous knowledges, knowledges located at the bottom of the teaching hierarchy. The women themselves internalized militaristic values (i.e., internalized a belief in hierarchy, control, and obedience) and humbly accepted their impoverished social and professional status (Mrvić-Petrović, 2000b). Jagoda and Mira, however, brought their families to Canada, providing their families with a decent life and claiming an agency even in the restrictive conditions of war, exile, and global militarism.

This chapter offers a re-vision of contemporary Canada (and Canada's educational system) not as a static and self-serving terrain but as a participant in transnational relations. It problematizes nationalist and state-bound definitions of teacher knowledge (or any other knowledge) and argues that the main issues of forced migration and refugee women's professional displacement lie in the systems of patriarchy, militarism, and imperialism that work across time and space. The assumptions and prejudices about refugee women teachers that are reflected in militaristic values such as othering, surveillance, and a belief in hierarchy are salient in shaping women's lives. Non-recognition of international teaching credentials and work experiences, as well as distrust towards non-Canadian teachers and pedagogies, is rooted in the country's monolithic and hierarchal approach to teaching and teacher education (see Hanson, Chapter 7 of this volume, for a discussion of international gender training strategies and challenges). Such an approach ignores the fact that there are multiple and situated knowledges and perspectives, thereby downplaying the contribution of refugee women teachers to teaching, learning, and teacher education in Canada (Ratković, 2011, 2013, 2014).

Jagoda's and Mira's narratives challenge the Canadian immigration, settlement, and teacher re-certification policies and practices that reflect militaristic values and attitudes. Current colonial politics of imposing

Canadian or Western concepts and issues onto refugee studies, teacher education, and teaching in a globalizing world must be contested. This work could be done through locating, exploring, and honouring transnational spaces and pedagogies already flourishing on Canadian soil.

AUTHOR'S NOTE

I would like to thank Dr. Susan A. Tilley for her guidance in conceptualizing, writing, and completing this chapter; her critical insights, her input in refining my writing, and her encouragement have been precious to me. Thanks are also due to Dr. Nancy Taber, who was a source of precious advice in the process of finalizing the chapter.

REFERENCES

Arat-Koc, S. 2005. The disciplinary boundaries of Canadian identity after September 11: Civilizational identity, multiculturalism, and the challenge of anti-imperialist feminism. *Social Justice, 32*(4), 32-49.

Aydemir, A., & Skuterud, M. (2005). Explaining the deteriorating entry earnings of Canada's immigrant cohorts: 1965-2000. *Canadian Journal of Economics, 38*(2), 641-671.

Ayuttacorn, A. (2012, July). *The body politics and politics of bodies: In case of female flight attendants.* Paper presented at the International Conference on International Relations and Development (ICIRD) 2012: Towards an ASEAN Economic Community (AEC)—Prospects, Challenges and Paradoxes in Development, Governance and Human Security, Chiang Mai, Thailand.

Bailey, N., Brown, G., & Wilson, C. (2002). The baby brigade: Teenage mothers and sexuality. *Journal of the Association for Research on Mothering, 4*(1), 101-110.

Bartky, S.L. (1998). Foucault, femininity, and the modernization of patriarchal power. In R. Weitz (Ed.), *The politics of women's bodies: Sexuality, appearance, and behaviour* (pp. 25-45). New York: Oxford University Press.

Bolton, M. (2000). *The third shift: Managing hard choices in our careers, homes, and lives as women.* San Francisco: Jossey-Bass.

Chang, G. (1994). Undocumented Latinas: The new "employable mother." In E.N. Glenn, G. Chang, & L.N. Forcey (Eds.), *Mothering: Ideology, experience, and agency* (pp. 259-285). New York: Routledge.

Clandinin, D.J., & Connelly, F.M. (2000). *Narrative inquiry: Experience and story in qualitative research.* San Francisco: Jossey-Bass.

Cockburn, C. (2007). *From where we stand: War, women's activism and feminist analysis*. London: Zed Books.

Connelly, F.M., & Clandinin, D.J. (1990). Stories of experience and narrative inquiry. *Educational Researcher, 19*(5), 2-14.

Connelly, F.M., & Clandinin, D.J. (Eds.) (1999). *Shaping a professional identity: Stories of educational practice*. New York: Teachers College Press.

Crittenden, A. (2001). *The price of motherhood: Why the most important job in the world is still the least valued*. New York: Henry Holt.

Dauvergne, C. (2005). *Humanitarianism, identity, and nation: Migration laws of Australia and Canada*. Vancouver: University of British Columbia Press.

Desai, N., & Krishnaraj, M. (2004). An overview of the status of women in India. In M. Mohanty (Ed.), *Class, caste, gender* (pp. 296-319). New Delhi: Sage Publications.

Dlamini, S.N., Anucha, U., & Wolfe, B. (2012). Negotiated positions: Immigrant women's views and experiences of employment in Canada. *Affilia: Journal of Women and Social Work, 27*(4), 420-434. doi: 10.1177/0886109912464479.

Dlamini, S.N., & Martinovic, D. (2007). In pursuit of being Canadian: Examining the challenges of culturally relevant education in teacher education. *Race, Ethnicity and Education, 10*(2), 155-175.

Ebert, T. (1993). Ludic feminism, the body, performance, and labour: Bringing "materialism" back into feminist cultural studies. *Cultural Critique, 23*, 5-50.

Editorial: Math education: Mom, what's a "times table"? [Editorial]. (2014, March). *Globe and Mail*. Retrieved on March 28, 2014 from www.theglobeandmail.com

Eisenstein, Z. (2007). *Sexual decoys: Gender, race and war in imperial democracy*. London: Zed Books.

Elliott, A., & Drake, S. (1999, December). *Concentric storying: A vehicle for professional development in teacher education*. Paper presented at the Ontario Educational Research Council.

Enloe, C. (2004). *The curious feminist*. Berkeley: University of California Press.

Enloe, C. (2007). *Globalization and militarism: Feminists make the link*. New York: Rowman & Littlefield.

Fenwick, T. (2004). What happens to the girls? Gender, work and learning in Canada's "new economy." *Gender and Education, 16*(2), 169-185.

Foucault, M. (1995). *Discipline and punish: The birth of the prison*. New York: Pantheon.

Furman, R., Lietz, C., & Langer, C.L. (2006). The research poem in international social work: Innovations in qualitative methodology. *International Journal of Qualitative Methods, 5*(3), 24-34.

Gallagher, M. (2010). Are schools panoptic? *Surveillance & Society, 7*(3/4), 262-272.

Glenn, E.N. (1994). Social constructions of mothering: A thematic overview. In E.N. Glenn, G. Chang, & L.N. Forcey (Eds.), *Mothering: Ideology, experience, and agency* (pp. 1-29). New York: Routledge.

Glesne, C. (1997). That rare feeling: Re-presenting research through poetic transcription. *Qualitative Inquiry, 3*, 202-221.

Gouthro, P.A. (2005). A critical feminist analysis of the homeplace as learning site: Expanding the discourse of lifelong learning to consider adult women learners. *International Journal of Lifelong Education, 24*(1), 5-19.

Gouthro, P.A. (2009). Neoliberalism, lifelong learning, and the homeplace: Problematizing the boundaries of "public" and "private" to explore women's learning experiences. *Studies in Continuing Education, 31*(2), 157-172.

Hart, M. (2001). *The poverty of life-affirming work: Motherwork, education, and social change.* Westport, CT: Greenwood Press.

Hays, S. (1996). *The cultural contradictions of motherhood.* New Haven, CT: Yale University Press.

Hennessy, R. (2000). *Profit and pleasure: Sexual identities in late capitalism.* London: Routledge.

Hewett, H. (2006). Talkin' bout a revolution: Building a mothers' movement in the Third Wave. *Journal of the Association for Research on Mothering, 8*(1/2), 34-54.

Hewett, H. (2009). Mothering across borders: Narratives of immigrant mothers in the United States. *Women's Studies Quarterly, 37*(3/4), 121-139.

Hill Collins, P. (2000). *Black feminist thought: Knowledge, consciousness, and the politics of empowerment.* New York: Routledge.

hooks, b. (2004). *The will to change: Men, masculinity, and love.* New York: Atria Books.

Hunter, B. (2000). *Home by choice: Raising emotionally secure children in an insecure world.* Sisters, OR: Multnomah.

Jabal, E., & Rivière, D. (2007). Student identities and/in schooling: Subjection and adolescent performativity. *Discourse: Studies in the Cultural Politics of Education, 28*(2), 197-217.

Johnston, D., & Swanson, D. (2003). Invisible mothers: A content analysis of motherhood ideologies and myths in magazines. *Sex Roles, 49*(1/2), 21-33.

Kaličanin, P., Lečić-Toševski, D., Bukelić, J., & Ispanović-Radojković, V. (1994). *The stresses of war and sanctions.* Belgrade: Institute for Mental Health.

Lewin, E. (1994). Negotiating lesbian motherhood: The dialectics of resistance and accommodation. In E.N. Glenn, G. Chang, & L.N. Forcey (Eds.), *Mothering: Ideology, experience, and agency* (pp. 333-354). New York: Routledge.

Mahler, S.J., & Pessar, P.R. (2001). Gendered geographies of power: Analyzing gender across transnational spaces. *Identities, 7*(4), 441-459.

McCormack, C. (2000a). From interview transcript to interpretive story: Part 1—Viewing the transcript through multiple lenses. *Field Methods, 12*(4), 282-297.

McCormack, C. (2000b). From interview transcript to interpretive story: Part 2—Developing an interpretive story. *Field Methods, 12*(4), 298-315.

McCormack, C. (2001). *The times of our lives: Women, leisure and undergraduate research* (Unpublished doctoral dissertation). University of Wollongong, New South Wales, Australia.

McCormack, C. (2004). Storying stories: A narrative approach to in-depth interview conversations. *International Journal of Social Research Methodology, 7*(3), 219-236.

Medic, D. (2007). *Foreign trained teachers: The emergence of the right to practise their profession in Ontario* (Unpublished master's thesis). Brock University, St. Catharines, ON.

Mohanty, C.T. (2006). US empire and the project of women's studies: Stories of citizenship, complicity and dissent. *Gender, Place and Culture: A Journal of Feminist Geography, 13*(1), 7-20.

Mojab, S. (1999). De-skilling immigrant women. *Canadian Women Studies, 19*(3), 123-128.

Mojab, S. (2000). The power of economic globalization: De-skilling immigrant women through training. In R.M. Cerver, A.L. Wilson, & associates (Eds.), *Power in practice: Adult education and the struggle for knowledge and power in society* (pp. 23-41). San Francisco: Jossey-Bass.

Mrvić-Petrović, N. (2000a). Separation and dissolution of the family. In V. Nikolić-Ristanović (Ed.), *Women, violence and war: Wartime victimization of refugees in the Balkans* (pp.135-150). Budapest: Central European University Press.

Mrvić-Petrović, N. (2000b). Social acceptance and the difficulty of adapting to a new environment. In V. Nikolić-Ristanović (Ed.), *Women, violence and war: Wartime victimization of refugees in the Balkans* (pp. 171-186). Budapest: Central European University Press.

Myles, J., Cheng, L., & Wang, H. (2006). Teaching in elementary school: Perceptions of foreign trained teacher candidates on their teaching practicum. *Teaching and Teacher Education, 22*, 233-245.

Nicholson, L.J. (1999). *The play of reason: From the modern to the postmodern*. Ithaca, NY: Cornell University Press.

O'Reilly, A. (2004). Introduction to A. O'Reilly (Ed.), *Mother outlaws: Theories and practices of empowered mothering* (pp. 1-28). Toronto: Women's Press.

O'Reilly, A. (2006). *Rocking the cradle: Thoughts on motherhood, feminism and the possibility of empowered mothering*. Toronto: Demeter Press.

O'Reilly, A. (2010). Outlaw(ing) motherhood: A theory and politic of maternal empowerment for the twenty-first century. In A. O'Reilly (Ed.), *Twenty-first-century motherhood: Experience, identity, policy, agency* (pp. 366-380). New York: Columbia University Press.

Parenti, M. (2002). *To kill a nation: The attack on Yugoslavia.* New York: Verso.

Phillion, J. (2003). Obstacles to accessing the teaching profession for immigrant women. *Multicultural Education, 11*(1), 41-45.

Ratković, S. (2011). Transitions from exile to academia: Stories of refugee women teachers from the former Yugoslavia. *Power and Education, 3*(3), 196-209.

Ratković, S. (2013). The location of refugee female teachers in the Canadian context: "Not just a refugee woman!" *Refuge: Canada's Journal on Refugees, 29*(1), 103-114.

Ratković, S. (2014). *Teachers without borders: Experiences, transitions, and identities of refugee women teachers from Yugoslavia* (Unpublished doctoral dissertation). Brock University, St. Catharines, ON.

Razack, S. (1998). Policing the borders of nation: The imperial gaze in gender prosecution cases. In S. Razack (Ed.), *Looking white people in the eye: Gender, race, and culture in courtrooms and classrooms* (pp. 88-129). Toronto: University of Toronto Press.

Reardon, B. (1996). Militarism and sexism: Influences on education for war. In R. Burns & R. Aspeslagh (Eds.), *Three decades of peace education around the world.* New York: Garland Publishing.

Richardson, L. (1992). The consequences of poetic representation. In C. Ellis & M.G. Flaherty (Eds.), *Investigating subjectivity: Research on lived experience.* Newbury Park, CA: Sage.

Richardson, L. (1994). Nine poems. *Journal of Contemporary Ethnography, 23*(1), 3-13.

Risman, B. (1998). *Gender vertigo: American families in transition.* New Haven, CT: Yale University Press.

Rothman, B.K. (1994). Beyond mothers and fathers: Ideology in a patriarchal society. In E.N. Glenn, G. Chang, & L.N. Forcey (Eds.), *Mothering: Ideology, experience, and agency* (pp. 139-160). New York: Routledge.

Ruddick, S. (1989). *Maternal thinking: Toward a politics of peace.* Boston: Beacon.

Scheper-Hughes, N. (1996). Maternal thinking and the politics of war. *Peace Review: Journal of Social Justice, 8*(3), 353-358.

Teelucksingh, C., & Galabuzi, G.R. (2005, November). Impact of race and immigrants status on employment opportunities and outcomes in the Canadian labour market. *Policy Matters, 22,* 1-13.

Trebilcot, J. (Ed.). (1983). *Mothering: Essays in feminist theory.* Totowa, NJ: Rowman & Allanheld.

Walsh, S.C., & Brigham, S.M., with members of the Women, Diversity, & Teaching Group (2007). Internationally educated female teachers who have immigrated to Nova Scotia: A research/performance text. *International Journal of Qualitative Methods, 6*(3), 1-28.

Walsh, S., Brigham, S., & Wang, Y. (2011). Internationally educated female teachers in the neoliberal context: Their labour market and teacher certification experiences in Canada. *Teaching and Teacher Education, 27*(3), 657-665.

9 ✕ ✕ ✕ ✚ ✕

AN INVISIBLE WEB

Examining Cyberbullying, Gender, and Identity
through Ethnodrama

Gillian L. Fournier

IN ONTARIO, CANADA, the Accepting Schools Act (Ontario, 2012), has
brought attention to cyberbullying in schools (Cyberbullying Research
Center, 2013; Kauffman & Landrum, 2013, p. 204; Mas, 2013; Teitel, 2012).
In 2012 the Ontario education minister, Lauren Broten, amended the
Education Act with Bill 13, which acknowledged cyberbullying as an
emergent technological phenomenon (Collins & Patterson, 2004) and
addressed a need for the prevention of and intervention into bullying in
schools. It also recognized the interconnectedness of online and off-line
adolescent identities (Wilson, 2006) and the impact that online activity
might have on students' well-being. The Accepting Schools Act echoes
recent research by suggesting that positive social change is enhanced by
the fostering of critical consciousness in youth (Freire, 2011; Garber, 2010;
O'Farrell 2010; Österlind, 2011; Taft, 2011).

As a secondary-school drama teacher in Ontario, I was interested in using drama for social intervention (DSI) to engage teenaged girls in an exploration of cyberbullying. DSI involves the use of drama techniques to address issues of social justice (Boal, 2008; Conrad, 2004; Lepp, 2011). I conducted a study that employed these qualitative arts-based procedures as a unique "alternative" (Creswell, 2012, p. 274) to qualitative research. The study (my master's thesis, see Fournier, 2014) took place in a medium-sized independent school in southwestern Ontario. The following questions were at the heart of my research: How do teenaged girls define cyberbullying? In what ways do teenaged girls experience cyberbullying?

The findings of this study are reported in the form of an ethnodrama. Ethnodrama is a recent method of presenting research findings (McCall, 2000) by "dramatiz[ing] significant selections of narrative through interviews, participant observation field notes, [and] journal entries" (Saldaña, 2006, p. 3). Bresler (2006) argued that qualitative research should have a "living presence," engaging researchers "in a dynamic, intimate dialogue that the research's audience can consequently also experience" (p. 61). Denzin (2003) highlighted ethnodrama's ability to "[put] culture into motion" (p. 8), bringing to life social phenomena existing within social performances. Most notably, ethnodrama uses the "language and words of 'the other'…to 'explain' the worlds of 'the other'" (Mienczakowski, Smith, & Morgan, 2002, p. 38).

Participants included a convenience sample of four girls in grades 11 and 12; the girls were aged 16 to 18 years old at the time of the study. They participated in nine extracurricular study sessions from January to April 2013. During these sessions the girls engaged in DSI activities with the intention of producing a collective creation. This goal did not come to fruition because the girls decided not to perform their work. Throughout the sessions I collected data through field notes, participant journals, interviews, and participant artifacts, achieving triangulation (Creswell, 2012, p. 259).

In the following, I explore cyberbullying as a social phenomenon that reinterprets existing definitions of traditional bullying. I also examine the interplay between cyberbullying, education, gender, and militarism. I then discuss the relationship between DSI and cyberbullying and present the findings of the study via selections of the ethnodrama "Cyberbullying: An Invisible Web." The ethnodrama communicates the following findings: (a) girl identity online consists of many disconnected avatars, demonstrating a need for educators to understand better the ways in which girls exist online as multiple, separate avatars; (b) cyberbullying discourses beg re-evaluation to reflect better the multiple avatar identities of girls; and (c) there is a need for preventative approaches to cyberbullying education that incorporate affective-empathy building (Ang & Goh, 2010).

Cyberbullying as a Social Phenomenon

Limited research exists about cyberbullying as a relatively new field of study. Existing literature emphasizes a need for further exploration of the issue, especially when discussing cyberbullying and adolescent girls. Current research separates cyberbullying from traditional bullying by examining the unique ways in which cyberbullying engages Internet technologies to oppress victims (Bauman, Toomey, & Walker, 2013; Erdur-Baker, 2010; Kauffman & Landrum, 2013). Hinduja and Patchin (2009) defined bullying as "repeated and deliberate harassment directed by one in a position of power toward one or more," involving "physical threats or behaviours...or indirect and subtle forms of aggression" (p. 185).

As a more contemporary social phenomenon (Kauffman & Landrum, 2013; Pelfrey & Weber, 2013), cyberbullying tends to resist the traditional, "typical" definitions of bullying (Bauman et al., 2013; Erdur-Baker, 2010). Collins and Patterson (2004, p. 33) identified electronic mail, instant messaging (IM), text messaging (SMS), message boards, voting or polling booths, and flaming—"sending angry, rude, or obscene messages" (Cyberbullying Research Center, 2013)—as common cyberbullying techniques. Cyberbullying behaviours may include "sending text or voice messages, pictures, or videos directly to victims, or simply posting such material on publicly available websites" (Kauffman & Landrum, 2013, p. 204).

Sbarbaro and Enyeart Smith (2011) recognized that the anonymity of cyberspace differentiates cyberbullying from traditional bullying. "[The] inability of the perpetrator to observe the target's immediate reaction... [creates] the absence of time and space constraints" (Bauman, 2010, p. 805) and, thus, may lead perpetrators to have "greater feelings of disinhibition" (Underwood & Rosen, 2011, p. 17). "Although cyberbullying begins anonymously in the virtual environment...it creates a hostile physical school environment where students feel unwelcome and unsafe...[reducing] equal opportunities to learn" (Shariff, 2005, p. 460).

Stern (2007) suggested that cyber-citizens undergo identity construction in a new way, by "lying...using technology to manipulate conversation...changing tone to manipulate conversation...and simply disclosing information about oneself that makes a particular impression" (p. 38). Given the rapidly developing nature of cyber-technologies, and thus cyber-citizenship (2007), cyberbullying requires special attention as a new vehicle for social violence among school-aged youth, especially as it functions differently from traditional bullying (Pelfrey & Weber, 2013).

Cyberbullying pervades schools regardless of Internet accessibility in the home. In a rural American study, Bauman (2010) found that availability of Internet access, speed, consistency, and technology-sharing in a household were factors contributing to the "digital divide" or gap in the accessibility of cyber-technologies for young people. Despite this divide, most students still identified themselves as avid cyber-technology users. Furthermore, Bauman discovered a direct relationship between age and the likeliness to engage with cyber-technologies, with cyber engagement increasing from grades 5 through 8 across genders.

A significant relationship exists between the frequency of cyber-technology use and cyberbullying (Erdur-Baker, 2010). Sbarbaro and Enyeart Smith (2011) discovered that as the grade level increased, so did incidents of "seeing others cyberbullied, being cyberbullied while [playing online video games]...and posting mean or hurtful comments about someone" (p. 148). Sbarbaro and Enyeart Smith recognized a need for further research to examine grade-specific cyberbullying behaviours. As a pervasive phenomenon in schools (Bauman, 2010), cyberbullying appears to increase as students progress through each grade level (Sbarbaro & Enyeart Smith, 2011).

What must be addressed is the fact that cyber-technology users are engaging in a fundamentally militarized space (see Magnusson and Mojab, Chapter 1 of this volume, for a discussion of alternative reality games; and Lane, Chapter 2 of this volume, for a discussion of social networking). Turse (2008) revealed that Internet and cellphone providers are intrinsically linked to the US Department of Defense, and corporations producing both software and hardware, like Apple and Microsoft, also hold contracts with the department. Ben-Porath (2006) suggested that "the culture of war and militarism is a patriarchal culture" (p. 91). If militarism is recognized as permeating the "lived" world, then online culture is also patriarchal—as a mirror of "lived" culture. Furthermore, Enloe (2007) argued that "women and men do not become militarized in identical ways." This begs for cyber spaces and cyberbullying to be examined as they relate uniquely to gender.

The intersection of gender and violence online has been a topic of much discussion in the media. The deaths of teenagers in two Canadian provinces, Amanda Todd in British Columbia (Teitel, 2012) in 2012, and Rehtaeh Parsons in Nova Scotia (MacDonald, 2014) in 2013, are examples of fatalities resulting from gendered violence online. Their stories of victimization are not unique, falling in line with others, like Ontario teenager Julia Kirouac (*w5*, 2012) who went to the media for support after an ex-boyfriend had distributed naked photographs of herself.

Most current research examining links between gender and cyberbullying is inconclusive (Ang & Goh, 2010; Hinduja & Patchin, 2009; Ringrose & Renold, 2010; Smith & Slonje, 2010). In addition to grade level, gender is a proposed factor affecting individual engagement with cyberbullying, despite discrepancies in existing research that addresses the topic (Ang & Goh, 2010; Beckman, Hagquist, & Hellström, 2013). Bauman (2010) suggested that, like race or ethnicity, gender is an influential factor in cyberbullying, one that is "essentially unexamined" (p. 807). Similarly, Schoffstall and Cohen (2011) noted a scarcity of research identifying the relationship between gender and cyberbullying, and stated that studies claiming to show a relationship exhibit mixed results.

Smith and Slonje (2010) suggested that because cyberbullying exhibits characteristics of indirect bullying, for example, "not done face-to-face" (p. 256), researchers might look to cyberbullying as a site of increased female involvement. This suggestion draws on traditional bullying literature that assumes female passivity (i.e., no engagement in overt displays of aggression), projecting these ideologies onto online engagement (Ringrose & Renold, 2010). Hinduja and Patchin (2009) problematized this argument by proposing that girls might behave passively as a result of being shaped by hegemonic ideologies of gender. They suggested that girls find freedom from "[social] constraints in cyberspace" (p. 52), and called for a re-examination of girl engagement online.

In an ethnographic study of two United Kingdom schools, Ringrose and Renold (2010) examined girls and boys separately to identify the ways in which bullying discourses involved "complex gendered/classed/sexualized/racialized power relations embedded in children's school-based cultures" (p. 573). Their findings suggested that bullying incidents transgress "normative performances of young masculinity and femininity" (p. 577). However, "'normative cruelties' of doing gender" (p. 577) are reinforced through the differentiation of gender expectations and the legitimization of gendered behaviours.

Boy and girl participants performed social "cruelties" (Ringrose & Renold, 2010, p. 577) differently, in ways that were "'intersected' by...axes of identity and power" (p. 591), such as race and sexuality. In interviews, teenaged girls viewed "meanness" as "part of the normative cruelties of 'doing' girl" (p. 585). Asserting that the "just be friends" (p. 587) approach to girl conflict resolution trivializes and normalizes their experiences of conflict, Ringrose and Renold demanded a "critical overhaul" (p. 591) of bullying research to address better the individual gendered experiences and attitudes towards bullying.

Drama as Social Intervention, and Cyberbullying

Extensive literature supports the use of DSI to deal with issues of social justice, including bullying. Current research demands new methods of addressing cyberbullying that are holistic and build critical consciousness in adolescents (Ang & Goh, 2010; Cassidy & Jackson, 2005; Taft, 2011). As a qualitative researcher, Saldaña (2011) argued that the arts can surpass the expressive limitations of typical research methods. Creswell (2012) also suggested that arts-based research offers a unique approach to qualitative investigations (p. 274). The arts may allow for the broader expression of research findings and, thus, the production of knowledge (Eisner, 2008; Greene, 1995; Saldaña, 2011; Siegesmund & Cahnmann-Taylor, 2008), thereby challenging hegemonic ideologies (Barone & Eisner, 2012; Finley, 2008; Sanders, 2006).

For many years drama has been implemented as a means of fostering moral development in youth (Rabin, 2009; Winston, 1996). In particular, DSI has been used to address global social conflict (Lepp, 2011) in countries such as Africa (Heap & Simpson, 2005; Mangeni, 2006, p. 234; Sutherland, 2006) and Brazil (Freire, 2011; Nogueira, 2006). In prisons worldwide DSI has been used with convicts to explore forms of institutionalized violence (Balfour, 2000), to facilitate self-exploration and reflection (Ramamoorthi, 2006), and to teach problem-solving skills (Conrad, 2004).

In schools internationally DSI has given young people a voice in their exploration of social issues (Bryanston, 2001; Conrad, 2004; Nelson, Colby, & McIlrath, 2000; Nicholson, 2003). DSI allows students to further engage with curriculum (Hatton, 2004; Zatzman, 2005) and generates a unique ownership of language and expression (Edell, 2013). In both cognitive and affective domains, it focuses on the student's individual growth throughout and beyond DSI activities (Gonzalez, 2002).

Boal's (2008) Forum Theatre has been used as a DSI technique, locally and internationally, with children and youth to address bullying, gendered violence, and other issues of social change (Belliveau, 2006; Clark, 2009; Kloeble, 2012; Mixed Company Theatre, n.d.; Österlind, 2011). Furthermore, the Seoul Agenda (UNESCO, 2010) affirmed the importance of the arts by setting three goals for arts education. The third goal is of greatest relevance to this study: to "apply arts education principles and practices to contribute to resolving the social and cultural challenges facing today's world" (p. 8), including "remarkable advances in technology" (p. 2). DSI is an effective technique to support critical thinking and social justice among adolescents (Clark, 2009; Conrad, 2004; Hatton, 2004; Heap & Simpson, 2005; Lepp, 2011). By applying DSI techniques to foster critical reflection, I hoped to address cyberbullying in a way that would not only generate equity and inclusivity but also foster meaningful learning for student participants.

Presenting Cyberbullying as an Ethnodrama

Campbell and Conrad (2006) proposed that ethnodrama "raises more questions than it provides answers" (p. 377), "put[ting] culture into motion" (Denzin, 2003, p. 8). The ethnodrama, titled "Cyberbullying: An Invisible Web," reduced data from my research to what was "essential and salient" (Saldaña, 1999, p. 62), in order to highlight five themes and offer multiple perspectives (Creswell, 2012, p. 259). The emergent themes were (a) I Can't Share That, (b) Cyberbullying Is, (c) One Girl Is Many Avatars, (d) Danger Zone, and (e) I Know It; I Don't Want to Feel It. Characters represented five voices in the data: Salvatore, Andy, Rin, Robin, and Miss F as the researcher.

Each of the girls' scripted lines either was taken verbatim from transcripts and handwritten arifacts or represented a quotation recorded in my field notes; however, in scene 2, when the girls brainstorm what cyberbullying is, the girls' language was modified for clarity, while sensitivity towards their true voices was maintained as much as possible.

Campbell and Conrad (2006) suggested that, in ethnodrama, "characters and incidents [are] shaped by the researcher['s] perspec[tive], sympathetic to the predicament of the youth and optimistic for positive change" (p. 377). As the researcher, I remained aware of my omnipresent voice in the ethnodrama; thus, the Miss F character speaks primarily in questions derived directly from the inductive interview questions, weekly journal prompts, and researcher field notes. In this way, her character's voice is meant to merely facilitate the journey of the other characters.

The set and production elements in the ethnodrama are minimal. The script only requires four chairs and a small selection of handheld props. Throughout the ethnodrama each of the five emergent themes is made explicit with the use of projection technology to identify scene titles and emergent subthemes (Rogers, Frellick, & Babinski, 2002). In the script the girls and researcher take turns manipulating the projector with a remote control to visually represent their ownership of the research findings. Throughout the play, "big pad" oversized sticky notes are posted on a flat upstage and written upon to emphasize particular words that emerge from the data. The soundtrack that is used throughout the ethnodrama showcases selections from Robin's playlist for the girls' collective creation.

Below are selections from the ethnodrama; the script presents the results of the research that are most relevant to this particular discussion.

Throughout the ethnodrama some stage directions and dialogue were omitted, while the original meaning and intentions of study participants were maintained. Omitted content is identified by an ellipsis in parentheses.

In the omitted first scene of the ethnodrama the girls express their discomfort at performing a collective creation for an invited audience; instead, they decide to share their creative work with each other. Below are selections from scenes 2 to 5 of the ethnodrama, in which the aforementioned creative pieces are shared.

Cyberbullying: An Invisible Web

Characters.
ROBIN: Grade 11 girl with dark hair, wearing clothing with pockets
SALVATORE: Grade 11 girl, wearing clothing with pockets
ANDY: Grade 11 girl with hair long enough to be put in a ponytail; she wears a hair-elastic on her wrist, and clothing with pockets
RIN: Grade 12 girl who is shorter than the others, with blonde hair
MISS F: Researcher who carries a clipboard and a pen at all times; she wears clothing that will allow her to move on and off stage, into the audience

Scene 2: Cyberbullying Is

Cyberbullying in the abstract.
[For each of the following lines there is a handwritten projection of the girl's text.
SALVATORE presses a button on the remote control, and "Cyberbullying is..."
is projected upstage.]
ROBIN & ANDY: (...) Cyberbullying is...´

SALVATORE: An anonymous person

ANDY, SALVATORE, ROBIN, & RIN: Judging

SALVATORE: People by covering themselves with

ANDY, SALVATORE, ROBIN, & RIN: Lies

ROBIN & ANDY: And

ANDY, SALVATORE, ROBIN, & RIN: Fake names

SALVATORE: In a big, invisible web of hurt *[crossing downstage, away from the others]* it is something that the

ROBIN & ANDY: Victim

SALVATORE: (...) Feels

ANDY, SALVATORE, ROBIN, & RIN: Guilty and humiliated

SALVATORE: About, and the

ROBIN & ANDY: Offender

SALVATORE: Feels

ANDY, SALVATORE, ROBIN, & RIN: No guilt

SALVATORE: Cyberbullying should be treated

SALVATORE & RIN: The same as regular bullying

SALVATORE: But it is harder to get caught or punished when it is online. When they

SALVATORE & RIN: Forget there is a

ANDY, SALVATORE, ROBIN, & RIN: Real!

SALVATORE & RIN: Person

SALVATORE: On the

SALVATORE & RIN: Other side

SALVATORE: They become that

SALVATORE & RIN: Phone call at night

SALVATORE: From a

ANDY, SALVATORE, ROBIN, & RIN: Perfect "stranger" determined to make your life a living hell. Cyberbullying is easy to do.

RIN: *[Crossing to SALVATORE]* And almost a joke

ROBIN: (...) It is a virtual reality

RIN: That feels way too real

ANDY, SALVATORE, ROBIN, & RIN: People can interpret it in different ways

ANDY & ROBIN: *[Looking at each other]* Even if it is unintentional

SALVATORE & RIN: It is still there because

ANDY, SALVATORE, ROBIN, & RIN: People get carried away

ANDY: *[Sarcastically, with some honesty]* Cyberbullying is BAD

ANDY, SALVATORE, ROBIN, & RIN: It is suicide

ANDY & ROBIN: It is the cuts on my wrists.

ROBIN: Cyberbullying is

ANDY, SALVATORE, ROBIN, & RIN: *[All crossing to meet centre]* Like a crime scene

ANDY & ROBIN: A murderer with no face

ANDY, SALVATORE, ROBIN, & RIN: *[Canon:]* Feels | like | no | escape

ANDY & ROBIN: A demonic clown out of place

ANDY, SALVATORE, ROBIN, & RIN: *[Sitting together]* Like a never-ending nightmare

SALVATORE & RIN: An infinite hallway full of laughter

ROBIN: *[Whisper]* The empty silence of unspoken words

ANDY & ROBIN: A child crying

SALVATORE & RIN: 'Cause it *hurts*

ROBIN: *[Whispers in RIN's ear]* A horrible secret

RIN: *[Whispers in SALVATORE's ear]* A *locked* door

SALVATORE: *[With increasing volume]* A constant, nagging voice saying

ANDY: *[Whispers in SALVATORE's ear]* You're not good enough

ROBIN: *[Loud and "creepy"]* It smells like a starry night glazed with the eerie sigh of mist

ANDY, SALVATORE, ROBIN, & RIN: Tastes like metal, old pennies in your mouth

ROBIN: Like dried tears

ALL: *[SALVATORE, RIN, and ANDY rise, slowly]* Inescapable, inerasable...It causes everything to go

ROBIN: *[Whispering]* Silent

ANDY & ROBIN: *[ROBIN remains seated, ANDY backs away from SALVATORE and RIN, upstage; shouting]* Your whole world crumples down.

ROBIN: *[Clutching her stomach]* A sinking feeling in your stomach...Left alone

ANDY, SALVATORE, & RIN: Forever. Angered by other people *[taunting]* like a room of teens cursing at you feels

SALVATORE & RIN: *[With emphasis, stopping themselves and ANDY]* Very unfair

ANDY & ROBIN: The story of a journey

ALL: *[Slow and taunting]* A nightmare...*[ROBIN rises. All shout, crossing to the audience, pointing]* and you're the victim!

SALVATORE & RIN: *[Taunting]* And no one will save you—you're

ANDY, SALVATORE, ROBIN, & RIN: *[With emphasis, still taunting]* Completely and utterly

ROBIN: *[Broken]* Alone.

ANDY: *[Backing up and crossing upstage. She appears to be avoiding the content because she is uncomfortable with it.]* Cyberbullying is like...

[RIN, ROBIN, and SALVATORE continue, to each other, without ANDY.]

RIN: (...) *[Taking the remote control from SALVATORE: she presses a button on the remote control, and the image of a diary appears.]* Cyberbullying is like a diary. A diary is a place for thoughts, ideas, and beliefs. A diary could become blackmail, like cyberbullying content. It takes words and turns them against you. It plays with your feelings.

[ROBIN presses a button on the remote control, and an image of a nazar appears.]

ROBIN: Cyberbullying is like a nazar: an "evil eye." It represents the bravery of Horus, whose eye was cut out, and protection in Muslim and Jewish faiths. If the eyes are the windows of the soul, a person's life and memories can be seen through their eyes. Online, a person cannot physically see through words like they can see in real life. Online you can tell a lot about a person by what they say instead of what they look like. Eyes also represent spectators who protect the bully and witness what occurs. The eyes of society prefer not to see

these incidents. Like a nazar, the computer screen protects cyberbullies. [ROBIN ends downstage right.]

[ROBIN presses a button on the remote control, and an image of a sleep mask
appears.]

SALVATORE: Cyberbullying is like a blind-fold. The victim is blind to
the source of the bullying and who sees it. The bully is blind to the
victim's reaction and the pain she has caused her victim. The victim
is blind to how witnesses react. Are they laughing? Are they angry
with the person who wrote it? Do they even care? It is dangerous. Not
seeing the damage they are causing, allows them to be even more
destructive. (...)

Experiences with cyberbullying.

[(...) ALL speak directly to the audience, as if speaking in an interview with
MISS F.]

ANDY: In elementary school I was bullied a bit—over the Internet.

ROBIN: I've been cyberbullied before and I know how it feels.

SALVATORE: I've never experienced cyberbullying.

ANDY: It wasn't really...anything huge, just, I dunno, on pictures
or something on Facebook, my classmates wouldn't write nice
comments.

ROBIN: I wrote a story on the Internet about my life and friends, and I
described everything as realistically as I could. Somebody found the
story and didn't like their description.

SALVATORE: Like...I think I've heard of people saying that they've got
like, rude messages from people.

ROBIN: They figured out that I wrote the story. It was a big mistake. All
my friends were mad at me because, to them, I was the mean one.

ANDY: I don't remember what they said...exactly. Just...[shrugs] yeah.

SALVATORE: The rude messages people got were never like—really, really
bad. They're normally just...mean. [Crosses to stand with ROBIN and
RIN downstage right.]

ROBIN: *[To SALVATORE]* When it happened to me, it was horrible because it was cyberbullying, plus physical bullying, plus psychological bullying. It was like, everything all at the same time.

ANDY: *[Standing]* It just really hurt my self-confidence. I kind of...locked everything out...and I became a lot quieter. *[Pauses]* I don't really use Facebook anymore. (...)

Reactions to cyberbullying.

[ANDY remains upstage but is not included in the following dialogue.]

RIN: *[To SALVATORE and ROBIN]* Cyberbullies just want to make themselves cooler...or do not understand what they are doing. I think it's stupid. Maybe they have been bullied at school. But, when they're alone, next to their computer and typing, it's slightly different. They feel they can do whatever they want.

[ANDY presses a button on the remote control, and the projection turns off.]

ROBIN: If it's hatred they have for you, they just can't hide it.

RIN: People cyberbully because they think the Internet is more private than it is.

SALVATORE: I don't want to make the Internet seem bad. It can be good. It is so helpful sometimes.

ROBIN: It's, like, a misunderstanding, sometimes...it can be. Somebody misunderstands something you said, and then a whole fight starts out of nothing...sometimes. (...)

SALVATORE: If someone were to message you something rude, you could just show it to your friends. And most people at this school are pretty nice. So, like, if someone were to show me a really rude message from someone, I wouldn't like the person anymore who wrote the message. And most people would do that. Or they might even, like, call them out on it. So, not very many people do it. Like, I don't see very much cyberbullying here.

RIN: For me, cyberbullying wasn't so real. Yeah, it's happening to some people, yeah because they're stupid, actually, to do this stuff...Like when you hear that someone put pictures of themself somewhere,

you're like, "Oh my God, you guys are so stupid!" Really! But now...
you try to understand why they actually did that. Maybe something
happened to them, and they need attention. Because of this, they're
getting bullied. (...)

ROBIN: Cyberbullying has always been bad, but knowing what other
people think about it, I guess my understanding kinda changes. (...)

A story about cyberbullying.

SALVATORE: We have Tasha.

[RIN waves and puts on the pair of sunglasses.]

SALVATORE: Jeff.

[ROBIN waves and puts on the baseball cap.]

SALVATORE: And Andy can play Ashley for me.

*[ANDY waves and puts her hair up in a ponytail with the hair-elastic on her
wrist.]*

RIN: Tasha is mean! *[She playfully makes a "mean" face.]*

ANDY: Ashley's a tomboy. *[ANDY awkwardly adjusts her clothes, then laughs
under her breath.]*

ROBIN: And Jeff's a meathead. *[She crosses her arms, as though she were a boy
trying to show off his arms.]*

SALVATORE: Tasha and Jeff are dating, but they don't really get along.

*[Dialogue in the role-play among Tasha, Jeff, and Ashley occurs centre stage.
Other action occurs downstage right and left.]*

RIN: *[As Tasha]* I really think we should go shopping; all of the new
clothes are out for the summer. There's this dress I really want.
So-and-so wore it in a magazine I read, and—

ROBIN: *[As Jeff. Not paying attention to Tasha. ROBIN exaggerates her masculinized gestures.]* There's a soccer game on tonight. My favourite team
is playing, and they're up against some crazy competition.

RIN: *[As Tasha, exaggerating her feminized gestures]* But you're not listening.
So-and-so wore it and—

ROBIN: *[As Jeff]* So this game tonight—

SALVATORE: This is really getting too sexist. Okay. *[To MISS F]* Then Jeff
meets Ashley, who also really likes soccer.

ANDY: *[As Ashley, she mimes dribbling a soccer ball. She stops to look at
ROBIN.]* Hey.

ROBIN: *[As Jeff, looking at ANDY]* I'd tap that.

SALVATORE: So they go out to a café and watch the game.

ANDY & ROBIN: *[As Ashley and Jeff, standing, arms stretched in the air, as if
watching a TV screen]* GOAL!

SALVATORE: Tasha gets upset and posts an unflattering photo of Ashley
on Facebook.

RIN: *[As Tasha]* Jeff, have you seen this photo? What a loser!

ROBIN: *[As Jeff]* She is totally ruining my rep! I'm done with her.

RIN: *[As herself]* Hold on, Tasha was so upset she started sharing photos?
I don't get it.

ROBIN: *[As herself]* I think Jeff needs to be more boyish. *[She tucks her hair
up under her baseball cap.]*

MISS F: Let's stop for a second. What do you think Ashley should do?

SALVATORE: If someone posted a photo of me, I wouldn't ignore it.

RIN: Something needs to happen for Ashley to protect herself.

SALVATORE: A cat fight?

ROBIN: *[As Jeff]* I'm a meathead. I'd enjoy that.

SALVATORE: *[Nearly laughing]* I'll fight you!

ROBIN: *[As Jeff]* Oh yeah? *[Laughs]*

MISS F: Let's freeze here. How can we fix the problem?

SALVATORE: Ashley could stand up and risk becoming the victim.
Well...Ashley wouldn't fix the problem. She could stop doing things
online so there is less of an audience for the bully.

ROBIN: How about this: Jeff doesn't care about the post. *[As Jeff, miming
looking at a photo on Tasha's computer screen]* If I find her too ugly or too
annoying tonight, then I'll get rid of her and go back to Tasha.

ANDY: Wow, I feel really judged!

SALVATORE: Ashley is a different kind of victim; she's not "girly." Ashley
should call a friend for advice.

ANDY: *[Nodding, as Ashley]* We're the only ones who can work this out.

ROBIN: I'll play Ashley's friend...Erica. *[ROBIN takes off the baseball cap. As Erica]* Did you see the photo on Facebook?

ANDY: *[As Ashley]* Yeah. I don't know what I'm going to do.

ROBIN: *[As Erica]* You know it was Tasha who posted it right?

ANDY: *[As Ashley]* What?

ROBIN: *[As Erica]* You should really do something about it.

ANDY: *[As Ashley]* I'm going to tell Jeff that she is the one who posted it!

ROBIN: Okay, and Jeff can give her one more chance and see that he loves her.

SALVATORE: Or Tasha could feel bad and take the photo off Facebook.

RIN: Erica could tell the principal!

[ANDY, SALVATORE, RIN, and ROBIN pause, searching for a solution.]

SALVATORE: We didn't come up with a solution. Not a good one.

RIN: Most stories about cyberbullying end badly. (...)

Scene 3: One Girl Is Many Avatars

[MISS F places the basket on the floor downstage centre, then presses a button on the remote control, and turns off the projection. (...) SALVATORE, RIN, ROBIN, and ANDY all pull out the objects relevant to her avatar from the basket. RIN takes the elf ears, blonde wig, and cape. ROBIN takes the pirate hat, sword, and pistol. SALVATORE takes the tutu, clown nose, and cigarette. ANDY takes the heavy, laced boots, spray paint, and cross. (...)]

Girl avatars.

RIN: (...) I have an avatar in an online game called *Allods*. She looks similar to me; however, in this game you can pick a different race, so I picked elf. *[Puts on the elf ears]* She has long, blonde hair *[puts on the wig]* and a lot of clothes, which are mostly dresses. *[Puts on the cape]* I don't like to wear them in real life, except when I have to wear a skirt at school. Also she has a different name and is much taller than I am [laughs].

ROBIN: On IMVU (an alternate, kind of, virtual reality online) my avatar is a pirate named Mika [puts on the hat]. She has long, black hair, emerald-green eyes, full red lips, and she usually wears corsets, swords [holds up her sword], guns [holds up her pistol], tight black pants and thigh-high boots. I guess that's the basic appearance of my character. She's the pirate captain of a steampunk ship who goes on adventures with her friends. Surprisingly Mika looks like me, except for the colours of her hair and eyes. I try to stay as close as myself as possible.

SALVATORE: My avatar is half Tumblr and half Facebook. On Facebook I am "pure" [puts on the tutu] because it's a space where you creep people, judge others, and are expected to conform. On Tumblr I'm more...weird [puts on the clown nose]. Tumblr shows the inside of your head. You can include images and ideas that you like but don't have to know what it means. [She takes an awkward drag on the fake cigarette, shrugs, and laughs.] On Tumblr you reblog content based on your instincts. You can tell a lot about who a person is by looking at what they "like" or reblog.

ANDY: [Sits on the floor and puts on the heavy, laced boots] My avatar probably seems more rebellious and more confident than I am. I portray a much darker side of me on Tumblr. [Puts the cross around her neck] It's a little crazy and confusing, which not a lot of people will understand [shakes the can of spray paint, takes off the lid, and mimes spray painting a wall downstage, making the "psss" sound of the paint], but that is how people online see me because that is how I have allowed them to see me.

RIN: The game world is totally different from the world I have on VK... [realizing that she has to explain the acronym] the Russian Facebook. On this social media page the avatar is basically my picture, or me with someone else. [Shrugs] Sometimes I use Photoshop to correct the photo.

ROBIN: On Facebook I usually make profile pictures out of my drawings, but Beaker from the Muppets is my current profile pic. I rarely post statuses. Facebook is only a way of talking to my friends and family in Mexico.

ANDY: On Tumblr, people mainly post pictures: I use the upside-down cross symbol a lot. You pick your own URL and customize the theme and colours. I think my theme is set as "soft grunge." Tumblr content is reposted and not original, although users have the ability to include new content. It is ultimately a way of collecting emblems of your interests, not ideas or items you are necessarily committed to.

SALVATORE: (...) You could Google me and you'd find...things that I do for sports, or whatever, and then you'd think I'm, like, a sporty person, rather than being, like, oh, that person also likes art and schoolwork. (...) On Tumblr I'm a lot different than I am on Facebook. I just think that it's, like, different—parts, like sides of me. There's so many different...places where I'm different aspects of me.

Online identities are different from real life.

SALVATORE, ANDY, RIN, and ROBIN: Online identities are different from real life.

ANDY: Because Tumblr is like the inside of your head, it's scary to let someone see it. It is more personal, and the pictures you choose say more than comments and posts on Facebook. It is uncomfortable to have people you know follow you on Tumblr because it is so personal and you are worried to share these "inner workings" of your brain with people you know. When you tell a friend your Tumblr link, you freak because it's so personal. It's frightening to think about what they will think. So most followers on Tumblr are strangers. It's easier to be personal and intimate with strangers or very, very close friends online.

RIN: If your online friends don't know you personally, you can create a lot of images of who you are.

ANDY: My avatar online is not like I am in reality. It's a smarter and more mature version of myself, or the self that I portray in person. Online I am more creative, deeper, and more artsy through the images I choose to show on the Internet. That's because, on the Internet, you *choose* how you want people to see you by monitoring and controlling what you show them. Whereas in person, they see you as they want to see you, and make their own judgements.

RIN: Your online image fluctuates through the ways in which you communicate, including how quickly you respond to messages, how appropriate your response is, and the tone of your written words.

ANDY: Online, people always feel more comfortable, including myself, because, really, you could be anyone or anything you want. Everyone makes themselves appear a certain way that, pretty much, always isn't true to themselves.

ROBIN: When I go online I try to stay as true to my real self as I can. I feel like I'd be cheating on myself if I didn't.

[RIN, ANDY, and SALVATORE turn to look at her sideways, acknowledging that she is in a pirate costume. ROBIN smiles and shrugs.]

RIN: [Gesturing to what she is wearing] Online, I am not my true self. It's like a black-and-white photo.

ROBIN: Not your true colours?

[RIN removes her avatar items and returns them to the basket.]

ANDY: [Sitting to remove her heavy, laced boots] We all have that in common, that our avatars aren't really true to who we are. (...)

Scene 4: Danger Zone

MISS F: [Standing upstage] Okay, then what advice would you have for someone *like* you about cyberbullying? (...)

SALVATORE: The Internet can be detrimental. It can suck you in and give you problems with your social skills.

RIN: These days most people have Internet friends.

SALVATORE: And sometimes people use the Internet to say things they wouldn't usually say in person.

ROBIN: Although handy, these people can be deceiving. Don't get me wrong; there's also nice people roaming the Internet, but not all of them are all that innocent. Beware of cyber friends.

RIN: These Internet friends live far away from you, and maybe you will never even see each other. If you and he do not really know each other...it can be very dangerous to have one of these friends.

ROBIN: Stay clear from random cyber strangers! You don't want to be like Little Red Riding Hood now, do you?

SALVATORE: People who cyberbully do not have the courage to speak their thoughts face to face.

ROBIN: Sometimes online is better than face to face and fist to fist.

ANDY: A major part of human communication is body language, and by having a screen in front of you rather than the actual person, it allows you to hide a lot. If you so choose...When I talk to people online, even my friends, I become more confident and say more witty things. It also makes it easier to lie...because, as I said before, body language is a huge factor in communication. When a person is lying, there are signs you pick up on, that you can physically see.

RIN: Online, communication is different, from how it is in real life. I thought about it...before, how like we try to chat with each other... like even with our friends. It's slightly different if we were talking by Skype, or if we're like, talking like, natural, like we are talking right now. So it's slightly different. Online you have the time to think about what you want to write, or what you want to say.

ROBIN: You can tell a person by what they say instead of what they look like online. You see who they truly are through what they say.

RIN: And people put their whole lives online, their feelings and ideas, the bad and sad moments of life are now public. But they do not receive sympathy from their audience.

SALVATORE: The cyberbully forgets there is a *real* person on the other side getting hurt. The Internet is a sort of barrier between human communication, like a wall where you can't see the other person's reactions to what you are saying. You can't even hear the emotions in their voice. (...)

Scene 5: I Know It; I Don't Want to Feel It

Improved understanding of self rather than cyberbullying.

ROBIN: From this study, I've learned that cyberbullying is bad, obviously... (...)

RIN: (...) I kind of get, understand, why it's happening. So like, people are jealous, as usual bullying, but in the Internet...I don't think I get a sense of how it *feels*...but I don't want to *feel* this at all. (...)

ANDY: I've learned that there are different perspectives on cyberbullying. And, just...that there are different ways that people can be cyberbullies for different reasons.

RIN: We actually didn't learn about *someone*...using these activities, like, we try to work together and like organize everything everyone thought and try to become...of one opinion with each other. So I think it's helpful. We try to agree with each other.

ROBIN: I like expressing my feelings through writing, acting, and art, like we used in the study. I felt like I told a bit of my past. Maybe some of these girls haven't gone through what I have, but I still feel like it helps them understand me.

RIN: The role-play was helpful because I could actually think about why the people made the choices they did. (...)

ANDY: Other people's perspectives helped my understanding of cyberbullying, because everyone sees things differently.

RIN: In school, at the beginning of the year we were shown movies that talked about cyberbullying. For me, it was not so real...and now...you try to understand why they actually did that. So, this kind of stuff, it's coming closer...and you actually start to care about it.

SALVATORE: It was weird to talk so much about how we felt and focus on one topic for so long. But I realized that cyberbullying can come in many different instances or forms. I found this out from the stories.

ANDY: I've just become more aware. Kind of—just...talking about cyberbullying with other people makes you think about it more and, I don't know, just makes it...more real. (...)

SALVATORE: It made me, not worried, but, like, it kinda made me more *aware* of what I'm doing online. Like when I'm talking to people, or if I call them something on Facebook. Now I'm kinda...thinking I should be more aware of what they're thinking when they read that comment. Not that I *meant* to call them anything mean, but it could be taken in a bad way. (...)

Hopes for others.

MISS F: Well...before we finish...How do you think you could make a change to incidents of cyberbullying?

ANDY: *[Presses a button on the remote control, and "Hopes for others" is projected upstage.]* Stop being a bystander and stand up for the victims of cyberbullying if you see they can't stand up for themselves.

SALVATORE: I can stop being the bystander. When I see others being mean to people online, I could report it or comment back saying that what they are saying is wrong. I could stand up and risk becoming a victim too, or I could just stop doing things online so there is less of an audience for the bully.

RIN: I think the victim needs to stop being shy and stand up for themselves.

[(...) ANDY presses a button on the remote control, and "Dear Someone Like Me..." is projected upstage. The lights fade out upstage. Only ANDY, SALVATORE, RIN, and ROBIN are lit downstage.]

ANDY: Dear Someone Like Me:

SALVATORE: The Internet is great. It is awesome for talking to your friends or finding inspiration.

RIN: I hope you are not spending all day long on the Internet. If so, go out and find a hobby. *[Laughs]*

SALVATORE: The Internet connects almost the entire world.

ROBIN: But although the world can be cold and misleading, there is also a bright side to it all. *[(...) She writes and speaks the last part of her line, recording the line in large font on one of the sticky notes.]* Don't worry. You'll be fine.

RIN: I know life is much better than you think. *[Crosses upstage, takes a marker, like ROBIN, and records her line on a different sticky note.]*

SALVATORE: People like cyberbullies are not worth your time. *[Crosses upstage, takes a marker and records her line on another sticky note.]*

ROBIN: I know it can be tough, but you'll see that light shines even in the darkest of places. *[Writes "even in the darkest of places" on another sticky note. To ANDY]* With a little help from your friends, anything is possible.

SALVATORE: *[Drawing a heart on an empty sticky note]* With love

RIN: *[Drawing a heart, like SALVATORE]* With love

ROBIN: *[Drawing a heart]* Love

SALVATORE: *[Putting the cap on her marker and turning to the audience]* Salvatore.

RIN: *[Turning to the audience]* Rin

ROBIN: *[Turning]* Robin

ANDY: *[Looking back to the other girls]* And Andy *[presses a button on the remote control, and "Love, Someone Like You" is projected on all of the sticky notes that do not have writing.]*

ANDY, ROBIN, RIN, and SALVATORE: Someone Like You.

[The instrumental introduction to "Crawling" by Linkin Park plays on loop. Lights fade to black. (...) End scene]

Discussion

In the following discussion I will address three of the major findings in this study. First, I will examine the girls' definition of cyberbullying as a social phenomenon, then I will move on to discuss their reported experiences with cyberbullying. I will follow by interrogating the girls' apparent, affective disengagement. Finally, I will explore how girl identity manifests as multiple avatars online.

Defining cyberbullying.

The girls revealed a multifaceted definition that fundamentally views cyberbullying as an inherently "bad" behaviour that resultantly "others" the perpetrator (JanMohamed, 1985, p. 59). The ostracizing of the cyberbully was evident in the girls' language throughout the study, namely in the comments referring explicitly to the cyberbully as "bad," and "cowardly." To the girls, cyberbullies were intangible, faceless "keyboard warriors." This perception arises despite the fact that three of the four girls revealed that their experience of cyberbullying had been as either a victim or a bystander. Furthermore, Salvatore, Andy, and Robin all connected their experiences of cyberbullying to peers whom they knew off-line. Bauman (2010) problematizes these self-identified roles, having suggested that "of students who were involved in cyberbullying, the vast majority were involved as both bullies and victims" (p. 827).

The girls in this study may have found more comfort in discussing cyberbullying on the level of abstraction, rather than real-life contexts (this is clear in scene 2 of the ethnodrama). Abstraction may have permitted the girls to explore this potentially controversial topic with greater ease.

Girls' experiences of cyberbullying.

I was surprised to find the girls so hesitant to share their personal experiences of cyberbullying. Only Andy identified herself as a victim of cyberbullying, briefly and broadly outlining her experiences of classmates' negative comments posted on her now-closed Facebook page. Inversely, Salvatore shared that she was unaware of schoolmates being cyberbullied and explained that her peer group would act against cyberbullying behaviours by speaking back to the cyberbully online. Alternatively, Robin outlined an experience in which she felt she had been bullied after she was accused of cyberbullying her peer. In this data none of the participants identified herself as solely a "bystander" or "cyberbully" in her experiences.

It seems that there is a lack of clarity in the language used by the girls to discuss their experiences. This might connect to the concept of the cyberbully as the "other" (JanMohamed, 1985, p. 59). In the context of this study, the girls may have been hesitant to use traditional language that might implicate themselves as either a perpetrator of this type of violence or a bystander.

The ways in which the girls ostracized the cyberbully throughout the study flowed into their descriptions of the Internet and specific online spaces. The Internet became a dangerous, wilderness-type space that housed "keyboard warriors"; Rin suggested that "Internet friends" became dangerous oppressors, and Robin compared her "Someone Like Me" to Little Red Riding Hood. In these descriptions it seems that the Internet is a space in which the girls expected to find oppressors; however, the supposed facelessness of cyberbullies was complicated by the way in which the girls emphasized their perceptions of off-line consequences. There is a divide between the way in which the girls understood cyberbullying and the way in which their real-life experiences fit into this definition.

Affective disengagement.

To support ethical practices in the exploration of this sensitive subject matter, DSI techniques employ distancing devices (Edell, 2013; Eriksson, 2011) to serve as a buffer between the girls' creative work and the cyberbullying content. Eriksson defines distancing as "the awareness of fiction...to function as protection" (p. 66). Providing distance is meant to allow participants to engage in a way that saves them from any unwanted vulnerability, while genuinely interacting with the research topic. However, distancing was apparent in the girls' demonstration of empathy throughout the study.

Ang and Goh (2010) separate empathy as "(affective empathy), which is the ability to experience and share the emotions of others," and as "(cognitive empathy), which is the ability to understand the emotions of others" (p. 388). The girls demonstrated cognitive empathy, understanding the feelings of others, especially when exploring perspectives; however, they did not demonstrate significant evidence of affective empathy. This was made explicit in Rin's comment: "I don't think I get a sense of how [cyberbullying] feels...but I don't want to feel this at all." Ang and Goh suggested that "girls, regardless of their levels of cognitive empathy,...reported similar and indistinguishable levels of cyberbullying behaviour" (p. 395). This would imply that, despite reporting an improved understanding of cyberbullying and demonstrating cognitive empathy, the study may not have had a notable impact on cyberbullying behaviour.

Girl identity manifests as multiple avatars online.

In this study, girls conceptualized their online identities as multiple, disconnected avatars (de Zwart & Lindsay, 2012; Stermitz, 2008), as illustrated in scene 3 of the ethnodrama. Davis (2010) argued that "the internet provides individuals with even more options for identity experimentation" than they have off-line (p. 150), echoing Adrian's (2008) assertion that "[virtual worlds] make...[a] multiplicity of identity actionable" (p. 368). Online environments appear to facilitate "liquid identity" (p. 368). Adrian also proposed that "what is changing [with online worlds] is not the 'self,' which remains unitary, but the effortlessness with which the 'self' can manipulate its appearances in different physical spaces" (p. 368).

The girls demonstrated this concept when creating and discussing their avatar images. Salvatore placed her Facebook and Tumblr identities on extremes of a continuum, from composition to psychological intimacy. Robin described herself as a steampunk pirate captain and separated this identity from her Facebook profile picture of Beaker from the Muppets. Rin described her identity as elf-like in a role-playing game but discussed her need to identify her boyfriend and interests on vк (a social media program like Facebook). Andy suggested that Google would reveal elements of her school involvements and family's public presence but that her Tumblr account truly revealed her inner thoughts.

Davis (2010) argued, "Blogging allows [girls] to disclose certain thoughts and feelings that they otherwise would not have the opportunity or inclination to share in other contexts" (p. 162) and that "intimacy can also be maintained through blogging" (p. 158). Salvatore and Andy both expressed their discomfort with sharing their Tumblr pages with friends and acquaintances. The girls were clear that Tumblr allowed them to share their personal ideas and interests without the fear of feeling the consequences of judgement. They are only "followed" by very close friends or complete strangers on Tumblr, despite the fact that these girls conceptualize the Internet as a predatory space with faceless oppressors.

The girls identified their disconnected avatars as different from their "true" off-line selves. What are the implications of these identities? Stermitz (2008) suggested that the "liquidity" of identity online is a way for girls to "choose and change between body concepts and fragments and therefore ques[tion] [ideologies] in their repressivity" (p. 538). Thus, liquid identity might be viewed as a source of empowerment for teenaged girls. Alternatively, I wonder what this liquidity is indeed empowering girls to do. Furthermore, how does this affect the ways in which girls build identity off-line in real-life spaces, even if their avatars are distinctly different from their off-line selves?

Implications for Researchers and Educators

The multiplicity of girl-avatar identities demands that researchers re-evaluate cyberbullying language, supporting the "critical overhaul" of "anti-bullying discourses" argued by Ringrose and Renold (2010, p. 591). I propose that the cyberbully, victim, and bystander discourses do not account for the multiplicity of roles assumed by girls online. Ringrose and Renold maintained that current language "support[s] heteronormative power...constructing binaries that pathologise the bully often in gendered, but also racialised and class-specific ways" (p. 590). This is also reinforced by Sbarbaro and Enyeart Smith's (2011) demand "to further identify influential factors revolved around bullying and cyberbullying" (p. 150).

Educators need to recognize the multiplicity of girls' online (avatar) identities. The understanding that girls perceive themselves as having many separate identities should influence how we educate them about online safety, as well as inform the ways in which we understand the complexities of girls' experiences with cyberbullying. This notion returns to a need for a working language that better addresses the realities of girls' avatar identities in the cyberbullying context (Ringrose & Renold, 2010). If "violence is normalised through the blurring of boundaries between games, play-fighting and violence" (Ringrose & Renold, 2010, p. 580), thus, with the continuing employment of cyberbullying discourses that are no longer appropriate, cyber-violence is normalized in the blurring of divisions between girls' online spaces and identities. The traditional "bully-victim" concept needs to be fleshed out so that the current realities for girls can be better addressed.

Another implication for educators is that girls have particular sites of safety online. In this study the girls made clear the communities in which they were comfortable sharing more intimate details about their personalities and ideas (e.g., Tumblr). Teachers and administrators must be aware that girls may be more comfortable sharing intimate personal details with strangers online than they may be with close friends and acquaintances. It appears that girls assume that the anonymity of their online audience creates a safe space for expression. This is clearly problematic when considering the militarization of cyberspaces (Ben-Porath, 2006; Enloe, 2007; Turse, 2008).

Finally, it appears that there is a need to incorporate empathy building into cyberbullying programs in schools. Ang and Goh (2010) argued that "empathy training and education should be included in cyberbullying intervention programs" (p. 395). In this study, girls suggested that discussing incidents of cyberbullying from the news media (in awareness programs) did not empathetically engage students. Furthermore, Ringrose and Renold (2010) argued that "dominant 'bully discourses' employed to make sense of and address conflict offer few resources or practical tools for addressing and coping with everyday, normative aggression and violence in schools" (p. 575).

Ben-Porath (2006) suggested that "schools can work with the students, engaging their critical capacities, emotions and imagination, to envision alternative possible futures" (p. 91). I encourage teachers and administrators to refocus and reconceptualize the ways in which we educate students about cyberbullying in order to address better these disengaging discourses and generate affective empathy in students.

REFERENCES

Adrian, A. (2008). No one knows you are a dog: Identity and reputation in virtual worlds. *Computer Law and Security Report, 24,* 366-374.

Ang, R., & Goh, D.H. (2010). Cyberbullying among adolescents: The role of affective and cognitive empathy, and gender. *Child Psychiatry & Human Development, 41,* 387-397.

Balfour, M. (2000). Drama, masculinity and violence. *Research in Drama Education, 5*(1), 9-21.

Barone, T., & Eisner, E.W. (2012). *Arts based research.* Los Angeles: Sage.

Bauman, S. (2010). Cyberbullying in a rural intermediate school: An exploratory study. *Journal of Early Adolescence, 30*(6), 803-833.

Bauman, S., Toomey, R.B., & Walker, J.L. (2013). Associations among bullying, cyberbullying, and suicide in high school students. *Journal of Adolescence, 36*(2), 341-350.

Beckman, L., Hagquist, C., & Hellström, L. (2013). Discrepant gender patterns for cyberbullying and traditional bullying: An analysis of Swedish adolescent data. *Computers in Human Behavior, 29*(5), 1896-1903.

Belliveau, G. (2006). Using drama to achieve social justice: Anti-bullying project in elementary schools. In L.A. McCammon & D. McLauchlan (Eds.), *Universal mosaic of drama and theatre: The IDEA 2004 dialogues* (pp. 325-335). Ottawa: IDEA.

Ben-Porath, S.R. (2006). *Citizenship under fire: Democratic education in times of conflict.* Princeton, NJ: Princeton University Press.

Boal, A. (2008). *Theatre of the oppressed* (C.A. McBride, M.-O.L. McBride, & E. Fryer, Trans.). London: Pluto Press.

Bresler, L. (2006). Toward connectedness: Aesthetically based research. *Studies in Art Education, 48*(I), 52-69.

Bryanston, C. (2001). The children. *Drama Magazine* (Winter), 29-35.

Campbell, G., & Conrad, D. (2006). Arresting change: Popular theatre with young offenders. In L.A. McCammon & D. McLauchlan (Eds.), *Universal mosaic of drama and theatre: The IDEA 2004 dialogues* (pp. 375-391). Ottawa: IDEA.

Cassidy, W., & Jackson, M. (2005). The need for equality in education: An intersectionality examination of labeling and zero tolerance practices. *McGill Journal of Education, 40*(3), 435-456.

Clark, J. (2009). Acting up and speaking out: Using theatre of the oppressed and collective memory work as alternative research methods and empowerment tools in work with girls. *Agenda: Empowering Women for Gender Equity, 79*, 49-64.

Collins, L., & Patterson, J. (2004). Cyber bullying: The new frontier. *Teaching and Learning, 1*(3), 32-34.

Conrad, D. (2004). Popular theatre: Empowering pedagogy for youth. *Youth Theatre Journal, 18*, 87-106.

Creswell, J.W. (2012). Educational research: Planning, conducting, and evaluating quantitative and qualitative research (4th ed.). Boston: Pearson.

Cyberbullying Research Center. (2013). Retrieved from http://cyberbullying.us

Davis, K. (2010). Coming of age online: The developmental underpinnings of girls' blogs. *Journal of Adolescent Research, 25*(1), 145-171.

Denzin, N.K. (2003). *Performance ethnography: Critical pedagogy and the politics of culture.* Thousand Oaks, CA: Sage.

de Zwart, M., & Lindsay, D. (2012). My self, my avatar, my rights? Avatar identity in social virtual worlds. In D. Riha (Ed.), *At the interface / probing the boundaries: Frontiers of cyberspace* (pp. 81-100). Amsterdam: Rodopi B.V.

Edell, D. (2013). "Say how it is": Urban teenage girls challenge and perpetuate stereotypes through writing and performing theatre. *Youth Theatre Journal, 27*(1), 51-62.

Eisner, E. (2008). Art and knowledge. In J.G. Knowles & L.C. Ardra (Eds.), *Handbook of the arts in qualitative research: Perspectives, methodologies, examples, and issues.* Los Angeles: Sage.

Enloe, C. (2007). *Globalization and militarism: Feminists make the link.* Lanham, MD: Rowman & Littlefield.

Erdur-Baker, Ö. (2010). Cyberbullying and its correlation to traditional bullying, gender and frequent and risky usage of internet-mediated communication tools. *New Media & Society, 12*(1), 109-125.

Eriksson, S.A. (2011). Distancing. In S. Schonmann (Ed.), *Key concepts in theatre/drama education* (pp. 65-71). Rotterdam: Sense.

Finley, S. (2008). Arts-based research. In J.G. Knowles & A.L. Cole (Eds.), *Handbook of the arts in qualitative research: Perspectives, methodologies, examples, and issues.* Los Angeles: Sage.

Fournier, G.L. (2014). *How are girls' attitudes toward cyberbullying affected by drama for social intervention?* (Unpublished master's thesis). Brock University, St. Catharines, ON. Retrieved from http://hdl.handle.net/10464/5390

Freire, P. (2011). *Pedagogy of the oppressed* (30th anniversary edition, M. Bergman Ramos, Trans.). New York: Continuum International.

Garber, E. (2010, Fall). Global and local: Rethinking citizenship in art and visual culture education. *Encounters on Education, 11,* 117-133.

Gonzalez, J.B. (2002). From page to stage to teenager: Problematizing "transformation" in theatre for and with adolescents. *Stage of the Art, 14*(3), 17-21.

Greene, M. (1995). Art and imagination: Reclaiming the sense of possibility. *Phi Delta Kappan, 76*(5), 5.

Hatton, C. (2004). On the edge of realities: Drama, learning and adolescent girls. *Drama Australia Journal NJ, 28*(1), 87-102.

Heap, S., & Simpson, A. (2005). A lesson for the living: Promoting HIV/AIDS competence among young Zambians. *Youth Theatre Journal, 18*(1), 89-101.

Hinduja, S., & Patchin, J.W. (2009). *Bullying beyond the schoolyard: Preventing and responding to cyberbullying.* Thousand Oaks, CA: Corwin Press.

JanMohamed, A. (1985). The economy of Manichean allegory: The function of racial difference in colonialist literature. *Critical Inquiry, 12,* 59-87.

Kauffman, J.M., & Landrum, T.J. (2013). *Characteristics of emotional and behavioral disorders of children and youth* (10th ed.). Boston: Pearson.

Kloeble, C. (2012, June). *Far from the heart: Report of the effectiveness of forum theatre as an educational tool regarding youth dating violence and sexual assault in Saskatchewan schools.* Unpublished report, University of Regina Community Research Unit, University of Regina, Saskatchewan.

Lepp, M. (2011). Drama for conflict management: DRACON international. In S. Schonmann (Ed.), *Key concepts in theatre/drama education* (pp. 99-104). Rotterdam: Sense.

MacDonald, M. (2014, February 29). Nova Scotia court issues first cyberbullying prevention order. *National Post.* Retrieved from http://news.nationalpost.com

Mangeni, P. (2006). Negotiating learning contexts: Some experiences of culture, power, and gender in working with multi-cultural communities through theatre for development. In L.A. McCammon & D. McLauchlan (Eds.), *Universal mosaic of drama and theatre: The IDEA 2004 dialogues* (pp. 233-243). Ottawa: IDEA.

Mas, S. (2013, July 23). Proposed cyberbullying law draws NDP support. *CBC News.* Retrieved from www.cbc.ca

McCall, M.M. (2000). Performance ethnography: A brief history and some advice. In N.K. Denzin & Y.S. Lincoln (Eds.), *Handbook of qualitative research* (2nd ed., pp. 421-433). New York: Sage.

Mienczakowski, J., Smith, L., & Morgan, S. (2002). Seeing words—hearing feelings: Ethnodrama and the performance of data. In C. Bagley (Ed.), *Dancing the data* (pp. 34-52). New York: Peter Lang.

Mixed Company Theatre. (n.d.) Retrieved from www.mixedcompanytheatre.com

Nelson, B., Colby, R., & McIlrath, M. (2000). "Having their say": The effects of using role with an urban middle school class. *Youth Theatre Journal, 15,* 59-66.

Nicholson, H. (2003). Acting, creativity and social justice: Edward Bond's *The Children. Research in Drama Education, 8*(1), 9-23.

Nogueira, M.P. (2006). A mosaic of community theatre practices in Southern Brazil. In L.A. McCammon & D. McLauchlan (Eds.), *Universal mosaic of drama and theatre: The IDEA 2004 dialogues* (pp. 269-278). Ottawa: IDEA.

O'Farrell, L. (2010). Introduction. *Encounters on education, 11,* xi-xiii.

Ontario. (2012). The Accepting Schools Act, an act to amend the Education Act with respect to bullying and other matters. c. S.O. 2012 C.5. Retrieved from http://ontla.on.ca/web/bills/bills_detail.do?locale=en&BillID=2549

Österlind, E. (2011). Forum play: A Swedish mixture for consciousness and change. In S. Schonmann (Ed.), *Key concepts in theatre/drama education* (pp. 247-251). Rotterdam: Sense.

Pelfrey, W.V., Jr., & Weber, N.L. (2013). Keyboard gangsters: Analysis of incidence and correlates of cyberbullying in a large urban student population. *Deviant Behavior, 34*(1), 68-84.

Rabin, C.L. (2009). The theatre arts and care ethics. *Youth Theatre Journal, 23,* 127-143.

Ramamoorthi, P. (2006). Freedom space: Drama therapy with prisoners in Madurai. In L.A. McCammon & D. McLauchlan (Eds.), *Universal mosaic of drama and theatre: The IDEA 2004 dialogues* (pp. 367-374). Ottawa: IDEA.

Ringrose, J., & Renold, E. (2010). Normative cruelties and gender deviants: The performative effects of bully discourses for girls and boys in school. *British Educational Research Journal, 36*(4), 573-596.

Rogers, D., Frellick, P., & Babinski, L. (2002). Staging a study: Performing the personal and professional struggles of beginning teachers. In C. Bagby & M.B. Cancienne (Eds.), *Dancing the data* (pp. 53-69). New York: Peter Lang.

Saldaña, J. (1999). Playwriting with data: Ethnographic performance texts. *Youth Theatre Journal, 13,* 60-69.

Saldaña, J. (2006, July). *An introduction to ethnodrama: Autoethnography as monologue.* Workshop presented at the American Alliance of Theater and Education (AATE) annual conference, Chicago.

Saldaña, J. (2011). *Fundamentals of qualitative research: Understanding qualitative research.* New York: Oxford University Press.

Sanders, J.H., III. (2006). Performing arts-based education research: An epic drama of practice, precursors problems and possibilities. *Studies in Art Education, a Journal of Issues and Research, 48*(1), 89-107.

Sbarbaro, V., & Enyeart Smith, T.M. (2011). An exploratory study of bullying and cyberbullying behaviors among economically/educationally disadvantaged middle school students. *American Journal of Health Studies, 26*(3), 139-151.

Schoffstall, C.L., & Cohen, R. (2011). Cyber aggression: The relation between online offenders and offline social competence. *Social Development, 20*(3), 587-604.

Shariff, S. (2005). Cyber-dilemmas in the new millennium: School obligations to provide student safety in a virtual school environment. *McGill Journal of Education, 40*(3), 457-477.

Siegesmund, R., & Cahnmann-Taylor, M. (2008). The tensions of arts-based research in education reconsidered: The promise for practice. In M. Cahnmann-Taylor & R. Siegesmund (Eds.), *Arts-based research in education: Foundations for practice* (pp. 231-244). New York: Routledge.

Smith, P.K., & Slonje, R. (2010). Cyberbullying: The nature and extent of a new kind of bullying, in and out of school. In S.R. Jimerson, S.M. Swearer, & D.L. Espelage (Eds.), *Handbook of bullying in schools: An international perspective* (pp. 249–262). New York: Routledge.

Stermitz, E. (2008). World of female avatars: An artistic online survey on the female body in times of virtual reality. *Leonardo, 41*(5), 538–539.

Stern, S.T. (2007). *Instant identity: Adolescent girls and the world of instant messaging.* New York: Peter Lang.

Sutherland, A. (2006). Making visible the invisible: Drama as voice for youth at risk in a South African context. In L.A. McCammon & D. McLauchlan (Eds.), *Universal mosaic of drama and theatre: The IDEA 2004 dialogues* (pp. 337–346). Ottawa: IDEA.

Taft, J.K. (2011). *Rebel girls: Youth activism and social change across the Americas.* New York: NYU Press.

Teitel, E. (2012, October 29). Cyberbullying: Bullied to death. *Maclean's, 125*(42), 68–70.

Turse, N. (2008). *The complex: How the military invades our everyday lives.* New York: Metropolitan Books.

Underwood, M.K., & Rosen, L.H. (2011). Gender and bullying: Moving beyond mean differences to consider conceptions of bullying, processes by which bullying unfolds, and cyberbullying. In D.L. Espelage and S.M. Swearer (Eds.), *Bullying in North American schools* (2nd ed., pp. 13–22). New York: Routledge.

UNESCO. (2010). *Seoul agenda: Goals for the development of arts education.* Second World Conference on Arts Education. [PDF document].

W5. (2012, September 21). Sext-ed: Inside the sexting sub-culture of teens. Retrieved from www.ctvnews.ca

Wilson, B. (2006). Ethnography, the internet, and youth culture: Strategies for examining social resistance and "online-offline" relationships. *Canadian Journal of Education, 29*(1), 307–328.

Winston, J. (1996). Emotion, reason and moral engagement in drama. *Research in Drama Education, 1*(2), 189–200.

Zatzman, B. (2005). Staging history: Aesthetics and the performance of memory. *Journal of Aesthetic Education, 39*(4), 95–103.

10 ✖ ✖ ✖ ✚ ✖

War Games

School Sports and the Making of Militarized Masculinities

Roger Saul

EVERY YEAR OVER HALF OF ALL Canadian high-school students participate in organized sports (Canadian Heritage, 2013; Ifedi, 2008). For male high-school students in Canada, upon whom this chapter focuses, the benefit is clear: a vast body of research suggests that sports participation promotes a range of physical and mental-health advantages, as well as encourages social gains like co-operation, friendship, communicative competencies, and positive school engagement (see Clark, 2009). Yet alongside these claims there exists an alternative body of scholarship that emphasizes the contested cultural meanings and contributions of sports to modern societies (see Coakley & Donnelly, 2009). Among other functions, it seeks to complicate the uncritical championing of the individual and social benefits of sports to the lives of young people. In this chapter I draw on three bodies of knowledge—cultural studies of sport, masculinity studies, and equity studies—to advance the particular claim that embedded in sports participation is a set of militaristic values, often implicit, that can have deleterious effects when transferred to educational contexts, especially for those on the margins of inclusion within these contexts. In particular, I focus on the way in which the endorsement of sports cultures in schools brings militaristic values to bear on social constructions of gender, and on masculinity in particular. In this respect, I suggest that sports are a well-placed delivery vehicle for the propagation of a militaristic "gender order" in schools (Connell, 2005).

Sports are a repository of projected, sanctioned, and celebrated militaristic values. In male sports subcultures in particular, these values are closely intertwined with socially endorsed ideas about what constitutes appropriate performances of gender. The successful male athlete is often one who has internalized tribalism, aggression, conflict resolution through competition, acquiescence to hierarchy, and the social validation of strength and bravery through uses of force (see Kidd, 2013; Klein & Sorenson, 2002; Schnyder, 2012; Wellard, 2002). All who participate in the athletic enterprise—student athletes, as well as supportive parents, teachers, coaches, and administrators—arguably conspire to endorse these militaristic values, even if unwillingly or unknowingly. In view of the pervasive social discourses on the positive benefits of sports participation, in what follows I explore a counter-discourse framed around the following questions: What *else* is learned by male students who participate in school sports? What kinds of interests are advanced or impeded by this alternative learning? Who is affirmed or denied by this learning? And why would educational stakeholders be wise to take notice of this alternative school-sports discourse?

To answer these questions I proceed along three tracks. I begin by drawing from cultural studies of sport literature to situate the legitimacy of the claim that, in modern societies, sports often function as a proxy endorsement of militarism (Jansen & Sabo, 1994; Jenkins, 2013). I next focus on how this now established sports-militarism connection can play out in schools in ways that sanction an impoverished view of masculinity—by privileging rigid expressions of maleness over fluid ones, favouring some socio-cultural male groupings over others, and placing all males in positions of uneven dominance over females (Butler, 1990, 1994; Connell, 2005, 2012). Lastly, drawing on the case of black, male, student athletes, I argue that the result of this sports-enabled inscription of rigid gender roles is that it works against the full inclusion of many Canadian males into school life. Notably, those young males on the margins of achieving endorsed masculine ideals—visible minorities, sexual minorities, the economically disadvantaged—often suffer within the school communities that prize the achievement of said ideals through sports.

Sports and Militarism

Adherence to Higate and Hopton's (2005) definition of militarism as the celebration of military tradition in national politics and popular culture (p. 443) illustrates that there is perhaps no greater conduit for the public celebration of military culture in modern life than sports participation and spectatorship. In this respect, making explicit the connection between militarism and sports—in discourse, in history, in institutional practices, and in popular culture—is a necessary first step in exploring how the values of militarism are supported by attention to sports in schools and societies.

What Jansen and Sabo (1994) have called the "sport/war metaphor" (p. 1) has merged contemporary understandings of both sports and war in the modern popular imagination, whereby sports talk is commonly delivered through a vernacular of war terminologies; to speak of war is now often to speak of sports. Only a cursory glance at most Canadian sporting events will reveal anthems being sung and flags being raised, before antagonistic sides "square off," "do battle," "design offences and defences," "attack," "blitz," "bomb," and so on. Jenkins (2013) calls this lexical connection the "sport-war intertext" and claims that it has the effect of rendering athletic contests and institutions as a "patriotic theatre...meant to promote a sense of national unity.... encouraging a coercive patriotism...help[ing] to sell wars through the pageantry of sport" (p. 3). The monstrosities of war, so often the inconspicuous veneer behind public expressions of nationalism, thus find an ally in sports, which "sanitize the atrocities of war" (Jansen & Sabo, 1994, p. 7) in promoting nationalist symbols and ideals (Kelly, 2012).

One need not look far to find these connections expressed, with frequency, in popular media. A significant finding in this regard comes from Messner, Dunbar, and Hunt (2000) as part of a larger study of the way televised sports and their accompanying advertisements support particular cultural constructions of masculinity (I explore such constructions later on). Their textual analysis of televised sports revealed that on average, at a rate of roughly five times per hour of sports commentary, sports commentators "used martial metaphors and language of war and weaponry to describe sports action" (p. 388). A most common occurrence here was the fusing of "the distinctions between values of nationalism with team identity and athletic aggression with military destruction" (p. 389). Similar instances of connection are likewise rampant in media, whether in the contemporary popular cultural trend of emphasizing a symbiosis between sports cultures on the one hand and militarized gang cultures on the other (Leonard, 2010), or in the common recourse to military imagery in post-game professional athlete interviews (King, 2008).

That said, the connection between militarism and sports in Canada and elsewhere runs deeper than mere lexical commonalities. In fact, there is ample reason to claim that "the mixing of metaphors of sport and war [has] played a historically unique social, rhetorical, and ideological role" and provided a "semiotic system and set of cultural values to advance and justify...respective plans, actions and interests" of militarism (Jansen & Sabo, 1994, p. 1). What the preceding suggests, in other words, is that the "sport-war intertext" (Jenkins, 2013) performs a function that is far from innocent; it works to position sports as an ideological support for the military state, as well as a material support for the maintenance of stability and order within it, and it has long done so (King, 2008).

The history, development, and growth of modern sports cultures bear out this assertion. Since at least the 19th century, nationalist agendas have focused on the promotion of sports participation as a strategy for creating order and a common version of morality among disparate peoples—many of them newly subjugated peoples within imperialist and expansionist contexts—as well as a complicity with patriotic ideals (Coakley & Donnelly, 2009; Huggins, 2012). Kidd (2013) sources the creation of modern sports practices to mid-19th-century Britain, when a common sports culture of the kind that would be recognized today spread through "emigration, emulation and imperialism" (p. 554). It is important to note here that the practices and ideals emphasized by this culture of play—social interaction structured by precise rules, consent to externally mandated standards of fairness, performance hierarchies, mannered aggression, co-operation towards a common goal, and displays of gentility in the face of adversity—are constructs of modern sports. Ancient sports, now popularized and mythologized through stories of ancient Greece and early Olympiads, were, however, founded on presumptions that today would be hardly recognizable (Kidd, 2013).

Of ancient sports Kidd (2013) writes, "They were extremely violent. The combative events, which were the most popular spectacles, were conducted with little regard for safety or fairness. There were no weight categories to equalize strength and size, no rounds and no ring. Bouts were essentially fights to the finish" (p. 554). He continues: "Performance for itself—pursuing the personal best despite one's placing—was meaningless to them....There were no team events, because competitors did not want to share the glory of victory. No competitor would have congratulated an opponent for a fairly fought or outstanding triumph. Today's handshake would have seemed an act of cowardice to them" (p. 554). This juxtaposition between modern and ancient signifies that those values often championed as being inherent to sports participation are not transcendent. They are born of particular social conditions and constructed for particular purposes, primarily as means of enforcing and "fostering respect for the established order" (Kidd, 2013. p. 555).

In elite schools, which were key nation-building institutions in 19th-century Britain for inculcating these ordering qualities, we see even more concrete ties between sports and nationalist or militaristic ideals for those boys who participated in them (emphasis here is on *boys*, as girls were dissuaded from athletic competition). Sports, Kidd (2013) writes, were consciously regarded "as educational, preparing boys and young men for careers in business, government, colonial administration, and the military by instituting physical fitness and mental toughness, obedience to authority and loyalty to the 'team'" (p. 555). Within such contexts militaristic ideals were likewise reinforced via sport through overt imperatives to discipline the body (Terret, 2011) and celebrate the values of war (Tinson, 2011). In time, as working-class males were invited into athletic spheres, sports were used—perhaps not surprisingly given all of the above—to regulate class relations by "inviting" all participants into the sphere of middle-class values and practices (Kidd, 2013).

In this respect, it is important to note of sports-militarism connections that, just as these are not merely lexical, they are not merely historical or stuck in the past. On the contrary, they continue to be in evidence today in a variety of public institutions in Canada, including schools. A most notable recent example concerns Canadian Interuniversity Sport, the governing body of university sports in Canada, which was recently sponsored by the Canadian Department of National Defence (see Kelly, 2012). The initiative, part of Operation Connection, allowed the Canadian military "a presence at all university sporting events and access to target recruits" (Kelly, 2012, p. 2). Here as earlier, the underlying lesson is that sports, so much a part of the fabric of Canadian life, are not ideologically neutral, nor are Canadians' engagements with them.

School Sports and Militarized Masculinity

Having established that militaristic values find a language, a support structure, and a means of dissemination through sports cultures, the remainder of this chapter considers the effect of this connection on educational life. What socially valued forms of masculinity does sports participation—understood as endorsing a set of militarized values—favour within school communities?

My central claim in the following sections is that it favours rigid constructions of masculinity, the enactments of which are available for practice by some but not by others, and the effects of which reinforce gender hierarchies and contribute to countless pathologies for all those wrapped up in what Connell (2005) has called a "gender order." The militarized male—actualized through the elevation of sports culture in Canadian schools, but not limited to it—has many recognizable, socially valued attributes. He is portrayed as strong, stoic, heroic, emotionally invulnerable, self-sufficient, a patriarch, a breadwinner, a protector, and one who is willing to risk personal safety for the good of his community (Higate & Hopton, 2005; Johnson, 2010). He is rarely overwhelmed, and he is always ready to fight for a worthy cause.

Contemporary projections of this archetype abound. Canadians are given ample opportunity to consume images of this militarized male in film and on television, to read about how he is rewarded as a leader of industry, and to honour his historical memory as essential to Canadian national, social, and individual well-being (Taber, 2013, 2014; see also Taber, introduction to this volume; Haddow, Chapter 3 of this volume). More so, his accomplishments can be witnessed daily on a multitude of athletic playing fields, including those of our schools, where, in uniform and under the charge of a coach's orders, he often enacts many of the just-mentioned projections against the backdrop of applause and encouragements from a supportive school community. While those in this community may not overtly discriminate against males who do not fit the militarized male archetype, and who do not wish to fit it—which is to say nothing of those females who are excluded from accessing the privileges afforded by its enactments—they discriminate implicitly when they choose to validate this archetype at the expense of a diversity of subjectivities that might otherwise comprise "maleness."

To understand better the ways in which certain social constructions of masculinity are legitimated and enacted in schools, and in which school sports operate as a staging ground for the validation of archetypal (i.e., militarized) forms of masculinity, it is instructive to look to a few key gender theories that provide a useful language for doing so. Drawing from these theories can further serve as a useful prelude to thinking about some of the consequences of these constructions on student life.

The notion of "hegemonic masculinity" and its deployment in schools is paramount here (Connell, 2005). Defined by Connell (2005) as "the masculinity that occupies the hegemonic position in a given pattern of gender relations, a position always contestable" (p. 76), hegemonic masculinity refers to the most valued institutional and cultural interpretation of maleness within any given set of social relations (Leach, 1994). By extension, the notion that a gender order exists in schools, as it would anywhere, refers to the way in which social relations in schools tend to reinforce symbolic orders and meanings about what it means to be appropriately male or female (Swain, 2005). In this context, the school, the one ubiquitous institution that all Canadian youth must encounter, comprises a key institutional space in which boys learn to be men.

But what exactly do they learn along these grounds? Connell (2005) suggests that gendered *hierarchies* impose themselves upon us in any multitude of social contexts, and that males are by necessity forced to learn to exist within them. We have seen how hegemonic masculinity occupies the top position in a given pattern of gender relations (whereby hegemonic males—usually white, middle-class, able-bodied, and able-minded—enjoy material and symbolic privileges over other males and females). Other forms of masculinity within Connell's (2005) conceptual hierarchy include "complicit masculinity" (males who distance themselves from direct displays of power but accept their gender privilege); "subordinated masculinity" (males variously excluded from the masculine "circle of legitimacy," i.e., "wimps," "nerds," "sissies"); and "marginalized masculinity" (males well positioned by their gender but unfailingly denied access to the upper echelons of the gender order owing to markers like race, class, and ethnicity) (pp. 76–81; see also Johnson, 2010).

These categories, at times called to task for being too overly deterministic (see Swain, 2005), nonetheless perform an important function: they rescue masculinity from the presumptions of biology and suggest that maleness is a socio-cultural construct rather than a natural state. Moreover, they open a space for thinking about the way that institutions like schools, not to mention school sports, are implicated in valuing particular constructions of masculinity over others. In this regard, Connell's categories of masculinity find a natural ally in the values embedded in the structure and functioning of most Canadian schools. Schools are exceedingly hierarchical spaces, places where students are regularly subjected to grading, sorting, and measuring mechanisms and are rewarded and punished in various forms of competition against each other (Bourdieu & Passeron, 1990). For this reason it should perhaps not come as a surprise that boys in schools might apply this same hierarchical valuing to all manner of gendered stock-taking and measurement against each other.

In such a context, sports become a key venue for legitimizing gendered hierarchies and elevating the values of hegemonic masculinity within schools. Here the spectre of militarism re-enters the discussion, for on the sports field the hegemonic male is the militarized male. He is the strongest male, as well as the fastest, shrewdest, most ruthless, most competitive, and most eager. And he of course enjoys cultural currency in realizing these hegemonic markers, in this way further cementing his own hegemony through acclaim from his peers, support from his teachers, and the garnering of publicity for himself and his school (James, 2005).

To the extent that such cultural currencies are afforded to the militarized male in schools, and ample research suggests that this is the case (see also Schnyder, 2012), what bears contemplating is how institutionally sanctioned and culturally rewarded forms of militarized masculinity push boys into the pursuit of particular ways of being. Put differently, at issue here is how pre-existing gendered roles precede lived gendered experiences in the making of men. This is of concern because it seems likely that a consequence of the prizing of militarized masculinity as a preferred form of hegemonic masculinity is a set of pathologies. In schools it is now a commonplace observation that those students most often suspended, disciplined, emotionally volatile, deemed at risk, and in need of "special" education are boys (Cappon, 2011). In this case, it does not seem a stretch to suggest a correlation between boys' struggles in schools and rigid notions of masculinity, whereby the rigidity of militaristic ideals, and the reward structure in place that encourages boys to perform gender in ways that align with these ideals (through school sports and otherwise), is perhaps precluding boys from fuller, more meaningful, and healthier explorations of what being male might mean within schools.

Butler's (1990, 1994) ideas about the relationships between gendered social roles and the subjects who enact them offer an interesting way forward in terms of addressing these preclusions. Drawing a distinction from the notion of gender performance—a popular constructionist perspective that imagines agentic males and females *choosing* to perform roles consonant with desired expressions of gender—Butler instead posits the notion of "performativity" as a more fitting theorization of how we enact and learn gender. According to performativity, individuals are never wholly unified gendered subjects who deliberately enact gender roles. Rather, individuals unwittingly become gendered through myriad processes of recursion, unconscious training, and forces of habit derived from socially and culturally sanctioned frames of reference. What this implies is that already-in-existence gender roles have primacy in the production of gender; said roles take on the function of producing, in individuals, the attributes they name.

Just as athletes are encouraged to rehearse sports skills until they are perfected, the suggestion here is therefore that so too are militarized, masculine roles subtly rehearsed and perfected as young males adopt and affirm athletic identities through sports participation (Sparkes, 2000). Yet Butler's notion of performativity represents the possibility of interrupting predominant social constructions of gender, because it engages the prospect of bringing unconsciously enacted gender roles into individual consciousness and collective discourse. Gender performativity resignifies social affinities towards rigid, militarized masculinity as a problem having to do with a failure of imagination; it suggests that we will only support more fluid experiences of gender in conjunction with the development of a more expansive and complex language for speaking about it. To the extent that being appropriately male is rigidly constructed and supported in schools, the implication is that our awareness of the workings of these constructions—brought to bear by giving them a language and putting them into discourse—can work to liberate us from them (see also Magnusson & Mojab, Chapter 1 of this volume, on making invisible gender relations visible).

Militarized Masculinity and Its Marginalizing Effects: The Case of Black, Male, Student Athletes in Canadian Schools

Mindful of the possibilities that theoretical interventions offer towards complicating perceptions and experiences of masculinity, the fact remains that in schools many young males are caught in a web of rigid gender constructions of the militarized variety discussed throughout, and they remain supported in these constructions within athletic realms in particular. The consequences of this on the experiences of students therefore need close and continued attention.

The fact that the sports-enabled inscription of rigid gender roles works against school inclusion for many males (Wellard, 2002), and that those males on the margins of masculine hegemony (racial and ethnic minorities, sexual minorities, the poor) are often accordingly disadvantaged within school communities, is by now no surprise (Kimmel, 2004). What is perhaps more striking about practices of masculine gender exclusion is an accompanying discriminatory practice (one that I focus on in what follows) that is especially insidious because it is much less talked about but has no less impact. I refer here to how educators often draw on militarized-sports discourses to promote the promise of school inclusion among male students, and to the effects of their doing so (James, 2003; Schnyder, 2012). That is, many young males on the margins of school are immanently sold on the social and educational "benefits" of sports-sanctioned hegemonic masculine ideals, and they endorse these ideals, but they are nonetheless denied the material means of achieving them within schooling and social orders that often leave little room for their inclusion (see also James, 2005: Majors, 1990). Put differently, marginalized male students are often prompted to play sports in order to attain greater inclusion within school life—indeed, through sports they learn many of the aforementioned militaristic values needed to succeed there—only to realize that the long-term dividends of their efforts do not pay off beyond the "war game" skills they have aimed to perfect.

A good way to concretize this assertion and to glean its workings in Canadian schooling contexts is through attention to the marginalization of one masculine subculture in particular. Black, male, student athletes in Canada, about whom I have previously written (Saul, 2006; Saul & James, 2006), offer an instructive example of a racialized subculture that is especially marginalized by short-sighted educator appeals towards encouraging sports participation, and help to show how the workings of intersecting oppressions factor into the marginalizing practices to which they are often subjected.

My earlier inquiries into the case of black, male, student athletes in Canada focused on a close reading of a popular weekly Toronto newspaper column that was devoted to reporting on them. I collected this weekly column—a repository of public information on student athlete experiences, interests, and aspirations, as well as on educator and media perceptions of the same—over the course of an entire school year. Applying methods of textual analysis, my study revealed a racialized philosophy of differentiation in reporting on males. For black, male students in comparison to others, media and those represented within it championed their chances for social mobility through sport out of a persistent inability to conceive of them outside of their athletic interests (Saul, 2006; Saul & James, 2006).

There is a long socio-historical legacy connecting black males to athletic success in North America, with sports serving as a contested racial terrain in which countless racial struggles and gains have been waged and achieved (Hartmann, 2000). Contemporary North American media likewise presents no shortage of success stories about black, male athletes, especially within socio-economically accessible sports (see Saul, 2006; Saul & James, 2006). However, we also have much evidence that in North American schools, and here the focus is on Canadian schools, black males often struggle against the standardized measures of achievement, graduation, and dropout rates (Dei, Mazzuca, McIsaac, & Zine, 1997; James, 2005).[1] An issue comes to the fore when educators combine these two variables—when they reason that, given the school disengagement of some black, male youth, an effective strategy is to encourage these males to join sports teams. Ample research suggests that this is seen as a viable option by many educators and that many black, male students are often sold on this very strategy (Edwards, 2000; James 2003, 2005; Solomon, 1989; Wetzel & Yaeger, 2000). One consequence is the adoption of aforementioned "athletic identities" among targeted black males, whereby one's sports role within the school context is elevated above all others (Sparkes, 2000).

Given earlier assertions about the supports and rewards tendered for successfully assuming these identities in schools and society, it is not hard to see the reason such roles would be appealing. In Canadian cities with significant black male populations, this appeal of adopting athletic identities as a means of negotiating school life often involves subcultures of young black males making tremendous sacrifices in trying to use sports as a gateway to school success, not just in the present but also with an eye towards future successes (Saul, 2006). Sports success therefore becomes a stand-in for school success as well as a means of achieving life aspirations, and the adoption of the cultural values that accompany this success—for one, an endorsement of the discourses and practices of militarism endemic to sports participation—becomes one of its offshoots. The problem is that the notion of achieving success through sports is an exceedingly fleeting abstraction for most, and its serious pursuit comes with few long-term, tangible benefits for all but a select group. The promises of hegemony, however problematic they might be, are nevertheless sold through this paradigm to significant numbers of black male youth on the margins of schooling success. Yet the means of achieving this hegemony most often remain deferred, a deferral that becomes accentuated once they are out of school, in a context where sports have long since been prioritized over studies (Edwards, 2000; Singer & May, 2011).

Raced and gendered oppressions therefore intersect here to create a "race logic" as concerns black, male, student athletes, one that is too often consented to by various educational stakeholders (Coakley & Donnelly, 2009). Assumptions are made about these males, the more problematic among them being the construction of black males as predisposed to make only very particular contributions to school life. The uglier underside of this characterization is a subtle form of racism (subtle because the characterization is celebrated), implying as it does an inverse relationship to intellectual capacities (Saul, 2006).

Militarism is again implicit in this race logic. In his ethnographic study of a public high school in the United States, Schnyder (2012) elucidates this connection. Among other findings, he suggests that schools can encourage in black males—through sports participation—a type of militarized, ultra-masculine performance that reinforces black males' own oppression under the guise of doing the opposite. About one young man he writes that "just as the coach implored young men to fight and define their masculinity along terms of warlike conflict, Rashad carried out this militaristic/violent ethos to other parts of his life" (p. 10). This coach used sports-war speak and sports contexts to motivate students in the pursuit of attaining culturally valued behaviours consonant with hegemonic, militarized masculinity (e.g., "real men don't quit and never give up fighting," p. 10). Yet this strategy really operated as a means of coercion whose effects were individually and socially debilitating.

The underlying consequence is a blame-the-victim discourse that often accompanies the educational struggles of marginalized males within schools. A "non-achieving" or "at-risk" marginalized male is constituted as a problem in need of improvement or of fixing. And, as in Schnyder's and others' examples (see Johnson, 2010), his shortcoming is often surmised to be that he has not fully embraced the values of his system and his society, that he needs to learn better how to fulfill the functions of being adequately male, and that he needs to adopt further the precepts of hegemonic masculinity. What is missing from this calculation is a systemic critique. Such a critique would need to posit that schools and societies reward exclusive forms of masculinity through the gender orders they define, and that perceived transgressions along these lines are committed by those who do not or cannot meet socially sanctioned markers of gendered power and privilege.

Conclusion

It is important for educators to consider the school-sports counter-discourse that I have described here, among more prevalent ones, in enacting just and equitable schooling relations in Canada. According to the terms of this discourse and its corresponding practices, militaristic values are embedded in sports participation, and these values help to valorize rigid masculine ideals to the detriment of all students who are inevitably wrapped in a commensurate gender order.

There is much at stake when school communities pay little attention to the discreet discourses and practices related to sports participation and pay little attention to the role of sports participation in perpetuating a gender order. Once made visible, these discourses and practices, not to mention the militarized ideals underpinning them, reveal compliances with student hierarchies that are rooted in gender differences. Those few hegemonic male students positioned at the top of the hierarchies enjoy a series of symbolic and material privileges in schools and otherwise. Yet their access to these privileges—whether through active pursuit or passive acquiescence—comes with a heavy social and educational price; successes and achievements are built here in a space where the elevation of some relies on the subjugation of others. Those subjugated, in this case students occupying subordinate places within these gender hierarchies—that is, all non-hegemonic males (such as the racialized black male student athletes described earlier), the poor, sexual minorities, females, and others—are the more immediate and consequential victims within this gender order. For such students, opportunities for attaining full and meaningful educational lives can be obstructed by barriers ranging from overt discrimination to myriad unnoticed struggles endemic to existence within a system that operates to discriminate against them (Kimmel, 2004). Given that the majority of Canadian students experience their educational lives as non-hegemonic males, continued inquiry into gender hierarchies and their often-invisible workings—whether through the lens of the school sports cultures described here or in any number of other examples detailed in this volume—is paramount. Only by deconstructing the workings of these hierarchies can new kinds of gender relations be imagined.

NOTE

1. Much has been written about the influences on these struggles, which can include the prevalence of exclusionary curricula and institutional racism, and about the effect of the low socio-economic status of many such students on school achievement (James, 2005).

REFERENCES

Bourdieu, P., & Passeron, J.C. (1990). *Reproduction in education, society and culture* (2nd ed.). London: Sage.

Butler, J. (1990). *Gender trouble: Feminism and the subversion of identity*. New York: Routledge.

Butler, J. (1994). Gender as performance: An interview with Judith Butler. Interview by Peter Osborn and Lynn Segal. *Radical Philosophy, 67*, 235-238.

Canada. Canadian Heritage. (2013). *Sport participation 2010: Canadian Heritage research paper*. Retrieved from http://publications.gc.ca

Cappon, P. (2011). *Exploring the "boy crisis" in Education*. Canadian Council on Learning. Retrieved from http://files.eric.ed.gov/fulltext/ED518173.pdf

Clark, W. (2009). *Statistics Canada: Kids' sports*. Retrieved from www.statcan.gc.ca

Coakley, J., & Donnelly, P. (2009). *Sports in society: Issues and controversies*. Whitby, ON: McGraw-Hill Ryerson.

Connell, R.W. (2005). *Masculinities* (2nd ed.). Berkeley: University of California Press.

Connell, R.W. (2012). *Gender: In world perspective* (2nd ed.). Cambridge: Polity Press.

Dei, G.J.S., Mazzuca, J., McIsaac, E., and Zine, J. (1997). *Reconstructing "dropout": A critical ethnography of the dynamics of Black students' disengagement from school*. Toronto: University of Toronto Press.

Edwards, H. (2000). Crisis of black athletes on the eve of the 21st century. *Society, 37*(3), 9-13.

Hartmann, D. (2000). Rethinking the relationships between sport and race in American culture: Golden ghettos and contested terrain. *Sociology of Sport Journal, 17*, 229-253.

Higate, P., & Hopton, J. (2005). War, militarism, and masculinities. In M.S. Kimmel, J. Hearn, & R.W. Connell (Eds.), *Handbook of studies on men and masculinities* (pp. 432-447). Thousand Oaks, CA: Sage.

Huggins, M. (2012). "Manufactured" masculinity. *Journal of Sport History, 39*(1), 147-156.

Ifedi, F. (2008). *Sports participation in Canada, 2005*. Culture, Tourism and the Centre for Education Statistics. Retrieved from www.statcan.gc.ca

James, C.E. (2003). It can't just be sports! Schooling, academics and athletic scholarship expectations. *Orbit, 33*(3), 33-35.

James, C.E. (2005). *Race in play: Understanding the socio-cultural worlds of student athletes.* Toronto: Canadian Scholars' Press.

Jansen, S.C., & Sabo, D. (1994). The sport/war metaphor: Hegemonic masculinity, the Persian Gulf War, and the new world order. *Sociology of Sport Journal, 11*(1), 1-17.

Jenkins, T. (2013). The militarization of American professional sports: How the sports-war intertext influences athletic ritual and sports media. *Journal of Sport and Social Issues, 37*(3), 1-16. doi: 10.1177/0193723512470686.

Johnson, B. (2010). A few good boys: Masculinity at a military style charter school. *Men and Masculinities, 12*(5), 575-596.

Kelly, J. (2012, November). Popular culture, sport and the "hero"-fication of British militarism. *Sociology* (online edition), 1-17. doi: 10.1177/0038038512453795.

Kidd, B. (2013). Sports and masculinity. *Sport in Society: Cultures, Commerce, Media, Politics, 16*(4), 553-564.

Kimmel, M.S. (2004). "I am not insane; I am angry": Adolescent masculinity, homophobia, and violence. In M. Sadowski (Ed.), *Adolescents at school: Perspectives on youth, identity, and education* (pp. 69-78). Cambridge, MA: Harvard Education Press.

King, S. (2008). Offensive lines: Sport-state synergy in an era of perpetual war. *Cultural Studies—Critical Methodologies, 8*(4), 527-539.

Klein, M.W., & Sorenson, S.B. (2002). Contrasting perspectives on youthful sports violence. In M. Gatz, M.A. Messner, & S.J. Ball Rokeach (Eds.), *Paradoxes of youth and sport* (pp. 197-206). Albany: SUNY Press.

Leach, M. (1994). The politics of masculinity: An overview of contemporary theory. *Social Alternatives, 12*(4), 36-39.

Leonard, D.J. (2010). Jumping the gun: Sporting cultures and the criminalization of Black masculinity. *Journal of Sport and Social Issues, 34*(2), 252-262.

Majors, R. (1990). Cool pose: Black masculinity and sports. In M.A. Messner & D.F. Sabo (Eds.), *Sport, men, and the gender order: Critical feminist perspectives* (pp. 109-114). Champaign, IL: Human Kinetics Books.

Messner, M.A., Dunbar, M., & Hunt, D. (2000). The televised sports manhood formula. *Journal of Sport and Social Issues, 24*(4), 380-394.

Saul, R. (2006). How Black male student athletes get stereotyped in Canada's schools. *Our schools, Our selves, 15*(2), 91-110.

Saul, R., & James, C.E. (2006). Framing possibilities: Representations of Black student athletes in Toronto media. *Canadian and International Education Journal, 35*(1), 63-79.

Schnyder, D.M. (2012) Masculinity lockdown: The formation of Black masculinity in a California public high school. *Transforming Anthropology, 20*(1), 5-16.

Singer, J.N., & May, R.A.B. (2011). The career trajectory of a black male high school basketball player: A social reproduction perspective. *International Review for the Sociology of Sport, 46*(3), 299-314.

Solomon, P. (1989). Dropping out of academics: Black youth and the sports subculture in a cross-national perspective. In L. Weis, E. Farrar, & H.G Petrie (Eds.), *Dropouts from school: Issues, dilemmas, and solutions* (pp. 79-93). Albany: SUNY Press.

Sparkes, A.C. (2000). Illness, premature career-termination, and the loss of self: A bibliographical study of an elite athlete. In R.L. Jones & K.M. Armour (Eds.), *Sociology of sport: Theory and practice* (pp. 13-32). Essex, UK: Pearson.

Swain, J. (2005). Masculinities in education. In M.S. Kimmel, J. Hearn, & R.W. Connell (Eds.), *Handbook of studies on men and masculinities* (pp. 213-229). Thousand Oaks, CA: Sage.

Taber, N. (2013). Learning war through gender: Masculinities, femininities, and militarism. In T. Nesbit, S. Brigham, N. Taber, & T. Gibb (Eds.), *Building on critical traditions: Adult education and learning in Canada* (pp. 123-132). Toronto: Thompson Publishing.

Taber, N. (2014). Generals, colonels, and captains: Discourses of militarism, education, and learning in the Canadian university context. *Canadian Journal of Higher Education, 44*(2), 105-117.

Terret, T. (2011). Prologue: Making men, destroying bodies: Sport, masculinity and the Great War experience. *International Journal of the History of Sport, 28*(3-4), 323-328.

Tinson, C. (2011). Review of *Not Just a Game. Radical Teacher, 90*, 69-71.

Wellard, I. (2002). Men, sport, body performance and the maintenance of "exclusive masculinity." *Leisure Studies, 21*(3-4), 235-247.

Wetzel, D., & Yaeger, D. (2000). *Sole influence: Basketball, corporate greed, and the corruption of America's youth*. New York: Warner.

CONCLUSION

Final Thoughts and Connecting Threads

Nancy Taber

THIS BOOK HAS ADDRESSED the ways in which gendered militarism is learned in Canada. The authors have explored gender as a social construct and a social relation that is inextricably linked to privileged performances of masculinity and femininity. Their work demonstrates that calling for *equal rights* is not enough. What, indeed, is the standard of equality to which one is matched? Militarized masculinity? A feminine beauty ideal? Western standards? Able bodies? Heteronormativity? Radical change is required in order to problematize the ways in which contending discourses of conservative and egalitarian gender relations work together to occlude marginalization (Taber, Chapter 4 of this volume). Therefore, there is a need to "make visible the *invisible* social relations" (Magnusson & Mojab, Chapter 1 of this volume, italics in original) and look past any "smokescreen[s] of inclusivity" (Mizzi, Chapter 6 of this volume). Enloe (2007) terms this developing a "feminist curiosity," explaining that "to insist upon posing questions about things that other people take for granted can be a political act" (p. 1). The authors in this book take a very political stance, arguing with a societal analysis that works for social justice. They are scholars and educators who engage learners and the public in a critique of the ways in which gender and militarism are inculcated in daily life.

The book demonstrates that Canadians interact daily with concepts, objects, spaces, and actions that are affected by gendered militarism, such as fairy tales, physical education and sport, social networking sites and cellphones, online gaming, and television programs and movies. They come into contact with the military at recruiting events, have their teaching credentials refused and abilities questioned, realize that soldiers are the most valued of citizens, and participate in international training that denigrates (or, at the very least, ignores) sexual minorities and treats all women as the same. Canadians learn to accept gendered militarism in educational contexts such as public pedagogies, compulsory schooling, teacher re-certification, citizenship tests, formal training, non-formal learning, adult education, and higher education. However, these same spaces are also sites of resistance. People simultaneously accept and challenge gendered militarism, consciously and unconsciously, as they go about their daily lives.

Magnusson and Mojab (Chapter 1) and Lane (Chapter 2) discuss how social movements work against militarism. Haddow (Chapter 3) argues for the use of critical military literacy to critique popular culture, while Castrodale (Chapter 5) implements a critical disability studies pedagogy. Mizzi (Chapter 6) calls for a rainbow audit of the Canadian military and any curriculum that the organization uses for training. Similarly, Hanson (Chapter 7) argues for a "feminist-inspired intersectional analysis" of gender training. Educators and scholars should continually ask, as Saul does (in Chapter 10, italics in original), "What *else* is learned?" not just, in his case, beyond sports skills but, in relation to the book as a whole, beyond what is apparent. What do prospective adult citizens and school children learn when studying citizenship documents that teach more than the rights and responsibilities of citizenship by promoting discourses of militarized masculinity (Taber, Chapter 4)? What do refugee teachers learn when it seems that a return to motherhood is the best way for them to integrate into Canadian society (Ratković, Chapter 8)? What do girls learn in relation to cyberbullying and their own identities as pertains to their schooling (Fournier, Chapter 9)? All the chapters demonstrate that a nuanced understanding of the complexity of gender, militarism, and learning is required in order to change the ways that people think and act.

I would like to end this book with something that I often ask students to create in my courses: a found poem based on the literature. In this case, I have taken phrases from each chapter that I think characterize the author's overall argument, provoke further thought, and provide threads from which to weave together the content of the book. This is not meant to reduce each author's chapter to a few lines, as her or his work is far too complex for that, but to comprehensively represent the book as a whole.

Gender, Militarism, Learning

Gender (and intersecting oppressions) as a societal construct
militarism as an overarching concept...connected to but not equated
with war and militaries
learning from a lifelong perspective.

Recognition, fear, and diminishing hope converge...immersed in a world
    of war games
eliminates the distinction between gaming fiction and warring
the *appearance* of equality and democracy...contrasts sharply against
    the *essence* of creating
militarized insecurity, subjugation, and violence
this, then, is not empowerment; it is a contradiction.

Little room for critical commentary

targeting young women for wedding advertisements

and young men for military employment

collaborative online communities...challenge patriarchy and advocate for peace.

Conscious and unconscious ideology in popular culture

potential to both reinforce dominant patriarchal and militaristic beliefs

opportunities for social and ideological resistance

simultaneously reinforce systems of oppression against women,

promote militaristic values among citizens

create a space for education and resistance.

Who Canadians are expected to be

and *what values* they are supposed to hold and enact

with a stroke of a pen...privileges men, masculinity, and war

Canada as a whole is presented as masculinized and militarized

problematize these discourses of citizenship.

What it means to be human...asking what a body can do

soldiers' bodies thus represent mouldable bodies that can be trained

in the service of their country

they are oxymoronically disposable and indispensable citizens

disability as an educational site of the possibility to challenge the conventional

taken-for-granted ableist ways of being and knowing in the world.

Non-normative gender role...effeminate mannerisms

discomfort and challenge

an implicit curriculum reinforces silence around homosexuality

changing the heteromasculinization of military systems.

Critical points and critical pedagogies of intervention

complexities of gender inequality

efforts to include masculinity...in training for gender equality...rejected male gender norms being so "given" that they go unnoticed

pedagogical interventions from the field of critical adult education...

    critically reflexive

facilitation...disrupting the power relationships that are inherent in

    conflict situations.

So intensively watched, judged, and disciplined in her classroom

that she internalized this gaze

monolithic and hierarchal approaches to teaching and teacher education

there are multiple and situated knowledges and perspectives

claiming an agency even in the restrictive conditions of war, exile, and

    global militarism.

Cyberbullying as a contemporary social phenomenon

one girl is many avatars...liquid identity...multiplicity of roles

empathy building

refocus and reconceptualise.

Sports...a key venue for legitimizing gendered hierarchies and elevating

    the values of

hegemonic masculinity within schools

marginalized male students...prompted to play sports in order to attain

    greater inclusion

long-term dividends...do not pay off beyond the "war game" skills

what is missing from this calculation is a systemic critique.

A nuanced understanding

complexity of gender, militarism, and learning

radical change is required.

CONTRIBUTORS

Mark Anthony Castrodale is an instructor of disability studies in education at King's College, University of Western Ontario, and an instructor of critical disability studies in education in the university's Faculty of Education, where he recently completed his PHD. He completed his bachelor of arts degree (honours) in geography at McMaster University, bachelor of education degree at Brock University, and a master of critical disability studies at York University. Mark Anthony's research interests include socio-spatial qualitative inquiry, mobile methodologies, geographies of disability, critical disability studies, critical policy analysis, Foucauldian analytics, addressing ableism in the academy, and examining the impacts of educational policies and practices on the lives of persons with disabilities in post-secondary educational contexts.

Gillian L. Fournier is a teacher of English and dramatic arts in southwestern Ontario. For her work with drama as social intervention and with cyberbullying she received the American Alliance for Theatre and Education's 2015 Distinguished Thesis Award Honorable Mention, as well as Brock University's Jack M. Miller Excellence in Research Award for 2014, and Master of Education Thesis Award for 2014. Since 2004, as a playwright and an educator, Gillian has been engaging youth in drama for social intervention.

Andrew Haddow is a student in the master of education program at Brock University. He completed his bachelor of arts degree (honours) in English and history at York University. His current research concerns the pedagogical implications of popular media in Canada, in relation to gender, identity, and foreign policy. Andrew's interests include international education, cultural capital, and the educational potential of film, television, and video games for both youth and adults. Upon the completion of his master of education, Andrew will be moving to Japan to teach English as a second language in the public school system, and he plans to return to Canada later to complete a doctorate.

Cindy Hanson is an associate professor and director of the Adult Education and Human Resources Development Unit at the University of Regina (Faculty of Education), Canada. She teaches and conducts research related to local and global applications of participatory, transformative, and intergenerational learning. Transnational activism in training for gender equality was the subject of her doctoral work, completed in 2009. Prior to this, she held consultancies in gender and education in over 15 countries, including work in Nepal and Ethiopia during times of conflict.

Laura Lane is a doctoral candidate in the Faculty of Education at Brock University. She completed a bachelor of arts degree in English language and literature, and a master of education degree in the socio-cultural contexts of education, at Brock University. Her research interests include forms of capital and privileged culture in university institutions; gender discourses in popular and digital media; educational possibilities of social media; technology in early-years classrooms; and discussion groups as sites for gender critique. Her research scope covers a variety of educational contexts from the early years to adult education. Laura is also a practising teacher with the Niagara Catholic District School Board and is certified to teach English and geography at the high-school level. She also teaches undergraduate courses in Brock University's Faculty of Education.

Jamie Magnusson is an associate professor of adult education and community development at OISE, University of Toronto. Her activism and scholarship on "precarity and dispossession" examine militarized financialization in terms of urban development and social justice themes, with particular attention to women, youth, and LGBTQ communities. Recent publications include "Precarious Learning and Labour in Financialized Times" (*Brock Journal of Education*, 2013); "Biosurveillance as a Terrain of Innovation in an Era of Monopoly Finance Capital" (*Policy Futures in Education*, 2013); "The Art of (Bio)Surveillance: Bioart and the Financialization of Living

Systems" (co-authored with Elisabeth Abergel, *Topia* special issue on *The Financialized Imagination*, 2014); and "Financialization" (2015), in S. Mojab (Ed.), *Marxism and Feminism*, London: Zed Books.

Robert C. Mizzi is an assistant professor in the Faculty of Education at the University of Manitoba. His current research interests largely focus on two areas: LGBTQ educators and educators who cross borders to work in foreign contexts. Robert examines the lives of these groups of educators in both K-12 and adult learning contexts. He has published over 35 chapters, articles, and reviews in journals and books, such as the *Journal of Homosexuality* and *Journal of Peace Education*. He has also published three books that focus on educator and social development, including the edited book *Breaking Free: Sexual Diversity and Change in Emerging Nations* (QPI Publications and Lambda Foundation). Robert is a research associate for the Arthur Mauro Centre for Peace and Justice (University of Manitoba) and the Perspectives editor (Adult Education) for the journal *New Horizons in Adult Education and Human Resource Development*.

Shahrzad Mojab, a professor of adult education and women's studies at the University of Toronto, is an academic activist, specializing in educational policy studies; gender, state, migration, and diaspora; women, war, violence, and learning; Marxist feminism; and anti-racism pedagogy. She is the editor of *Marxism and Feminism* (2015). Shahrzad co-edited with Sara Carpenter *Educating from Marx: Race, Gender and Learning* (2012); edited *Women, War, Violence, and Learning* (2010); co-edited with Nahla Abdo *Violence in the Name of Honour: Theoretical and Political Challenges* (2004); and co-edited with Himani Bannerji and Judith Whitehead *Of Property and Propriety: The Role of Gender and Class in Imperialism and Nationalism* (2001). Shahrzad has been the guest editor of the special issues of *Comparative Studies of South Asia, Africa, and the Middle East Journal*, on *Gender and Empire* (Summer 2010) and *Dissent: The Politics and Poetics of Women's Resistance* (2012); the *International Journal of Lifelong Education*, on women, war, and learning; and *Resources for Feminist Research*, on war and militarization.

Snežana Ratković is a science teacher from the former Yugoslavia who immigrated to Canada in 1998 after the Yugoslav wars. She works as a research officer in the Faculty of Education at Brock University. Her research focuses on forced migration and settlement, teacher identity, transnational and transdisciplinary teacher education, women's studies, research ethics, and social justice in education. In her doctoral research Snežana explored experiences, transitions, and identities of 10 refugee women teachers from Yugoslavia who had immigrated to Ontario and Quebec between 1993 and 1998. For this interdisciplinary and transnational research study she received the 2014 Jack M. Miller Excellence in Research Award and the 2014 Canadian

Association for the Study of Women in Education (CASWE) Graduate Student Award. Snežana has published in *The Reading Professor*; *Forum Qualitative Sozialforschung / Forum: Qualitative Social Research*; *South African Journal of Higher Education*; *Power and Education*; *Educational Action Research Journal*; *Studies in Higher Education*; *Refuge: Canada's Journal on Refugees*; and *Brock Education Journal*.

Roger Saul is an assistant professor in the Faculty of Education at the University of New Brunswick. His research and teaching focuses on educational foundations, cultural studies, and critical theory. His work has been published in the *International Journal of Learning and Media*; *Digital Culture and Education*; *The Journal of Popular Culture*; *Educational Studies*; and the *Canadian and International Education Journal*. Saul is co-editor of the book *Education in North America* (Bloomsbury Press, 2014).

Nancy Taber is an associate professor in the Faculty of Education at Brock University. She teaches in the areas of critical adult education, socio-cultural contexts of schooling, and learning gender in a militarized world. Her work often draws on her experiences serving in the Canadian military as a Sea King helicopter air navigator. Nancy's research includes a critique of militarism from the standpoint of military mothers, an analysis of the ways in which discourses of militarism intersect with academia in higher education, and an exploration of gendered issues of militarism in fiction and popular culture. Nancy is co-editor of *Building on Critical Traditions: Adult Education and Learning in Canada*. She is guest editor of an issue on the state of feminism in Canadian adult education for the *Canadian Journal for the Study of Adult Education*. Nancy has published in journals such as *Adult Education Quarterly*; *International Journal for Lifelong Education*; *Studies in Continuing Education*; *Canadian Journal for the Study of Adult Education, Gender and Education*; *Journal of Peace Education*; *Children's Literature in Education*; and *Qualitative Research*. She is currently co-editing a book, *Popular Culture as Pedagogy: Research in the Field of Adult Education*. Nancy is a member of the Canadian Association for the Study of Adult Education as well as the Niagara branch of the Canadian Authors Association. She is currently using the genre of fiction to explore the complexities of women's lives.

INDEX

as protectors, 25-26, 32, 65, 161
representation in citizenship
materials, 64, 66, 69-71, 72-74, 75,
76-77
and sports, 209-24
in *Urgent EVOKE*, 9-10
and video games, 52-53
and war, 28-29, 33-35, 89, 107, 149
on WILPF Facebook page, 37
See also Canadian Armed Forces; gay
men; gender roles; masculinity
Messner, M.A., 212
militarism
in *Buffy the Vampire Slayer*, 55-56
and Canadian army, 32-33, 34-35
in citizenship documents and
resources, 64-65, 69-71, 72, 73-78
and cyberbullying, 177
defined, XVIII, 148
and disability, 83, 90, 91-94, 99-101
and education, 66-67, 94, 165-66, 215-19
on Facebook, 25-26, 27, 32-35, 38
and feminism, 149
forcing gender roles, 28-30
found poem, 231-33
and gamefied learning, 2, 3
and government commemoration,
XVIII-XX
and hegemonic masculinity, 217-18
methods of combatting lessons of,
18-22
and motherhood, 148, 152-54
in popular culture, 44, 49-50, 53-54
recent advances of in US and Canada,
48-49, 51
and refugee women, 165
and relations of financialized
capitalism, 12-17
rhetoric of, 99-100
societal impact of, VIII-IX, 94-95
and sports, 210, 211-24
and *Urgent EVOKE*, 4, 5, 7-12, 18
and use of bodies, 88-90

values of, 83
and women, 49-50, 148, 149
See also Canadian Armed Forces; war
Mindry, D., 139
Mira (Yugoslav refugee), 156-58, 161-65
Miss Representation (film), 50
Mitchell, Joni, XX
Mojab, S., 20
Moncur, Bruce, 93
moral politic of engagement, 139
Moranis, Rick, 45
Mother Canada, XIX
motherhood, 148, 152-54, 162-64
Mukhopadhyay, M., 137
Mullins, Aimee, 91

nationalism, 213-14
neoliberalism, 47, 65
Never Forgotten National Memorial, XIX
Newsom, Siebel, 50
novels, 19-21, 54-55

objectification, 50
Once Upon a Time (TV show), XX-XXI
O'Reilly, J.D., 55
"other" groups/othering
and cyberbullying, 198, 199
and ethnodrama, 174
and the military, 111, 115, 118, 121, 148
and powerful exploiting the weak, 149
for refugees, 163

Pakistan, 133-34
panopticon, 151, 162, 164
Parent, Guy, 93
Parenti, M., 150
Parsons, Rehtaeh, 177
passport, 75
Patchin, J.W., 175, 178
patriarchy, 50, 55, 150-51, 152, 153, 165-66,
177
Patterson, J., 175-76
pedagogy. *See* education

performativity, 218-19

Peters, W., 56

Peterson, V.S., 83

popular culture, 43, 44, 45-46, 49-50, 54-59

Poulin, C., 111

Poyntz, S.R., 57

Province, Charles, 65

Queer as Folk (TV show), 56

queer knowledge, 116-17, 122

racism, 222-23

rainbow audit, 123-24

RAND Corporation, 5

rape, 17

Ratkovic, S., 156

Remembrance Day, 94

Renold, E., 178-79, 202, 203

Ringrose, J., 178-79, 202, 203

Robinson, B., 48

Rothman, B.K., 152

Runyan, A.S., 83

Sabo, D., 211

Saldaña, J., 179

Sandlin, J.A., 56

Sarkeesian, Anita, 51-52, 53

Sbarbaro, V., 176, 177, 202

Schnyder, D.M., 222-23

Schoffstall, C.L., 178

Second City Television (SCTV), 45-46

Second Life (video game), 6

Seoul Agenda, 180

September 11th terror attacks, 66

Sesame Street (TV show), 47

Shah, M.K., 138

Shildrick, M., 86

Sjoberg, L., 86, 87, 94

Slee, R., 96

Slonje, R., 178

Smith, Dorothy, 19

Smith, M., 112

Smith, P.K., 178

Snow White, XXI

Snow White and the Huntsman (film), XXI

social action, 27

social justice, 179-80

social media, 3, 32, 35-36, 38-39.
    See also Facebook

Somalia, 115

special education, 97

sports

    and education, 209-11, 223-24

    historical connection to militarism,
        211-14

    and marginalization of African-
        Canadians, 220-23

    and masculinity in schools, 212,
        215-19, 224

Stark, Justin, 93

Stermitz, E., 201

Stern, S.T., 176

subordinated masculinity, 217

suicide, 93

surveillance, 151-52, 162

Swift, J., 49

Taber, N., XV-XVII, 27, 54-55

Taylor, S., 88

television, XX-XXI, 45-46, 47, 49, 55-56

Terry, A., 90

Thomas, Dave, 45

Titchkosky, T., 87, 97

Todd, Amanda, 177

training for gender equality (TGE), 133-36

transformational learning, 136, 138-42

transgender, 116. See also LGBTQ

transnationalism, 165-66

transsexuals, 56

Tropes vs. Women in Video Games
    (video game), 52

True, J., 135

Tumblr, 191, 192, 201

Turse, N., 177

OTHER TITLES FROM THE UNIVERSITY OF ALBERTA PRESS

Building Sustainable Peace
Tom Keating & W. Andy Knight, Editors
978-0-88864-414-5 | $39.95 paper
978-0-88864-560-9 | $31.99 PDF
504 pages | Index, bibliography
Co-published by United Nations University Press
Political Science | Peace Studies

Not Drowning But Waving
Women, Feminism and the Liberal Arts
Susan Brown, Jeanne Perreault, Jo-Ann Wallace
& Heather Zwicker, Editors
978-0-88864-550-0 | $39.95 paper
978-0-88864-613-2 | $31.99 EPUB
978-0-88864-669-9 | $31.99 Kindle
978-0-88864-614-9 | $31.99 PDF
496 pages | 5 B&W photographs, introduction, notes,
bibliography, index
Feminism | Humanities | Women's Studies

Weaving a Malawi Sunrise
A Woman, A School, A People
Roberta Laurie
978-1-77212-086-8 | $39.95 paper
978-1-77212-113-1 | $31.99 EPUB
978-1-77212-114-8 | $31.99 Kindle
978-1-77212-115-5 | $31.99 PDF
440 pages | 29 B&W photographs, 1 map, notes, index
Wayfarer Series
Women's Studies | International Education | Development